Web3 for Students: From Zero To Blockchanin Hero

Anshuman Mishra

Published by Anshuman Mishra, 2025.

📓 About the Book: *Web3 for Students: From Zero to Blockchain Hero*

In a world where technology is evolving faster than ever, *Web3* is not just a buzzword — it's a revolution.

"Web3 for Students: From Zero to Blockchain Hero" is a student-friendly, practical, and easy-to-understand guide specially designed for young learners who want to understand the **future of the internet** — including **blockchain, cryptocurrency, NFTs, smart contracts**, and **decentralized applications (DApps)**.

Written in a simple, engaging language with zero jargon, this book helps students, teenagers, and young tech enthusiasts **understand and participate** in one of the most **transformational shifts** in digital technology — even if they have no prior technical knowledge.

Whether you're a high school student, a university learner, or someone simply curious about **Bitcoin, NFTs, or earning from crypto**, this book will make you confident in navigating the Web3 space.

✹ What This Book Covers

- ⬥ The evolution from Web1 to Web3
- ⬥ Fundamentals of **blockchain technology**
- ⬥ Understanding and using **cryptocurrencies** like Bitcoin & Ethereum
- ⬥ Step-by-step guide to **buying, selling, and storing crypto**
- ⬥ Deep dive into **NFTs** and how to create, sell, or collect them
- ⬥ Introduction to **smart contracts and DApps** with examples
- ⬥ Career paths in the Web3 space: from developers to community managers
- ⬥ Real-world projects, tools, and platforms every student should know
- ⬥ Practical tips, safety guidelines, and responsible use of Web3

◎ Who Should Read This Book?

- ✓ **School and college students** who are curious about emerging tech
- ✓ **Non-technical learners** who want to understand crypto and NFTs
- ✓ **Aspiring entrepreneurs** looking to explore digital assets and smart contracts
- ✓ **Creative individuals** (artists, musicians, gamers) wanting to earn through Web3

- ☑ **Educators and parents** who want to introduce young minds to futuristic technology

---

☑ Benefits of Studying This Book

💡 Benefits	🔍 Details
🎓 **Easy-to-Understand**	Designed for beginners; no prior tech background needed
💼 **Career-Focused**	Explores job roles, freelancing, and earning opportunities
🔨 **Hands-On Learning**	Includes practical activities: create NFTs, deploy smart contracts
🌐 **Global Perspective**	Covers international platforms, communities, and tools
🛡 **Security Awareness**	Teaches how to stay safe from scams and hacks in crypto
📈 **Future-Ready Skills**	Prepares students for careers in Web3, blockchain, and DeFi
🎮 **Fun and Interactive**	Play-to-earn games, NFT art creation, student projects
🧰 **Toolkits & Resources**	Lists of free tools, tutorials, communities, and cheat sheets

---

☐ Learning Outcomes

After reading this book, students will be able to:

- ☑ Explain blockchain, NFTs, and cryptocurrency in simple terms
- ☑ Use real tools like MetaMask, OpenSea, and Etherscan
- ☑ Mint their own NFTs and test simple smart contracts
- ☑ Understand how Web3 is disrupting traditional industries
- ☑ Prepare a beginner's Web3 portfolio or resume
- ☑ Join communities, DAOs, or start their own crypto-based projects

---

💬 Final Note

"Web3 for Students" is not just a book — it's an **entry ticket** into the internet of the future. If you want to be **career-ready**, **tech-smart**, and **digitally independent**, then this book is the perfect companion on your Web3 journey.

No matter where you are — in your dorm room, school library, or coffee shop — **your blockchain journey starts here.**

📘 BOOK TITLE: *WEB3 FOR STUDENTS: FROM ZERO TO BLOCKCHAIN HERO*

YOUR PRACTICAL GUIDE TO MASTERING CRYPTOCURRENCY, NFTS & SMART CONTRACTS

📓 TABLE OF CONTENTS

ABOUT THE AUTHOR:

ANSHUMAN KUMAR MISHRA IS A SEASONED EDUCATOR AND PROLIFIC AUTHOR WITH OVER 20 YEARS OF EXPERIENCE IN THE TEACHING FIELD. HE HAS A DEEP PASSION FOR TECHNOLOGY AND A STRONG COMMITMENT TO MAKING COMPLEX CONCEPTS ACCESSIBLE TO STUDENTS AT ALL LEVELS. WITH AN M.TECH IN COMPUTER SCIENCE FROM BIT MESRA, HE BRINGS BOTH ACADEMIC EXPERTISE AND PRACTICAL EXPERIENCE TO HIS WORK.

CURRENTLY SERVING AS AN ASSISTANT PROFESSOR AT DORANDA COLLEGE, ANSHUMAN HAS BEEN A GUIDING FORCE FOR MANY ASPIRING COMPUTER SCIENTISTS AND ENGINEERS, NURTURING THEIR SKILLS IN VARIOUS PROGRAMMING LANGUAGES AND TECHNOLOGIES. HIS TEACHING STYLE IS FOCUSED ON CLARITY, HANDS-ON LEARNING, AND MAKING STUDENTS COMFORTABLE WITH BOTH THEORETICAL AND PRACTICAL ASPECTS OF COMPUTER SCIENCE.

THROUGHOUT HIS CAREER, ANSHUMAN KUMAR MISHRA HAS AUTHORED OVER 25 BOOKS ON A WIDE RANGE OF TOPICS INCLUDING PYTHON, JAVA, C, C++, DATA SCIENCE, ARTIFICIAL INTELLIGENCE, SQL, .NET, WEB PROGRAMMING, DATA STRUCTURES, AND MORE. HIS BOOKS HAVE BEEN WELL-RECEIVED BY STUDENTS, PROFESSIONALS, AND INSTITUTIONS ALIKE FOR THEIR STRAIGHTFORWARD EXPLANATIONS, PRACTICAL EXERCISES, AND DEEP INSIGHTS INTO THE SUBJECTS.

ANSHUMAN'S APPROACH TO TEACHING AND WRITING IS ROOTED IN HIS BELIEF THAT LEARNING SHOULD BE ENGAGING, INTUITIVE, AND HIGHLY APPLICABLE TO REAL-WORLD SCENARIOS. HIS EXPERIENCE IN BOTH ACADEMIA AND INDUSTRY HAS GIVEN HIM A UNIQUE PERSPECTIVE ON HOW TO BEST PREPARE STUDENTS FOR THE EVOLVING WORLD OF TECHNOLOGY.

IN HIS BOOKS, ANSHUMAN AIMS NOT ONLY TO IMPART KNOWLEDGE BUT ALSO TO INSPIRE A LIFELONG LOVE FOR LEARNING AND EXPLORATION IN THE WORLD OF COMPUTER SCIENCE AND PROGRAMMING.

Copyright Page

Title *Web3 for Students: From Zero to Blockchain Hero*

Author: Anshuman Kumar Mishra
Copyright © 2025 by Anshuman Kumar Mishra

All rights reserved. No part of this book may be reproduced, stored in a retrieval system, or transmitted in any form or by any means—electronic, mechanical, photocopying, recording, or otherwise—without the prior written permission of the author or publisher, except in the case of brief quotations in book reviews or scholarly articles.

This book is published for educational purposes and is intended to serve as a comprehensive guide for MCA and BCA students, educators, and aspiring programmers. The author has made every effort to ensure accuracy, but neither the author nor the publisher assumes responsibility for errors, omissions, or any consequences arising from the application of information in this book.

The Evolution of the Internet: Web1, Web2, Web3

The internet has undergone a significant transformation since its inception, evolving through three distinct phases: Web1, Web2, and Web3. Each phase represents a shift in how information is accessed, shared, and controlled.

◆ **Web1 – The Read-Only Web (1990s to early 2000s)**

Web1, the first generation of the internet, was characterized by its static and one-way nature. It was primarily a medium for consuming information, with limited user interaction.

- **Characteristics:**
  - **Only developers could create websites:** Creating and publishing content required technical expertise, limiting participation to a small group of individuals.
  - **Users could only read content:** Users were primarily passive consumers of information. There were no features for user-generated content, logins, or comments.
  - **No interaction or personalization:** Websites offered a fixed set of information, with little to no customization or personalized experiences.
- **Example:**
  - Imagine visiting a classic encyclopedia online. You could search for and read articles, but you couldn't edit them, discuss them with other readers, or save your favorite articles in a personalized way. A basic news website from 1998 exemplifies this: users could read headlines and articles, but features like liking, commenting, or sharing were absent. Early websites were often built using simple HTML, with limited styling and interactivity.

◆ **Web2 – The Read-Write Web (2004 onwards)**

Web2 marked a significant shift, enabling users to not only consume content but also to create, share, and interact with it. This era brought about the rise of social media, user-generated content, and interactive applications.

- **Characteristics:**
  - **Social media, blogs, e-commerce, cloud storage:** Web2 facilitated the development of platforms that allowed users to connect, share information, and conduct transactions online.
  - **Users can create accounts, upload photos/videos, and comment:** Users became active participants in the online ecosystem, contributing content, engaging in discussions, and building online communities.
  - **Data stored in centralized servers:** A key characteristic of Web2 is the centralization of data. User information and content are primarily stored on servers owned and controlled by large corporations.

- **Examples:**
  - Platforms like YouTube, Instagram, Facebook, Twitter, and Medium are prime examples of Web2. On YouTube, you can upload videos, subscribe to channels, and comment on videos. On Instagram, you can share photos and stories, follow other users, and engage with their content. Facebook allows you to create a profile, connect with friends, share updates, and join groups. These platforms thrive on user-generated content and interaction, but they also control the data associated with these activities.

◆ Web3 – The Read-Write-Own Web (Present & Future)

Web3 represents the next evolution of the internet, aiming to address the limitations of Web2 by introducing decentralization, user ownership, and trustless systems. It seeks to empower users with greater control over their data, identity, and digital assets.

- **Characteristics:**
  - **No single company owns your data:** In Web3, data is distributed across a network, rather than being stored in centralized servers controlled by a single entity.
  - **You control your identity and digital assets:** Users have greater autonomy over their digital identities and assets, which are often represented as tokens on a blockchain.
  - **You can earn from your content:** Web3 enables new models for content creation and monetization, allowing creators to earn directly from their work through mechanisms like cryptocurrency rewards and NFTs.
  - **Uses technologies like blockchain, cryptocurrency, smart contracts, and DAOs:** Web3 leverages these technologies to achieve its goals of decentralization, security, and user empowerment.
- **Examples:**
  - **Brave Browser:** This web browser rewards users with Basic Attention Tokens (BAT) for viewing privacy-respecting ads, giving users control over their attention and allowing them to earn from it.
  - **Audius:** This decentralized music streaming platform enables artists to connect directly with fans and earn cryptocurrency through tokenomics, bypassing traditional intermediaries.
  - **OpenSea:** This NFT marketplace allows users to buy, sell, and create non-fungible tokens, representing ownership of unique digital assets like art, collectibles, and virtual land.
  - **ENS (Ethereum Name Service):** ENS allows users to own human-readable domain names (like "yourname.eth") that are associated with their cryptocurrency wallets, simplifying the process of sending and receiving cryptocurrency and establishing a decentralized online identity.

✹ What Makes Web3 Revolutionary?

Web3 isn't just an upgrade; it represents a fundamental shift in the distribution of power in the digital world. It aims to move away from the centralized control of Web2 and empower individual users. Here's a detailed look at its key revolutionary aspects:

⚷ 1. Decentralization

- **Web2:** In the current Web2 paradigm, data is primarily stored on centralized servers owned and operated by large corporations. This gives these companies significant control over user information, making it vulnerable to censorship, single points of failure, and manipulation.
- **Web3:** Decentralization addresses this by distributing data across a network of computers (nodes) that are part of a blockchain. A blockchain is essentially a shared, immutable ledger that records transactions and information across this network.
- **Revolutionary Aspect:**
  - **No single point of control:** Data is not held by one entity, making it much harder for any single organization or individual to control or manipulate it.
  - **Increased resilience:** If one node in the network goes down, the data remains accessible from other nodes, enhancing reliability and reducing the risk of data loss.
  - **Censorship resistance:** It becomes significantly more difficult to censor information, as there's no central authority that can easily block or remove it.
- **Example:**
  - Imagine a decentralized social network built on a blockchain. Instead of your posts, profile information, and connections being stored on Facebook's servers, they are distributed across many computers in the network. If one computer fails, your data is still safe. No single entity can unilaterally decide to delete your account or censor your posts.

⚷ 2. Ownership & Identity

- **Web2:** In Web2, users typically create accounts on various platforms (e.g., Facebook, Google) and their digital identity and data are tied to these platforms. Users don't truly "own" their data; it's controlled by the companies providing the services.
- **Web3:** Web3 empowers users with greater control over their digital assets and identity through technologies like cryptocurrency wallets.
- **Revolutionary Aspect:**
  - **Self-sovereign identity:** Users can manage their digital identity without relying on centralized providers.
  - **True ownership of digital assets:** Users can own digital assets (like cryptocurrencies and NFTs) in a way that's similar to owning physical property.
  - **Reduced reliance on intermediaries:** Users can interact with applications and services without always needing to log in through or rely on large corporations.
- **Example:**

- With a cryptocurrency wallet (like MetaMask), you can store your cryptocurrencies and NFTs. This wallet is controlled by you, using a private key. You can use this wallet to interact with decentralized applications (dApps) without needing to create a traditional account or provide your personal information to each application. This gives you control over what data you share and with whom. You are not forced to "Log in with Google" or "Log in with Facebook," which gives those companies access to your data.

3. Trustless Systems

- **Web2:** In Web2, many interactions rely on trust in intermediaries. For example, when you buy something online, you trust the e-commerce platform and the payment processor to handle the transaction correctly.
- **Web3:** Web3 leverages smart contracts to create "trustless" systems.
- **Revolutionary Aspect:**
  - **Reduced need for intermediaries:** Smart contracts automate agreements and transactions, reducing the reliance on third parties.
  - **Increased transparency:** The rules of a smart contract are clearly defined in code, making them transparent and verifiable.
  - **Enhanced security:** Smart contracts are executed automatically and immutably, reducing the risk of fraud or manipulation.
- **Example:**
  - A smart contract can be used to automate the process of buying and selling a house. The contract can be programmed to transfer ownership of the property to the buyer once the payment is received and verified, without the need for a traditional escrow service. The code itself ensures that the rules are followed, eliminating the need to "trust" a middleman.

4. Financial Empowerment

- **Web2:** Traditional financial systems can be inaccessible to some, especially in developing countries, and often involve fees and intermediaries.
- **Web3:** Web3 offers new ways for users to participate in the digital economy and earn value.
- **Revolutionary Aspect:**
  - **Greater financial inclusion:** Anyone with an internet connection can potentially access and participate in these new financial systems.
  - **New earning models:** Users can earn money in various ways beyond traditional employment.
  - **Direct participation:** Users can directly participate in the governance and ownership of platforms and projects.
- **Examples:**
  - **Cryptocurrencies (Bitcoin, Ethereum):** These digital currencies enable peer-to-peer transactions without the need for banks, potentially reducing fees and increasing accessibility.

- o **NFTs (art, music, collectibles):** Creators can sell their digital creations directly to consumers, bypassing traditional intermediaries and potentially earning more from their work.
- o **Play-to-earn games:** These games reward players with cryptocurrency or NFTs for their participation, creating new economic opportunities.
- o **DAOs (Decentralized Autonomous Organizations):** These are community-led organizations with rules encoded in smart contracts, allowing members to collectively govern the organization and share in its success. Anyone can potentially participate and earn, even without a traditional bank account or formal employment.

☐ Real-World Use Cases You See Every Day

Web3 is rapidly moving beyond theoretical concepts and finding practical applications across various industries. Here's a breakdown of some emerging real-world use cases:

🎮 Gaming – Play and Earn

- **Web2:** Traditional online games often involve players spending money on in-game items, but these items are typically owned by the game developers and cannot be easily traded or used outside of that specific game.
- **Web3:** Play-to-earn (P2E) gaming leverages blockchain technology to give players true ownership of in-game assets.
- **Examples:**
    - o **Axie Infinity:** Players earn Smooth Love Potion (SLP) and Axie Infinity Shards (AXS) by playing the game. These tokens can be traded on cryptocurrency exchanges. In-game characters ("Axies") are represented as NFTs, meaning players own them and can trade them.
    - o **Decentraland:** This virtual world allows users to buy, sell, and develop virtual land (represented as NFTs). Players can create experiences, play games, and socialize within Decentraland, with opportunities to earn cryptocurrency.
- **How it works:** Game developers create in-game assets (characters, weapons, land, etc.) as NFTs. These NFTs are stored on a blockchain, and players acquire them through gameplay or by purchasing them. Players can then use these assets within the game and also trade them with other players, effectively turning gameplay into a potential source of income.
- **Impact:** P2E games are changing the gaming industry by:
    - o Empowering players with ownership.
    - o Creating new economic models within games.
    - o Potentially providing income opportunities, especially in developing countries.

🎨 Art and Music – Create and Monetize

- **Web2:** Artists and musicians often rely on intermediaries like galleries, record labels, and streaming services to distribute and monetize their work. These intermediaries can take a significant portion of the revenue and may limit the artist's control over their creations.
- **Web3:** NFTs offer a new way for artists and musicians to connect directly with their fans and monetize their work without intermediaries.
- **How it works:**
  - Artists can "mint" their digital artwork (images, videos, music) as NFTs on a blockchain. This creates a unique, verifiable record of ownership.
  - They can then sell these NFTs directly to collectors or fans on NFT marketplaces.
- **Impact:**
  - **Direct-to-fan model:** Artists can bypass traditional gatekeepers and build direct relationships with their audience.
  - **Increased revenue:** Artists can potentially earn more from their work by selling NFTs directly.
  - **New forms of artistic expression:** NFTs enable new forms of digital art and creative expression.
  - **Example:** A musician can release a song as an NFT. Fans who purchase the NFT not only own a piece of music but may also gain access to exclusive content, experiences, or future royalties.

💰 Finance – Decentralized Finance (DeFi)

- **Web2:** Traditional financial services are controlled by centralized institutions like banks, which can impose fees, restrict access, and lack transparency.
- **Web3:** DeFi aims to recreate traditional financial services (lending, borrowing, trading) on decentralized blockchains, making them more open, accessible, and transparent.
- **Examples:**
  - **Aave:** A lending and borrowing platform that allows users to lend and borrow a variety of cryptocurrencies without going through a traditional bank. Interest rates are determined by algorithms, and transactions are recorded on the blockchain.
  - **Uniswap:** A decentralized exchange (DEX) that allows users to trade cryptocurrencies directly with each other, without relying on a central exchange. Trades are facilitated by smart contracts, and liquidity is provided by users who earn fees.
- **How it works:** DeFi platforms use smart contracts to automate financial transactions. Users interact with these contracts using cryptocurrency wallets, enabling them to:
  - Lend and borrow cryptocurrency.
  - Trade cryptocurrencies.
  - Earn interest or fees.
- **Impact:**
  - Increased financial inclusion: DeFi can provide access to financial services for people who are unbanked or underbanked.
  - Greater transparency: Transactions are recorded on a public blockchain, making them auditable and transparent.
  - Reduced costs: By eliminating intermediaries, DeFi can potentially reduce fees and transaction costs.

☐ Digital Certificates

- **Web2:** Verifying the authenticity of documents like degrees, certifications, and licenses can be a cumbersome process, often involving contacting the issuing institution.
- **Web3:** Blockchain technology can be used to create tamper-proof digital certificates that are easily verifiable.
- **How it works:**
  - Universities, institutions, or organizations can issue digital certificates as records on a blockchain.
  - Each certificate is cryptographically secured, making it virtually impossible to alter or forge.
- **Impact:**
  - **Reduced fraud:** Tamper-proof certificates make it much harder to create fake credentials.
  - **Simplified verification:** Employers or other parties can instantly verify the authenticity of a certificate online, without contacting the issuing institution.
  - **Increased efficiency:** Streamlines the process of verifying credentials, saving time and resources.
- **Example:** A university can issue a student's degree as a digital certificate on a blockchain. The student can then share this certificate with potential employers, who can quickly and easily verify its authenticity by checking the blockchain record.

☐ Social Media 3.0

- **Web2:** Social media platforms are controlled by centralized companies that own user data, control algorithms, and can censor content.
- **Web3:** Decentralized social media platforms aim to give users more control over their data, content, and social networks.
- **Examples:**
  - **Lens Protocol:** A blockchain-based social graph developed by Aave, allows users to own their profiles and content, and control how they interact with other users.
  - **Mastodon:** While not strictly blockchain-based, Mastodon is a decentralized social network where users join independent servers, giving them more control compared to centralized platforms.
- **How it works:**
  - These platforms use blockchain or decentralized protocols to distribute data and control across a network of users, rather than relying on a central server.
  - Users may own their profiles and content as NFTs or through other blockchain-based mechanisms.
- **Impact:**
  - Reduced censorship: Content is less susceptible to censorship by a single entity.
  - Data ownership: Users have more control over their data and how it's used.
  - Algorithm transparency: Algorithms that determine content visibility can be more transparent and potentially controlled by the community.

☐☐ E-commerce & Loyalty

- **Web2:** E-commerce loyalty programs are often tied to specific platforms, limiting their utility.
- **Web3:** NFTs can be used to create more flexible and interoperable loyalty programs.
- **How it works:**
  - Web3 stores can issue NFTs as loyalty rewards to customers.
  - These NFTs can represent points, discounts, or other benefits.
- **Impact:**
  - **Interoperability:** Customers can potentially trade these NFTs or use them across different platforms or stores.
  - **Increased engagement:** NFTs can create more engaging and interactive loyalty programs.
  - **New marketing opportunities:** Businesses can use NFTs to create unique and collectible rewards.
- **Example:** An online retailer could issue NFTs to its most loyal customers. These NFTs could provide discounts, early access to sales, or exclusive merchandise. Customers could also trade these NFTs with other collectors or use them at partner stores.

⇐ Conclusion of Chapter 1

Web3 is not just about cryptocurrency. It's a **completely new internet** where **you have control, you own your digital life**, and **you can build, earn, and create freely** — from anywhere in the world.

This book is your **gateway to that future**. Whether you're an artist, coder, gamer, or curious student — this is where your **Web3 journey begins**.

30 MCQ QUESTIONS WITH ANSWER ON

1. Which web generation was primarily "read-only"? a) Web2 b) Web3 c) Web1 d) All of the above *Answer: c) Web1*

2. In Web1, who were the primary creators of website content? a) Users b) Companies c) Developers d) Governments *Answer: c) Developers*

3. Which of the following is a characteristic of Web1? a) Interactive content b) User-generated content c) Static web pages d) Centralized platforms *Answer: c) Static web pages*

4. Which web generation introduced social media and interactive applications? a) Web1 b) Web2 c) Web3 d) None of the above *Answer: b) Web2*

5. Which of the following is a key feature of Web2? a) Decentralization b) User-generated content c) Static web pages d) User data ownership *Answer: b) User-generated content*

6. In Web2, where is user data primarily stored? a) On the user's computer b) On decentralized networks c) On centralized servers d) On blockchain *Answer: c) Centralized servers*

7. Which of the following is an example of a Web2 application? a) A basic news website from 1998 b) YouTube c) A decentralized application (dApp) d) A blockchain *Answer: b) YouTube*

8. Which web generation is characterized as "read-write-own"? a) Web1 b) Web2 c) Web3 d) None of the above *Answer: c) Web3*

9. Which technology is a foundation of Web3? a) HTML b) JavaScript c) Blockchain d) CSS *Answer: c) Blockchain*

10. In Web3, who has greater control over their data? a) Large corporations b) Governments c) Users d) Internet service providers *Answer: c) Users*

11. Which of the following is a core principle of Web3? a) Centralization b) Intermediaries c) Decentralization d) Data control by single entities *Answer: c) Decentralization*

12. How is data primarily stored in Web3? a) On individual computers b) On company servers c) On blockchains d) In physical storage *Answer: c) On blockchains*

13. What is a key benefit of decentralization in Web3? a) Increased control by a single entity b) Reduced resilience c) Censorship resistance d) Single point of failure *Answer: c) Censorship resistance*

14. In Web3, users manage their digital assets using: a) Bank accounts b) Social media profiles c) Cryptocurrency wallets d) Email addresses *Answer: c) Cryptocurrency wallets*

15. What does Web3 offer in terms of digital identity? a) Identity controlled by companies b) Centralized identity management c) User-controlled identity d) No digital identity *Answer: c) User-controlled identity*

16. What are self-executing codes that remove the need for middlemen in Web3 called? a) Hypertext Markup Language b) Cascading Style Sheets c) Smart contracts d) JavaScript libraries *Answer: c) Smart contracts*

17. What is a key advantage of smart contracts? a) Increased need for trust b) Reliance on intermediaries c) Automated and transparent execution d) Centralized control *Answer: c) Automated and transparent execution*

18. Which of the following is a way users can earn in Web3? a) Traditional employment only b) Through centralized platforms only c) Cryptocurrencies and NFTs d) Only through bank accounts *Answer: c) Cryptocurrencies and NFTs*

19. What does NFT stand for? a) Non-Financial Transaction b) Non-Fungible Token c) New Financial Technology d) Network File Transfer *Answer: b) Non-Fungible Token*

20. What is a potential application of NFTs? a) Replacing physical currency b) Representing ownership of digital art c) Centralized data storage d) Traditional banking *Answer: b) Representing ownership of digital art*

21. What does DeFi stand for? a) Digital Finance b) Decentralized Finance c) Data Finance d) Distributed Finance *Answer: b) Decentralized Finance*

22. What is a goal of DeFi? a) To increase reliance on banks b) To create open and accessible financial systems c) To centralize financial control d) To eliminate digital currencies *Answer: b) To create open and accessible financial systems*

23. Which of the following is a characteristic of DeFi? a) Centralized control b) Lack of transparency c) Reliance on intermediaries d) Use of smart contracts *Answer: d) Use of smart contracts*

24. In Web3 gaming, what do players often own as NFTs? a) The game itself b) In-game assets c) The game company d) Other players' accounts *Answer: b) In-game assets*

25. How do artists benefit from NFTs? a) They rely solely on galleries. b) They earn directly from fans. c) They lose control of their work. d) They only sell physical art. *Answer: b) They earn directly from fans.*

26. Which of the following is a feature of Web3 social media? a) Centralized control b) Algorithm bias c) User data ownership d) Content censorship by a single entity *Answer: c) User data ownership*

27. What is a potential use of blockchain in digital certificates? a) Making them easier to forge b) Making them tamper-proof c) Centralized storage of certificates d) Eliminating the need for certificates *Answer: b) Making them tamper-proof*

28. How can Web3 stores use NFTs for loyalty programs? a) By issuing them as physical rewards b) By issuing them as digital rewards that can be traded c) By eliminating loyalty programs d) By restricting rewards to a single platform *Answer: b) By issuing them as digital rewards that can be traded*

29. Which of the following is a benefit of Web3 e-commerce loyalty programs? a) Reduced customer engagement b) Interoperability of rewards c) Centralized control of rewards d) Limited reward options *Answer: b) Interoperability of rewards*

30. Which of the following is NOT a core technology of Web3? a) Blockchain b) Cryptocurrency c) Smart contracts d) Centralized databases *Answer: d) Centralized databases*

10 MID SIZE QUESTIONS WITH ANSWER ON

1. Describe the key differences between Web1 and Web2, providing examples of technologies or platforms that exemplify each era.

- **Answer:**
    - **Web1 (Read-Only):** This was the internet's initial phase, characterized by static web pages and limited user interaction. Content creation was primarily restricted to developers.
        - **Key Differences:**
            - One-way communication.
            - Static content.
            - Decentralized, open protocols but limited user participation.
        - **Examples:** Personal websites, early search engines (Yahoo), static HTML pages.
    - **Web2 (Read-Write):** This era brought about interactive web applications and user-generated content, leading to the rise of social media and online platforms.
        - **Key Differences:**
            - Two-way communication.
            - Dynamic content.
            - Centralized platforms.
            - User participation and content creation.
        - **Examples:** Social media (Facebook, Twitter), video sharing (YouTube), e-commerce (Amazon).

2. Explain the concept of "centralization" in the context of Web2, and discuss its potential drawbacks. How does Web3 aim to address these drawbacks?

- **Answer:**
    - **Centralization in Web2:** Data and control are concentrated in the hands of a few large companies (e.g., Google, Facebook). These companies store user data on their servers and control access to it.
    - **Drawbacks:**
        - **Single point of failure:** If a company's servers go down, users lose access to their data and services.
        - **Data breaches:** Centralized databases are attractive targets for hackers.
        - **Censorship:** Companies can control what content is displayed and can censor user expression.
        - **Data exploitation:** Companies can monetize user data without users' full control or fair compensation.
    - **Web3's approach:** Web3 aims to address these drawbacks through decentralization. Data is distributed across a network of nodes (computers) on a blockchain, reducing reliance on central authorities and giving users more control over their data.

3. What are the core technologies that underpin Web3, and how do they contribute to its decentralized nature?

- **Answer:**
  - **Blockchain:** A distributed, immutable ledger that records transactions and data across a network of computers. It provides transparency, security, and decentralization.
  - **Cryptocurrency:** Digital currencies that operate on blockchain technology, enabling peer-to-peer transactions without intermediaries.
  - **Smart contracts:** Self-executing contracts with the terms of the agreement directly written into code. They automate processes and enforce agreements without the need for trust.
  - **Decentralized Autonomous Organizations (DAOs):** Organizations whose rules and governance are encoded in smart contracts, enabling community-led decision-making.

  These technologies contribute to decentralization by:

  - Distributing data across the network (blockchain).
  - Enabling peer-to-peer transactions (cryptocurrency).
  - Automating processes and removing intermediaries (smart contracts).
  - Facilitating distributed governance (DAOs).

4. Explain the concept of "user data ownership" in Web3, and contrast it with how user data is handled in Web2.

- **Answer:**
  - **User data ownership in Web3:** Users have greater control over their personal data. They can decide what data is collected, how it's used, and who can access it. This is often facilitated through technologies like blockchain-based identity solutions and self-custodial wallets.
  - **Web2 data handling:** In Web2, user data is primarily collected and stored by centralized companies. Users often have limited control over their data, and companies can monetize it through targeted advertising and other means.
  - **Contrast:** Web3 shifts the power dynamic, giving users more agency over their data, while Web2 places data control in the hands of large corporations.

5. Describe the concept of "trustless systems" in the context of Web3, and explain how smart contracts contribute to creating such systems.

- **Answer:**
  - **Trustless systems:** These are systems where users can interact with each other without needing to rely on trust in a central authority or intermediary.
  - **Smart contracts:** Smart contracts are self-executing agreements with the terms written directly into code. They automate the execution of these terms when predefined conditions are met.

- **Contribution:** Smart contracts enable trustless systems by:
  - Automating and enforcing agreements.
  - Making the rules of interaction transparent and verifiable in code.
  - Reducing the need for intermediaries to oversee transactions.
  - Ensuring that agreements are executed as coded, eliminating the risk of manipulation.

6. Discuss the potential of Web3 to enhance financial inclusion, providing examples of how it can benefit individuals who are underserved by traditional financial systems.

- **Answer:**
  - **Enhanced financial inclusion:** Web3 technologies, such as cryptocurrencies and DeFi, can provide access to financial services for individuals who lack access to traditional banking systems.
  - **Examples:**
    - **Cross-border payments:** Cryptocurrencies can facilitate faster and cheaper cross-border transactions, benefiting migrant workers sending remittances.
    - **Decentralized lending and borrowing:** DeFi platforms can offer lending and borrowing services to individuals without requiring traditional credit checks, potentially benefiting those with limited credit history.
    - **Access to financial services:** Individuals in developing countries with limited banking infrastructure can use cryptocurrency wallets to access a range of financial services.

7. Explain how Non-Fungible Tokens (NFTs) are changing the dynamics of digital content creation and ownership, particularly for artists and musicians.

- **Answer:**
  - **Changing dynamics:** NFTs are revolutionizing digital content creation by providing a way to represent ownership of unique digital assets.
  - **Impact on artists and musicians:**
    - **Direct-to-fan sales:** Artists can sell their work directly to fans, bypassing traditional intermediaries like galleries and record labels.
    - **Increased revenue:** Artists can potentially earn more from their creations by selling NFTs.
    - **New forms of monetization:** NFTs enable new revenue streams, such as royalties from secondary sales.
    - **Control and ownership:** Artists retain greater control over their work and its distribution.

8. Describe the core principles of Decentralized Finance (DeFi), and provide examples of DeFi applications that are becoming increasingly prevalent.

- **Answer:**
  - **Core principles:**

- Openness: Anyone can access and use DeFi protocols.
- Transparency: Transactions are recorded on a public blockchain.
- Decentralization: No single entity controls the system.
- Permissionless: No gatekeepers or intermediaries are required.
  - **DeFi applications:**
    - **Lending and borrowing platforms (Aave, Compound):** Users can lend and borrow cryptocurrencies.
    - **Decentralized exchanges (Uniswap, SushiSwap):** Users can trade cryptocurrencies directly with each other.
    - **Yield farming platforms:** Users can earn rewards by providing liquidity to DeFi protocols.

9. Discuss the potential benefits and challenges of using blockchain technology for digital certificates, such as academic degrees or professional certifications.

- **Answer:**
  - **Potential benefits:**
    - **Tamper-proof:** Blockchain-based certificates are extremely difficult to forge.
    - **Verifiability:** Employers and institutions can easily verify the authenticity of certificates.
    - **Efficiency:** Streamlines the verification process, saving time and resources.
    - **Accessibility:** Certificates can be easily accessed and shared online.
  - **Challenges:**
    - **Adoption:** Widespread adoption by institutions is needed.
    - **Standardization:** Lack of universal standards for blockchain-based certificates.
    - **Cost:** Implementing blockchain solutions can have upfront costs.
    - **Privacy:** Ensuring the privacy of certificate holders' data on a public blockchain.

10. How is Web3 changing the landscape of social media, and what are the potential advantages of decentralized social networks compared to traditional platforms?

- **Answer:**
  - **Changing landscape:** Web3 is moving social media towards decentralized platforms where users have more control over their data and content.
  - **Potential advantages:**
    - **Reduced censorship:** Less control by a single entity.
    - **Data ownership:** Users own their data, not the platform.
    - **Algorithm transparency:** Algorithms can be open-source or community-governed.
    - **Increased user control:** Users have more control over their experience and interactions.
    - **Examples:** Platforms like Mastodon (partially decentralized) and Lens Protocol are exploring these concepts.

CHAPTER 2: BLOCKCHAIN SIMPLIFIED – THE BACKBONE OF WEB3

🔍 What is a Blockchain?

A Blockchain as a Distributed Digital Ledger

Imagine a traditional ledger, like an accounting book, used to record transactions. In a traditional system, this ledger is maintained by a single entity, such as a bank or a company. A blockchain, however, is a *distributed* digital ledger. This means:

- **Digital:** It exists in electronic form, not as a physical book.
- **Ledger:** It records transactions or data.
- **Distributed:** Instead of being stored in one central location, the ledger is copied and shared across a network of many computers.

As you mentioned, "millions of computers around the world maintain and verify it together." These computers are often referred to as "nodes." Each node in the network holds a copy of the blockchain.

Blocks and Chains

The term "blockchain" comes from how data is structured:

- **Blocks:** Data is not added to the ledger one entry at a time. Instead, data is grouped into "blocks." A block contains a batch of recent transactions or data.
- **Chain:** These blocks are linked together in a chronological order, forming a "chain." Each new block contains a reference to the previous block, creating a secure and immutable connection.

☐ Simple Analogy: The Decentralized Google Doc

Your analogy of a Google Doc is excellent for understanding the core concepts:

- **Anyone can see:** Like a public Google Doc, a blockchain is often publicly accessible. Anyone can view the data recorded on it.
- **Everyone agrees on the changes:** When someone wants to add new data (a transaction) to the blockchain, the network of computers (nodes) must reach a consensus to verify and validate that data. This ensures that only valid information is added.
- **Once you write something in it, it can't be erased:** Once a block of data is added to the blockchain, it becomes extremely difficult, if not practically impossible, to alter or delete it. This immutability is a crucial security feature.
- **Decentralized storage:** Unlike a Google Doc, which is stored on Google's servers, a blockchain is distributed across thousands of computers (nodes) globally. This means there's no single point of control or failure.

Key Properties of a Blockchain

To summarize, a blockchain has these key properties:

- **Decentralization:** Data is distributed across a network.
- **Immutability:** Once data is recorded, it's very difficult to change.
- **Transparency:** Transactions are often publicly viewable.
- **Security:** Cryptographic techniques secure the data and transactions.
- **Consensus:** The network of nodes agrees on the validity of new data.

💡 Example: Buying an NFT Art Piece

Your example of buying an NFT art piece effectively illustrates how a blockchain works in a real-world scenario:

- **Web2:** In a Web2 system, a centralized website (like an online art marketplace) would record the transaction in its database. The record is controlled by the website owner.
- **Web3:** In a Web3 system:
  - The transaction (Anshuman buying "CryptoArt #77" from Maya) is grouped with other transactions into a block.
  - This block is added to the blockchain.
  - The blockchain records details like:
    - Block #123456
    - Buyer (Anshuman)
    - Seller (Maya)
    - Asset ("CryptoArt #77")
    - Price (0.5 ETH)
    - Date (21-Apr-2025)
  - This block is permanently stored and linked to the previous block, creating a secure and auditable record.

In essence, a blockchain provides a secure, transparent, and decentralized way to record and verify information, enabling trustless interactions and new possibilities across various applications.

☐ How Decentralization Works

Centralized Systems (Web2)

In Web2, the internet is largely organized around centralized systems. This means:

- **Central Authorities:** Data, services, and control are concentrated in the hands of a few powerful organizations.

- **Examples:**
    - o **Google:** Controls search, email (Gmail), cloud storage (Google Drive), and more.
    - o **Amazon:** Dominates e-commerce and cloud computing (Amazon Web Services - AWS).
    - o **Banks:** Control financial transactions and hold customer funds.
    - o **Social Media Platforms (Facebook, Twitter):** Control user data, content distribution, and platform policies.

Decentralized Systems (Web3)

Web3 aims to move away from this model by distributing control and data across a network of participants.

- **No Single Owner:** In a truly decentralized system, no single person, company, or entity owns or controls the entire system.
- **Distributed Data and Verification:** Data and the responsibility for verifying it are spread across a network of users, often referred to as "nodes."

Understanding Nodes

A node is a computer or device that participates in the network. Each node may:

- Store a copy of the blockchain (in the case of a blockchain network).
- Help to validate transactions.
- Contribute to the network's security.
- Participate in the network's governance (in some systems).

How Decentralization Works in Practice

Here's a simplified view of how a decentralized system functions:

1. **Transaction/Data Creation:** A user initiates a transaction (e.g., sending cryptocurrency, creating an NFT) or generates data.
2. **Propagation:** This transaction/data is broadcast to the network of nodes.
3. **Verification:** Nodes in the network verify the validity of the transaction/data. This process involves complex algorithms and consensus mechanisms.
4. **Consensus:** The nodes reach an agreement (consensus) on the validity of the transaction/data.
5. **Recording:** Once verified, the transaction/data is recorded on the blockchain (or distributed ledger).
6. **Distribution:** The updated ledger is distributed to all the nodes in the network, ensuring that everyone has an identical copy.

⬚ Centralized vs. Decentralized: A Comparative Example

Your table provides a great comparison. Let's elaborate on each point:

Feature	Centralized (Web2)	Decentralized (Web3)
Owner	One company (e.g., Google)	Community of users
Data stored	Central server	Distributed across thousands of nodes
Hack risk	Single point of failure	Extremely hard to hack (requires a 51% attack)
Transparency	Not fully visible	100% transparent; anyone can verify

- **Owner:**
  - ○ **Centralized:** A company like Google owns its servers, databases, and the software that runs its services. They have the ultimate say in how the system operates.
  - ○ **Decentralized:** In a blockchain network, the "owner" is the collective community of users and nodes that maintain the network. No single entity has absolute control.
- **Data Stored:**
  - ○ **Centralized:** Data is stored on servers owned and controlled by the central authority. For example, your emails are stored on Google's servers, and your shopping history is stored on Amazon's servers.
  - ○ **Decentralized:** Data is distributed across a large number of nodes in the network. Each node holds a copy of (at least a portion of) the data. This eliminates the risk of a single point of failure.
- **Hack Risk:**
  - ○ **Centralized:** Centralized systems are vulnerable to attacks because they have a single point of failure. If a hacker gains access to the central server, they can potentially compromise a large amount of data.
  - ○ **Decentralized:** Decentralized systems are much more resistant to hacking. To compromise the network, an attacker would need to control a significant portion of the nodes (typically more than 50% in a blockchain network), which is extremely difficult and computationally expensive, known as a "51% attack."
- **Transparency:**
  - ○ **Centralized:** The inner workings of a centralized system are often opaque. Users have limited visibility into how their data is used or how algorithms operate.
  - ○ **Decentralized:** Blockchain networks are often highly transparent. All transactions are recorded on the public ledger, and anyone can verify them. The rules of the system are typically open-source and publicly auditable.

In essence, decentralization aims to create a more democratic and resilient internet, where power and control are distributed among users rather than concentrated in the hands of a few powerful entities.

🔑 Key Concepts of Blockchain

A blockchain operates on several fundamental concepts that work together to create a secure, transparent, and decentralized system. Let's explore these in detail:

🎁 1. Blocks

A blockchain is, at its core, a chain of blocks, and understanding what goes into a block is crucial.

- **What a Block Contains:**
  - **A list of transactions:** This is the primary data that the blockchain records. Transactions can represent anything from cryptocurrency transfers to the exchange of digital assets.
  - **A timestamp:** This records when the block was created, providing a chronological order for the transactions.
  - **A reference (hash) to the previous block:** This is a crucial element that links each block to the one before it, forming the "chain." It ensures the integrity and immutability of the blockchain.
  - **A unique hash (digital fingerprint) of its own:** Each block has a unique identifier, a cryptographic hash, that represents the block's data.
- **Block Formation and Addition:**
  - When a certain amount of transaction data is accumulated, it's bundled together into a new block.
  - Once the block is filled and validated, it's "locked" and permanently added to the chain.
  - This process continues, with each new block linking back to the previous one, creating a chain of blocks.
- **💡 Example:**
  - You've provided a good example:
    - **Block #01:**
      - 10:00 AM – A sent 1 ETH to B
      - 10:05 AM – C sent 0.5 ETH to D
    - This block contains two transactions and is assigned a unique hash.
    - **Block #02:**
      - 10:10 AM – E bought NFT #44
    - Block #02 contains a transaction, a timestamp, *and* a hash of Block #01. This hash is what creates the link between the two blocks.

☐ 2. Nodes

Nodes are the backbone of a blockchain network. They are the computers that maintain and operate the system.

- **Role of Nodes:**
  - **Store the full copy of the blockchain:** Each node typically stores a complete copy of the entire blockchain, ensuring that the data is distributed and redundant.

- **Validate and verify new transactions:** When a new transaction is initiated, nodes in the network check its validity. This involves verifying that the sender has sufficient funds and that the transaction is correctly formatted.
- **Keep the network running:** Nodes participate in the consensus process, which is how the network agrees on which transactions are valid and which blocks should be added to the chain. They also communicate with each other to keep the network synchronized.
- 💡 **Example:**
  - You used the example of 10,000 computers (nodes) spread across the world.
    - When you send cryptocurrency, your transaction is broadcast to these nodes.
    - Each node checks the transaction's validity (e.g., does the sender have enough funds?).
    - If a majority of the nodes agree that the transaction is valid, it is included in the next block.

🔐 3. Hashing

Hashing is a crucial cryptographic technique used in blockchains to ensure data integrity and security.

- **What is Hashing?**
  - A hash function is a mathematical algorithm that takes an input of any size (data) and produces a fixed-size output, called a hash.
  - The hash is like a unique "fingerprint" of the data.
  - Hash functions have specific properties:
    - Deterministic: The same input always produces the same hash.
    - One-way: It's computationally infeasible to reverse the process and get the original data from the hash.
    - Collision-resistant: It's extremely difficult to find two different inputs that produce the same hash.
- **Hashing in Blockchain:**
  - Each block in a blockchain contains the hash of the previous block, creating the chain.
  - Each block also has its own unique hash, calculated from the data within the block.
- **Data Integrity:**
  - If even a single bit of data within a block is changed, the block's hash will change completely.
  - Because each block's hash is included in the next block, any tampering with a previous block will change all subsequent hashes, making it immediately detectable.
- 💡 **Example:**
  - You provided a clear example:
    - Original data: "Anshuman paid Maya 0.5 ETH"
    - Hash: A1B2C3...

- Changed data: "Anshuman paid Maya 0.6 ETH"
- Hash: Z9Y8X7...
  - As you noted, this demonstrates how a tiny change in the data results in a completely different hash, ensuring that any data alteration is easily detectable.

☐ 4. Consensus Mechanism

Because a blockchain is maintained by a distributed network of nodes, there needs to be a way for these nodes to agree on the state of the blockchain and the validity of new transactions. This is where consensus mechanisms come in.

- **What is a Consensus Mechanism?**
  - A consensus mechanism is a set of rules and procedures that allows the nodes in a blockchain network to reach agreement on which transactions are valid and which blocks should be added to the chain.
  - It ensures that all nodes have a consistent and synchronized view of the blockchain.
- **Common Consensus Methods:**
  - **Proof of Work (PoW):**
    - Used by Bitcoin.
    - Nodes (called "miners") compete to solve a complex mathematical puzzle.
    - The first miner to solve the puzzle gets to add the new block to the chain and is rewarded with cryptocurrency.
    - Requires significant computational power and energy.
  - **Proof of Stake (PoS):**
    - Used by Ethereum 2.0 and other blockchains.
    - Nodes ("validators") stake a certain amount of their cryptocurrency to participate in the process of validating transactions and creating new blocks.
    - Validators are selected to create new blocks based on factors like the amount of cryptocurrency they stake and how long they have been staking.
    - More energy-efficient than PoW.
- 💡 **Example:**
  - Your analogy of 100 students in a class is helpful:
    - One student says, "Anshuman submitted the assignment."
    - Before the class record is updated, a majority (60+) of the students must agree, saying, "Yes, we saw it."
    - Only then is the record added.
  - In a blockchain, nodes perform this "agreement" process using the chosen consensus mechanism (PoW or PoS) to ensure that only valid transactions are added to the chain.

Decentralization: No Single Authority Controls Data

Reason: In Web2, our data and online interactions are largely controlled by centralized entities like social media platforms, search engines, and e-commerce giants. These companies own the servers, the data, and the rules. This centralization can lead to issues like censorship, data breaches, and a lack of user control.

Impact (Web3 empowered by Blockchain): Blockchain, by its very nature, is a distributed ledger technology. Data is not stored in a single location but is spread across a network of computers (nodes). This decentralization eliminates the single point of failure and control.

Example:

- **Cryptocurrencies like Bitcoin and Ethereum:** These are prime examples of decentralized systems. No single bank or government controls them. Transactions are verified by a distributed network of miners or validators.
- **Decentralized Social Media (DeSo) platforms:** Unlike traditional social media where a company owns your posts and profile, platforms built on blockchains allow users to own their content and data, making censorship much more difficult.
- **Decentralized Autonomous Organizations (DAOs):** These are organizations where rules and governance are encoded on a blockchain and decisions are made by token holders, rather than a central authority.

Transparency: Anyone Can See Transactions Anytime

Reason: In many traditional systems, transactions and data are opaque. We often have to trust intermediaries and have limited visibility into how things work behind the scenes.

Impact (Web3 empowered by Blockchain): Most blockchains are public and transparent. Every transaction recorded on the blockchain is publicly viewable and auditable. While the identities of the participants might be pseudonymous, the transaction history is immutable and accessible to anyone with an internet connection.

Example:

- **Checking Bitcoin transactions on a block explorer:** You can enter any Bitcoin address or transaction ID into a block explorer and see the entire history of transactions associated with it.
- **Supply Chain Management:** Blockchains are being used to create transparent supply chains where consumers can track the origin and journey of products, ensuring authenticity and ethical sourcing.
- **Decentralized Finance (DeFi) protocols:** All transactions and smart contract interactions on public blockchains like Ethereum are transparent, allowing users to verify the logic and activity of these financial applications.

Security: Tamper-Proof and Hard to Hack

Reason: Centralized databases are vulnerable to single points of attack. If a hacker gains access to the central server, they can potentially compromise vast amounts of data.

Impact (Web3 empowered by Blockchain): The cryptographic nature of blockchain, combined with its distributed consensus mechanisms, makes it incredibly secure and resistant to tampering. Once a transaction is recorded on the blockchain and confirmed, it is virtually impossible to alter or delete it. To tamper with the blockchain, an attacker would need to simultaneously control a majority of the network's nodes, which is computationally infeasible in most established blockchains.

Example:

- **The immutability of medical records:** Storing medical records on a secure blockchain could ensure their integrity and prevent unauthorized modifications.
- **Secure voting systems:** Blockchain-based voting systems can enhance transparency and security, making it harder to manipulate election results.
- **Non-Fungible Tokens (NFTs) and digital ownership:** The security of the underlying blockchain ensures the authenticity and ownership of digital assets represented by NFTs.

Trustless: No Need to Trust Anyone — Trust the System

Reason: Traditional online interactions often require trust in intermediaries. We trust banks to hold our money, social media platforms to manage our data, and online marketplaces to facilitate fair transactions.

Impact (Web3 empowered by Blockchain): Blockchain enables trustless interactions through the use of smart contracts. These are self-executing contracts with the terms of the agreement directly written into code. Because the code is transparent and runs on a decentralized network, parties can interact without needing to trust each other directly; they trust the code and the underlying blockchain network.

Example:

- **Decentralized Exchanges (DEXs):** On a DEX, you can trade cryptocurrencies directly with other users without needing to trust a central exchange to hold your funds. Smart contracts automatically execute trades when the agreed-upon conditions are met.
- **Escrow services on blockchain:** Smart contracts can act as impartial escrow agents, holding funds until both parties in a transaction fulfill their obligations.
- **Automated market makers (AMMs):** These DeFi protocols use smart contracts to automatically facilitate trading based on predefined algorithms, removing the need for traditional order books and intermediaries.

Ownership: You Truly Own Your Digital Identity, Tokens, and Assets

Reason: In Web2, our digital assets and identities are often tied to specific platforms. If a platform shuts down or changes its policies, users can lose access to their data and digital possessions.

Impact (Web3 empowered by Blockchain): Blockchain enables true digital ownership. Through cryptographic keys and non-custodial wallets, users have direct control over their digital assets, such as cryptocurrencies and NFTs. Your digital identity can also be more self-sovereign, not tied to a single platform.

Example:

- **Owning cryptocurrency in a non-custodial wallet:** You hold the private keys, giving you complete control over your funds, unlike keeping them on a centralized exchange.
- **NFTs representing ownership of digital art or collectibles:** When you own an NFT on a blockchain, your ownership is recorded on the immutable ledger and is not dependent on any single platform.
- **Decentralized Identity (DID):** Blockchain-based DID solutions aim to give users more control over their digital identities, allowing them to manage their data and selectively share information without relying on centralized identity providers.

In conclusion, blockchain technology provides the fundamental layers of decentralization, transparency, security, trustlessness, and ownership that are essential for realizing the vision of Web3. It's the bedrock upon which a more user-centric, open, and equitable internet is being built. Each of these reasons interlocks and reinforces the others, making blockchain not just a component of Web3, but truly its backbone.

⇽ Conclusion of Chapter 2

Blockchain is **more than just crypto**. It's the **foundation of Web3** — enabling freedom, privacy, and ownership in the digital world.

Understanding blockchain means you're understanding **how the future internet will run** — where power belongs not to Big Tech, but to **you**.

30 multiple-choice questions with answers covering the fundamentals of blockchain technology:

What is a Blockchain?

1. What is the primary function of a blockchain? a) To store data in a centralized database. b) To create a transparent and immutable record of transactions. c) To encrypt all internet communication. d) To manage social media accounts securely. **Answer: b)**

2. A blockchain is best described as a: a) Single, linear database controlled by one entity. b) Distributed, append-only ledger shared across a network. c) Cloud storage solution with enhanced security features. d) Type of advanced encryption algorithm. **Answer: b)**

3. What is the significance of the "chain" in blockchain? a) It refers to the physical cables connecting computers in the network. b) It indicates the chronological and linked nature of blocks of data. c) It describes the hierarchical structure of the network. d) It's a metaphorical term for the continuous flow of data. **Answer: b)**

4. Which of the following is a core characteristic of blockchain technology? a) Centralized control b) Immutability c) Easy editability d) Single point of failure **Answer: b)**

5. Blockchain technology was initially popularized by: a) Social media platforms b) Online retail companies c) Cryptocurrencies like Bitcoin d) Government agencies **Answer: c)**

6. What type of data is commonly stored on a blockchain? a) Only financial transactions b) Any type of digital information or record c) Primarily images and videos d) Personal identification details **Answer: b)**

7. The transparency of a public blockchain means that: a) The real identities of users are always visible. b) Anyone can view the transaction history. c) Data stored is unencrypted and easily readable. d) The blockchain is controlled by a public entity. **Answer: b)**

8. Which of the following is NOT a typical benefit of using blockchain technology? a) Increased security b) Enhanced transparency c) Faster transaction speeds in all cases d) Reduced need for intermediaries **Answer: c)**

9. What is the fundamental unit of data storage on a blockchain? a) A node b) A hash c) A block d) A consensus mechanism **Answer: c)**

10. What makes the data on a blockchain resistant to tampering? a) Strong encryption of individual data entries. b) The decentralized nature and cryptographic linking of blocks. c) The physical security of the servers hosting the blockchain. d) The constant monitoring by a central authority. **Answer: b)**

How Decentralization Works

11. What does decentralization mean in the context of blockchain? a) Data is stored on a single, powerful server. b) Control and data are distributed across multiple participants. c) All users have equal administrative privileges. d) The network operates without any rules or protocols. **Answer: b)**

12. In a decentralized blockchain network, who typically maintains and validates the blockchain? a) A single administrator or organization. b) A distributed network of computers (nodes). c) Government regulatory bodies. d) The original creators of the blockchain. **Answer: b)**

13. What is a key advantage of decentralization in blockchain over centralized systems? a) Faster processing speeds. b) Lower energy consumption. c) Increased resilience to censorship and single points of failure. d) Easier data modification and updates. **Answer: c)**

14. How does the distributed nature of a blockchain contribute to its security? a) It makes the physical hardware more difficult to access. b) Attacking one node is insufficient to compromise the entire network. c) It automatically encrypts data as it is distributed. d) It allows for easier detection of malicious activity by a central authority. **Answer: b)**

15. What role do individual computers (nodes) play in a decentralized blockchain network? a) Primarily data storage. b) Verifying transactions and maintaining a copy of the blockchain. c) Controlling user access and permissions. d) Developing new features for the blockchain. **Answer: b)**

Key Concepts: Blocks, Nodes, Hashing, Consensus

16. What is a "block" in the context of blockchain? a) A single transaction record. b) A container holding a batch of verified transactions. c) A unique identifier for a user on the network. d) A cryptographic key used for security. **Answer: b)**

17. How are blocks in a blockchain linked together? a) Through physical connections between the computers. b) By containing a cryptographic hash of the previous block. c) By a central server that maintains the order. d) Alphabetically based on the timestamp of the transactions. **Answer: b)**

18. What is a "node" in a blockchain network? a) A single transaction within a block. b) A computer connected to the blockchain network. c) A cryptographic algorithm used for hashing. d) The process of reaching agreement on the network. **Answer: b)**

19. What is "hashing" in blockchain technology? a) The process of encrypting all data on the blockchain. b) The process of converting input data of any size into a fixed-size string of characters. c) The method of organizing blocks in a chronological order. d) The algorithm used to verify transactions. **Answer: b)**

20. What is a key property of a cryptographic hash function used in blockchain? a) It's easy to reverse the hashing process to get the original data. b) Even a small change in the input data results in a significantly different hash. c) Different input data can easily produce the same hash value (collision). d) The hash output size varies depending on the input data size. **Answer: b)**

21. What is the purpose of including the hash of the previous block in the current block? a) To reduce the size of the blockchain. b) To create a secure and tamper-evident chain of blocks. c) To speed up the transaction verification process. d) To allow for easier editing of past transactions. **Answer: b)**

22. What is "consensus" in the context of blockchain? a) The agreement among all users on the network about the validity of transactions and the state of the blockchain. b) The process of encrypting data before it is added to a block. c) The method of distributing copies of the blockchain to different nodes. d) The rules governing the creation of new blocks. **Answer: a)**

23. Which of the following is a common type of consensus mechanism used in blockchain? a) Centralized voting system. b) Proof-of-Work (PoW). c) Client-server architecture. d) Hierarchical database management. **Answer: b)**

24. What is the role of miners in a Proof-of-Work (PoW) consensus mechanism? a) To validate user identities. b) To solve complex computational puzzles to add new blocks to the blockchain. c) To store and distribute copies of the blockchain. d) To regulate the transaction fees on the network. **Answer: b)**

25. What is a potential drawback of the Proof-of-Work (PoW) consensus mechanism? a) Low security and susceptibility to attacks. b) High energy consumption. c) Slow transaction processing times. d) Lack of transparency in the validation process. **Answer: b)**

26. What is the primary goal of a consensus mechanism in a decentralized blockchain network? a) To ensure fast transaction processing. b) To prevent double-spending and maintain the integrity of the blockchain. c) To reduce the computational power required to run the network. d) To allow for easy modification of past transactions when needed. **Answer: b)**

27. In a blockchain, what ensures that all nodes have a consistent and up-to-date copy of the ledger? a) Centralized data synchronization. b) The consensus mechanism. c) Strong encryption protocols. d) Physical connections between nodes. **Answer: b)**

28. What is the significance of the cryptographic hash in linking blocks? a) It makes it easy to rearrange the order of blocks. b) Any alteration to a previous block will change its hash and invalidate all subsequent blocks. c) It allows for efficient searching of data within the blockchain. d) It compresses the data stored in each block to save space. **Answer: b)**

29. Which of the following best describes the relationship between blocks and the blockchain? a) The blockchain is a single block that grows over time. b) The blockchain is a chain of interconnected blocks. c) Blocks are independent databases that are occasionally synchronized. d) Blocks are temporary storage units before data is moved to a central server. **Answer: b)**

30. How does the concept of "trustless" relate to blockchain technology? a) Users must inherently trust the creators of the blockchain. b) The system allows participants to interact without needing to trust each other directly due to the transparency and security enforced by the blockchain itself. c) Transactions are always anonymous and cannot be traced. d) There are no rules or regulations governing the use of the blockchain. **Answer: b)**

10 mid-size questions with answers covering the fundamentals of blockchain technology:

1. **Explain the core concept of a blockchain in simple terms and highlight its key differentiating factor from a traditional database. Answer:** At its core, a blockchain is a distributed and immutable ledger that records transactions across many computers. Unlike a traditional database, which is typically centralized and controlled by a single entity, a blockchain's data is spread across a network, making it transparent, resistant to tampering, and eliminating the need for a central authority to verify transactions.

2. **Describe how decentralization is achieved in a blockchain network. What are the primary benefits of this decentralized structure? Answer:** Decentralization in a blockchain is achieved by distributing the ledger and the responsibility for validating transactions across a network of independent computers (nodes). No single entity controls the data or the network. The primary benefits include increased security (no single point of failure), enhanced transparency (transaction history is often public), and greater resilience to censorship and manipulation.

3. **What is a "block" in a blockchain, and what kind of information does it typically contain? How is a new block added to the existing chain? Answer:** A "block" is a container that holds a batch of verified transactions, a timestamp, and a cryptographic hash of the previous block. This hash is crucial for linking blocks together chronologically and securely. A new block is added to the chain after network participants (e.g., miners or validators) reach a consensus on the validity of the transactions within the proposed block and the block itself, following the rules of the blockchain's consensus mechanism.

4. **Explain the role of "nodes" in a blockchain network. What different types of nodes might exist, and what are their general responsibilities? Answer:** Nodes are individual computers connected to the blockchain network that participate in maintaining and validating the blockchain. Different types of nodes can exist, such as full nodes (which hold a complete copy of the blockchain and participate in validation) and light nodes (which rely on full nodes for transaction verification). Their general responsibilities include receiving and broadcasting transactions, verifying transactions according to the network's rules, and maintaining a copy of the blockchain.

5. **What is "hashing" in the context of blockchain security? Describe the key properties of a cryptographic hash function that make it suitable for this purpose. Answer:** Hashing in blockchain involves using a cryptographic hash function to generate a unique, fixed-size "fingerprint" of a block's data. Key properties of these functions include: determinism (the same input always produces the same output), preimage resistance (it's computationally infeasible to find the original input from the hash), second preimage resistance (it's hard to find a different input that produces the same hash as a given input), and collision resistance (it's very difficult to find two different inputs that produce the same hash). These properties ensure the integrity of the data within each block and the secure linking of blocks.

6. **Describe the concept of "consensus" in a blockchain network. Why is it necessary, and what are the general principles that consensus mechanisms aim to achieve? Answer:** Consensus in a blockchain refers to the mechanism by which all or a majority of the nodes in the network agree on the validity of new transactions and the state of the blockchain. It's necessary to ensure that all participants have a consistent and trustworthy record of transactions, preventing fraud and double-spending. Consensus mechanisms aim to achieve agreement, fault tolerance (the network can still function even if some nodes fail or act maliciously), and immutability (once a transaction is agreed upon, it's very difficult to alter).

7. **Compare and contrast two common consensus mechanisms, such as Proof-of-Work (PoW) and Proof-of-Stake (PoS), highlighting their key differences in how consensus is achieved and their respective advantages and disadvantages. Answer:**
   - **Proof-of-Work (PoW):** Participants (miners) compete to solve complex computational puzzles. The first to find a solution gets to add the next block and is rewarded.
     - **Advantage:** Proven security track record (used by Bitcoin).
     - **Disadvantage:** High energy consumption.
   - **Proof-of-Stake (PoS):** Participants (validators) stake a certain amount of their cryptocurrency to have a chance to be selected to propose and validate new blocks. The probability of being selected is often proportional to the amount staked.
     - **Advantage:** More energy-efficient than PoW.
     - **Disadvantage:** Can potentially lead to centralization if wealth accumulates in the hands of a few.

8. **Explain how the linking of blocks using cryptographic hashes contributes to the immutability of a blockchain. What happens if someone tries to tamper with a transaction in an older block? Answer:** Each block contains a hash of the data within it and a hash of the previous block. This creates a chain where each block is cryptographically linked to the one before it. If someone tries to tamper with a transaction in an older block, the hash of that block will change. This change will then invalidate the hash recorded in the subsequent block, and so on down the chain. For the tampering to be successful, the attacker would need to recalculate the hashes of that block and all subsequent blocks, and also convince a majority of the network nodes that their altered chain is the correct one, which is computationally extremely difficult

9. **Discuss the concept of a "trustless" system in the context of blockchain. How does blockchain technology enable trustless interactions between parties who may not know or trust each other? Answer:** A "trustless" system in blockchain means that participants can interact and transact without needing to have inherent trust in each other or rely on a central intermediary. This is enabled by the transparency of the blockchain (rules and transactions are often publicly viewable), the immutability of the records (once a transaction is confirmed, it's very difficult to change), and the consensus mechanisms (ensuring agreement on the validity of transactions without relying on a single authority). The trust is shifted from individuals or institutions to the code and the distributed network itself.

10. **Beyond cryptocurrencies, what are some potential real-world applications of blockchain technology that leverage its key characteristics of decentralization, transparency, and immutability? Provide at least three distinct examples. Answer:**
    - **Supply Chain Management:** Tracking the origin and journey of goods to ensure authenticity, prevent counterfeiting, and improve transparency for consumers.
    - **Digital Identity:** Creating self-sovereign digital identities that give individuals more control over their personal data and reduce reliance on centralized identity providers.
    - **Voting Systems:** Developing more transparent and secure electronic voting systems to reduce the risk of fraud and increase voter confidence by providing an auditable and immutable record of votes.

CHAPTER 3: WHY STUDENTS MUST LEARN WEB3 TODAY

🎓 The Dawn of Web3: A World of Opportunities Awaits

The digital landscape is on the cusp of another monumental evolution, akin to the transformative power of the internet in the early 2000s and the mobile revolution of the 2010s. We are now witnessing the birth pangs of **Web3**, the next iteration of the internet. This isn't merely a fleeting trend; it's a fundamental shift in how we interact with the digital world, and for students stepping into this era, it presents an unparalleled opportunity to shape the future.

Whether your passion lies in coding, design, gaming, writing, or entrepreneurship, Web3 is not a niche corner of the internet – it's an expansive frontier offering avenues for everyone to contribute and thrive. Understanding and engaging with Web3 early on will equip you with the skills and knowledge to become the leaders and innovators of tomorrow.

🚀 1. The Exploding Realm of Web3 Career Opportunities

The emergence of Web3 has already sparked the creation of entirely new job roles – positions that were unimaginable just half a decade ago. The global demand for professionals with Web3 skills is experiencing an unprecedented surge, signaling a vibrant and rapidly expanding job market.

Let's delve deeper into some of the popular career roles within the Web3 ecosystem:

☐ Popular Career Roles in Web3:

| Job Role | What You Do | Example | Detailed Explanation only for direct connection to the blockchain network. | NFT Creator/Strategist | Design and market NFT collections | Create and sell NFT art on OpenSea | This role involves the artistic creation and strategic marketing of Non-Fungible Tokens (NFTs). An NFT creator might be a digital artist, musician, or any individual or brand looking to tokenize unique digital or physical assets. The strategist aspect involves understanding the NFT market, community building, and developing effective marketing campaigns to drive the value and adoption of the NFT collection. Platforms like OpenSea serve as marketplaces where these NFTs are bought and sold. For instance, a digital artist could create a series of unique digital paintings and sell them as NFTs to collectors, while a musician could tokenize exclusive songs or experiences. The strategist would then work on building hype and community around these creations.

🎨 2. Unleashing Innovation, Creativity, and Income Potential in Web3

Web3 represents a fundamental shift in the power dynamics of the internet. Unlike the Web2 era, where large corporations like Facebook, YouTube, and Instagram act as gatekeepers and central authorities, Web3 empowers individual creators and users with unprecedented control and ownership. This paradigm shift unlocks new avenues for innovation, fuels creativity, and establishes direct pathways for income generation, independent of traditional employment structures.

The Core Differences from Web2:

- **You Own Your Content:** In Web2, the content you create on platforms often belongs to the platform itself. They dictate the terms of use, monetization, and can even remove your creations. Web3, leveraging blockchain technology, allows you to truly own your digital assets. Whether it's artwork tokenized as an NFT or a blog post hosted on a decentralized platform, you have verifiable ownership and control over its distribution and use.
- **You Get Rewarded for Your Work:** Web3 introduces novel ways to directly monetize your contributions. Instead of relying solely on platform-driven advertising or centralized payment systems, creators can earn through mechanisms like direct sales of NFTs, cryptocurrency rewards for participation in decentralized communities, or revenue sharing models built into decentralized applications (dApps). This direct connection between value creation and value capture empowers individuals.
- **You Can Build Your Own Brand – Without Needing a Boss:** The decentralized nature of Web3 fosters a creator economy where individuals can build their own brands and communities directly. You are not bound by the hierarchical structures of traditional companies. Your reputation and success are built on your skills, contributions, and the value you provide to the ecosystem, rather than on climbing a corporate ladder.

💡 **Example 1: NFTs (Non-Fungible Tokens) – Tokenizing Creativity**

🎨 Consider the inspiring story of a **15-year-old artist from India** who transformed her digital artwork into **Non-Fungible Tokens (NFTs)** and remarkably **earned ☐30 lakh ($36,000)**. This exemplifies the democratizing power of NFTs.

Detailed Breakdown:

- **What are NFTs?** NFTs are unique digital assets that represent ownership of a specific item or piece of content. This could be anything from digital [1] art, music, videos, virtual real estate, [2] to collectibles. Each NFT is recorded on a blockchain, ensuring its uniqueness and verifiable ownership.
- **The Process:** The young artist likely created digital artwork using software like Procreate or Adobe Photoshop. She then used an NFT marketplace platform (like OpenSea, Rarible, or a local Indian platform) to "mint" her artwork as an NFT. Minting is the process of turning a digital file into a unique asset on the blockchain.
- **Selling and Earning:** Once minted, the NFT was listed for sale on the marketplace. Collectors and enthusiasts, recognizing the value or artistic merit of her work, purchased it using cryptocurrency. The smart contract associated with the NFT can even be programmed to give the original creator a percentage of any future resale value, ensuring ongoing income.

- **Impact:** This example highlights how Web3, through NFTs, bypasses traditional art market gatekeepers (galleries, agents) and allows creators, regardless of age or location, to directly connect with a global audience and monetize their talent.

💡 Example 2: Play-to-Earn Gaming – Earning While You Play

🎮 Games like **Axie Infinity** have pioneered the **Play-to-Earn (P2E)** model, where players can earn real cryptocurrency and valuable in-game assets (often tokenized as NFTs) simply by playing the game.

Detailed Breakdown:

- **How it Works:** In P2E games, players typically earn in-game tokens by completing tasks, winning battles, or developing their in-game characters and assets. These tokens can then be exchanged for other cryptocurrencies or fiat currency on crypto exchanges. In-game assets, like virtual land or unique characters, are often NFTs that can be bought, sold, and traded among players.
- **The Philippines Example:** The example of **students from the Philippines paying for their tuition using game income** is a powerful illustration of the economic opportunities P2E games can provide. In regions with lower average incomes, the earnings from these games can be substantial and life-changing.
- **Impact:** P2E gaming demonstrates how Web3 can blend entertainment with tangible economic benefits. It empowers players to not just be consumers of games but also active participants in a digital economy, earning rewards for their time and skill. This model has the potential to create new forms of digital employment and income generation.

💡 Example 3: DAOs (Decentralized Autonomous Organizations) – Collaborative Earning

🏛 Joining a **Decentralized Autonomous Organization (DAO)** like **"Bankless DAO"** offers a unique way to contribute your skills and earn cryptocurrency without the traditional constraints of employment. As a member, you can contribute as a writer, designer, moderator, or in various other roles based on your skills and the DAO's needs, and in return, you get paid in the DAO's native cryptocurrency.

Detailed Breakdown:

- **What are DAOs?** DAOs are community-led organizations governed by rules encoded on a blockchain (smart contracts). Decisions are made collectively by token holders through voting, rather than by a central authority.
- **Participation and Earning:** To become a contributor in a DAO, you typically join their online community (often on platforms like Discord or Telegram) and express your interest in contributing. DAOs often have specific working groups or projects you can join based on your skills. For example, Bankless DAO has working groups focused on writing newsletters, designing graphics, moderating discussions, and developing educational resources.

- **No Resume, No Interview:** Unlike traditional jobs, your entry into a DAO is primarily based on your willingness to contribute and the skills you bring to the table. There's often no formal resume submission or interview process. Your portfolio of work within the DAO and your level of participation speak for themselves.
- **Payment in Crypto:** Contributors are typically rewarded in the DAO's native cryptocurrency tokens. These tokens can have monetary value and can be exchanged for other cryptocurrencies or fiat currency. Holding these tokens also often grants you voting rights within the DAO, allowing you to participate in its governance.
- **Impact:** DAOs represent a new paradigm for work and collaboration. They empower individuals to contribute their skills to projects they believe in and earn rewards in a decentralized and transparent manner, fostering a sense of ownership and community.

💰 Income Potential in Web3 (Early Adopter Advantage)

The table below provides a glimpse into the potential income disparity between Web2 and Web3 roles, particularly highlighting the opportunities for remote and freelance work that perfectly suit students:

Skill	Web2 Monthly Salary (Local)	Web3 Monthly Earnings (Remote)
Coding	$500–$800	$1500–$5000
Design	$300–$600	$1000–$3000
Writing/Content	$200–$400	$800–$2000
Community/Mod	Volunteer-based	$500–$1500

Export to Sheets

Key Takeaways:

- **Global Reach:** Web3 opportunities are often remote and global, allowing you to work with projects and teams from anywhere in the world, potentially earning significantly more than local Web2 salaries.
- **Freelance Flexibility:** Much of the work in Web3 is project-based or part-time, offering students the flexibility to balance their studies with earning potential.
- **Early Adopter Advantage:** Just like early adopters of the internet and mobile technologies reaped significant benefits, students who learn and engage with Web3 now have a significant advantage in accessing these emerging and high-demand roles.

In essence, Web3 is not just a technological evolution; it's an economic and creative revolution that empowers individuals to own their creations, earn directly for their contributions, and build their own paths in the digital world, all without the traditional constraints of centralized platforms and hierarchical employment. For students, this presents an unprecedented opportunity to be at the forefront of this transformative era and shape their own futures.

☐ 3. How Web3 Will Shape the Future Economy: A Paradigm Shift

The advent of Web3 signals a profound transformation of the global economy, moving away from the centralized models that have dominated the internet era towards a more decentralized and user-centric system. This shift promises to redistribute power, wealth, and opportunities in unprecedented ways.

⬚ A Fundamental Shift: From Centralized to Decentralized Economy

The core distinction between Web2 and Web3 lies in the control and ownership of data and value:

- **In Web2, Companies Profit from Your Data:** The dominant business model of Web2 giants revolves around collecting, analyzing, and monetizing user data. Platforms like Facebook (now Meta), Google, and Amazon accumulate vast amounts of information about our online activities, which they then use for targeted advertising and other profit-generating activities. Users often have limited control over this data and the value it generates.
- **In Web3, You Control Your Data and Get Paid for Your Participation:** Web3 flips this model on its head. Built on blockchain technology, it empowers users to own their digital assets and data. Through cryptographic wallets and decentralized applications, individuals have greater control over their information and can potentially earn rewards for their engagement and contributions to various Web3 ecosystems. This could involve earning cryptocurrency for using a decentralized social media platform, contributing content to a Web3 knowledge base, or participating in the governance of a DAO.

💡 Examples of the Web3 Economy in Action:

Let's explore concrete examples of how this decentralized economy is taking shape:

🔐 Identity: Owning Your Digital Presence

- **The Web2 Problem:** In the current internet landscape, you need to create separate accounts with usernames and passwords for every website and application you use. This is cumbersome, compromises privacy, and leads to data silos controlled by individual platforms.
- **The Web3 Solution:** With Web3, you can own your digital identity through a **cryptographic wallet** like **MetaMask** or Trust Wallet. This wallet acts as your universal login and allows you to interact with various decentralized applications without the need for repetitive account creation. Your identity is tied to your wallet address (which can be pseudonymous), giving you more control over your data and how it's shared.
- **Example:** Imagine visiting a new decentralized social media platform. Instead of filling out a registration form, you simply connect your MetaMask wallet. The platform can verify your ownership of certain digital assets or your membership in specific communities directly from your wallet, without needing your personal details.

💼 Jobs: Borderless Opportunities Based on Skills, Not Degrees

- **The Web2 Limitation:** Traditional job markets often prioritize formal education and geographical location. Many opportunities are restricted by degree requirements and the need to be physically present in a specific office.
- **The Web3 Disruption:** Web3 opens up a global talent pool and emphasizes skills and contributions over traditional credentials. You can **work in DAOs** or for **global Web3 startups** remotely, contributing your expertise in areas like coding, design, writing, or community management, often without the prerequisite of a university degree. Your portfolio of work and your active participation within these ecosystems become your resume.
- **Example:** Consider a talented graphic designer in Ranchi. In Web2, their opportunities might be limited to local companies. In Web3, they can join a DAO focused on creating marketing materials for a decentralized finance (DeFi) protocol based in Europe, earning cryptocurrency for their contributions, all from the comfort of their home.

Money: Transacting with Crypto and Stablecoins

- **The Web2 Status Quo:** Our financial system is largely reliant on traditional banks and fiat currencies, which can involve intermediaries, fees, and geographical limitations.
- **The Web3 Alternative:** Web3 introduces **cryptocurrencies** like Bitcoin and Ethereum, as well as **stablecoins** (cryptocurrencies pegged to the value of traditional currencies like the US dollar), as alternative forms of money. These digital assets enable peer-to-peer transactions with potentially lower fees and faster settlement times, often without the need for traditional banking institutions.
- **Example:** A student freelancing for a Web3 project in another country can receive payment in a stablecoin directly to their crypto wallet. This transaction can be completed quickly and with minimal fees compared to traditional international bank transfers. They can then choose to hold the stablecoin, exchange it for other cryptocurrencies, or convert it to Indian Rupees through a cryptocurrency exchange.

Investment: Democratizing Access to Financial Opportunities

- **The Web2 Barrier:** Investing in early-stage companies, high-value art, or exclusive assets has traditionally been limited to accredited investors or those with significant capital.
- **The Web3 Democratization:** Web3 makes investment more accessible to everyone. **Tokenization** allows for fractional ownership of assets, meaning anyone can **invest in fractions of expensive art** as NFTs or participate in the early stages of Web3 projects by **investing in their native tokens**. This lowers the barrier to entry and allows a wider range of individuals to participate in wealth creation.
- **Example:** A student with a small amount of savings could purchase a fraction of a renowned digital artwork tokenized as an NFT. Similarly, they could invest in the early tokens of a promising decentralized application, potentially benefiting from its future growth.

Student-Driven Innovations: The Power of Early Engagement

The fact that many successful Web3 startups were founded by college students underscores the immense potential for young innovators in this space:

- **Lens Protocol:** Founded by Stani Kulechov (who also co-founded Aave), Lens Protocol is a **decentralized social media platform** built on the Polygon blockchain. It aims to be a Web3 alternative to platforms like Instagram, giving users ownership of their content, social graph, and monetization opportunities.
- **Mirror.xyz:** This is a **Web3 writing and blogging platform** that leverages blockchain technology to empower writers. Instead of relying on centralized platforms with their advertising models, writers on Mirror can **get paid in cryptocurrency** directly by their readers through crowdfunding, NFT sales of their articles, and other innovative monetization mechanisms.
- **Buildspace:** Founded by Farza TV, Buildspace is an educational platform focused on making learning Web3 accessible and engaging. It offers project-based learning where students **learn Web3 by building real-world projects and even get paid in crypto** for completing certain milestones. This incentivizes learning and fosters a practical, hands-on approach to Web3 development.

☞ **The Empowering Reality: You Don't Need VC Money – Just Skills and a Wallet**

These student-led startups highlight a crucial aspect of Web3: the reduced reliance on traditional venture capital (VC) funding in the early stages. With the ability to tokenize ideas, build communities directly, and earn through innovative mechanisms, aspiring entrepreneurs can bootstrap their projects with their skills and the support of the Web3 ecosystem, often starting with just a crypto wallet to receive and manage their earnings.

❋ **Why You Should Learn Web3 Today – A Summary of Benefits**

Reason	Benefit
💼 Future-proof careers	Be ahead of the curve, globally relevant
☐ Innovation playground	Build creative apps, games, communities
🪙 Earn while you learn	Freelance and remote gigs in crypto
🔑 Ownership & freedom	Control your identity, work, and money
☐ Global exposure	Work with international teams & projects

Export to Sheets

◎ **Action Plan for Students: Your Journey into Web3**

1. **Learn the Basics:** Start by understanding the foundational concepts of Web3, including blockchain technology, Non-Fungible Tokens (NFTs), and smart contracts. Numerous online resources, courses, and communities (like Buildspace) offer introductory materials.
2. **Create a Wallet:** Set up a non-custodial cryptocurrency wallet like MetaMask (for interacting with Ethereum and EVM-compatible blockchains) or Trust Wallet (for a

broader range of blockchains). This will be your gateway to interacting with Web3 applications.

3. **Build Your Profile:** Start showcasing your skills and interests on Web3-native platforms. GitHub is essential for developers, Mirror.xyz for writers, and explore decentralized social media platforms to build your online presence in the Web3 space.
4. **Join Communities:** Engage with relevant online communities on platforms like Discord, DAOs (find those aligned with your interests), and forums like LearnWeb3 DAO. These are invaluable spaces for learning, networking, and finding opportunities.
5. **Start Earning & Building:** Don't wait to become an expert. Begin creating, contributing to open-source projects, participating in DAO activities, and exploring freelance gigs in the Web3 space. Start earning cryptocurrency and building your portfolio.

The age of Web3 is not a distant future; it's unfolding right now. For students, embracing this technological and economic shift offers a unique chance to be pioneers, innovators, and leaders in the next era of the internet. The opportunities are vast, the barriers to entry are lower than ever, and the potential for impact is immense. The journey begins with learning and active participation.

✅ Conclusion:

"Students who learn Web3 today will not just get jobs — they will create jobs, build companies, and shape the next generation of the internet."

Web3 is not just about technology — it's about **opportunity, ownership, and empowerment**.

30 multiple-choice questions with answers covering career opportunities, innovation/creativity/income potential, and how Web3 will shape the future economy:

Career Opportunities in Web3

1. Which of the following is a key responsibility of a Blockchain Developer? a) Creating and marketing NFT collections. b) Analyzing cryptocurrency market trends. c) Building decentralized applications (dApps). d) Managing social media for Web3 projects. **Answer: c)**
2. What does an NFT Creator/Strategist primarily focus on? a) Securing blockchain code. b) Designing and marketing NFT collections. c) Analyzing crypto market data for investment decisions. d) Managing online communities for DAOs. **Answer: b)**
3. For which type of organization might a Crypto Analyst typically work? a) A traditional marketing agency. b) A decentralized autonomous organization (DAO). c) A centralized cryptocurrency exchange like Binance or Coinbase. d) A government regulatory body. **Answer: c)**

4. What is the main goal of a Web3 Marketer? a) Developing smart contracts. b) Promoting blockchain-based projects and brands. c) Auditing the security of Web3 platforms. d) Managing the technical infrastructure of a blockchain. **Answer: b)**
5. Which platform is often managed by a Community Manager in the Web3 space? a) A centralized database. b) A traditional email list. c) Discord or Telegram for a crypto project. d) A government website. **Answer: c)**
6. What is a defining characteristic of a Game Developer (Web3)? a) Primarily focusing on console-based games. b) Building play-to-earn games on blockchain platforms. c) Developing games that do not involve any digital assets. d) Working exclusively with traditional gaming studios. **Answer: b)**
7. The role of a Smart Contract Auditor is crucial for: a) Increasing the popularity of a crypto project. b) Ensuring the security and correctness of blockchain code. c) Designing the user interface of dApps. d) Managing the community engagement of a DAO. **Answer: b)**
8. How does a DAO Contributor typically participate in a decentralized community? a) By centrally controlling all decision-making processes. b) By passively observing discussions without any involvement. c) By actively contributing skills and voting on proposals. d) By solely investing financially without any other participation. **Answer: c)**
9. Web3 jobs are often characterized by which of the following features? a) Primarily requiring in-office presence. b) Limited to specific geographical locations. c) Frequently offering remote and global opportunities. d) Strictly requiring traditional academic degrees. **Answer: c)**
10. Learning Solidity programming is a key skill for which Web3 career role? a) NFT Creator/Strategist. b) Crypto Analyst. c) Blockchain Developer (especially on Ethereum). d) Web3 Marketer. **Answer: c)**

Innovation, Creativity & Income Potential

11. In Web3, who typically owns the content created by users? a) Large centralized platforms. b) The individual creators themselves. c) The blockchain network administrators. d) The initial investors in the Web3 project. **Answer: b)**
12. How can creators in Web3 directly benefit from their work? a) Solely through platform-based advertising revenue. b) By being rewarded with cryptocurrency and through direct sales of digital assets. c) Primarily through traditional copyright laws and enforcement. d) Only if their content is endorsed by major corporations. **Answer: b)**
13. What is a key characteristic of Non-Fungible Tokens (NFTs)? a) They are easily interchangeable and have the same value. b) They represent unique digital or physical assets with verifiable ownership. c) Their value is solely determined by centralized authorities. d) They cannot be bought or sold on open marketplaces. **Answer: b)**
14. Play-to-earn (P2E) gaming allows players to earn real value by: a) Only winning tournaments with large entry fees. b) Playing the game and earning in-game tokens or NFTs. c) Solely by streaming their gameplay on centralized platforms. d) By exploiting glitches in the game's code. **Answer: b)**
15. How do Decentralized Autonomous Organizations (DAOs) enable individuals to earn without traditional employment structures? a) By offering guaranteed monthly salaries regardless of contribution. b) By allowing members to contribute skills and get paid in

cryptocurrency based on their participation. c) By randomly distributing funds to token holders. d) By operating solely on volunteer labor with no monetary incentives. **Answer: b)**

16. What is a significant advantage for students looking for Web3 income opportunities? a) The requirement for extensive full-time commitments. b) The prevalence of freelance and part-time gigs. c) The need for expensive specialized equipment. d) The limited number of entry-level positions available. **Answer: b)**

17. Which of the following is a potential way for writers to earn in the Web3 ecosystem? a) Exclusively through traditional publishing houses. b) By getting paid in crypto for their content on platforms like Mirror.xyz. c) Primarily through likes and shares on centralized social media. d) Only by writing for established Web2 companies. **Answer: b)**

18. How does Web3 empower artists and creators compared to Web2? a) By increasing the control of centralized platforms over their work. b) By providing direct ownership and monetization possibilities. c) By limiting their audience to specific geographical regions. d) By making it harder to track and protect their intellectual property. **Answer: b)**

19. What is a key aspect of building a personal brand in Web3? a) Relying solely on endorsements from large corporations. b) Building a reputation based on your skills and contributions within decentralized communities. c) Primarily focusing on gaining followers on centralized social media. d) Maintaining anonymity and avoiding public engagement. **Answer: b)**

20. The income potential in Web3 for skilled individuals is often: a) Lower than traditional Web2 salaries for similar roles. b) Comparable to local Web2 salaries. c) Higher, especially for remote and freelance work. d) Entirely dependent on luck and market speculation. **Answer: c)**

How Web3 Will Shape the Future Economy

21. What is a fundamental shift in the economy driven by Web3? a) A move towards more centralized control of data. b) A transition from a decentralized to a centralized model. c) A shift from a centralized to a decentralized economy. d) No significant change in the underlying economic structure. **Answer: c)**

22. In Web3, who has greater control over their personal data compared to Web2? a) Large technology companies. b) Government regulatory bodies. c) Individual users themselves. d) The developers of blockchain protocols. **Answer: c)**

23. How do cryptographic wallets like MetaMask contribute to the Web3 economy? a) By centralizing user account information. b) By acting as a universal login and enabling ownership of digital identity. c) By restricting access to decentralized applications. d) By solely managing fiat currency transactions. **Answer: b)**

24. What is a potential benefit of Web3 for job seekers? a) A decreased demand for specialized skills. b) Limited opportunities outside of traditional corporate structures. c) Access to global job opportunities in DAOs and Web3 startups, often without strict degree requirements. d) A greater emphasis on geographical limitations for employment. **Answer: c)**

25. The use of cryptocurrencies and stablecoins in Web3 aims to provide: a) A more regulated and centrally controlled financial system. b) An alternative to traditional banking with potentially lower fees and faster transactions. c) A system solely focused on

large institutional investors. d) A less transparent and less secure method of financial exchange. **Answer: b)**

26. How does Web3 potentially democratize investment opportunities? a) By limiting investment to accredited and wealthy individuals. b) By making it easier for anyone to invest in tokens and fractionalized assets. c) By increasing the control of venture capital firms over early-stage projects. d) By making investment decisions solely based on centralized financial institutions. **Answer: b)**

27. Lens Protocol is an example of a Web3 startup focused on: a) Decentralized finance (DeFi). b) Decentralized social media. c) Play-to-earn gaming. d) Blockchain infrastructure. **Answer: b)**

28. What is the primary function of Mirror.xyz in the Web3 ecosystem? a) A platform for trading NFTs. b) A Web3 writing and blogging platform where writers can earn crypto. c) A decentralized cryptocurrency exchange. d) A tool for auditing smart contract security. **Answer: b)**

29. Buildspace facilitates the growth of the Web3 economy by: a) Providing venture capital funding to new startups. b) Educating individuals and paying them to build Web3 projects. c) Centralizing the development of blockchain protocols. d) Regulating the activities of decentralized autonomous organizations. **Answer: b)**

30. A key characteristic of the future economy shaped by Web3 is: a) Increased reliance on centralized intermediaries. b) Greater user control over data, identity, and value. c) A decrease in global collaboration and remote work. d) Limited opportunities for individual innovation and entrepreneurship. **Answer: b)**

10 mid-size questions with answers covering career opportunities, innovation/creativity/income potential, and how Web3 will shape the future economy:

1. **Discuss the evolving landscape of career opportunities in the Web3 space. Identify three distinct job roles and explain the core responsibilities and required skills for each. How do these roles differ from traditional Web2 counterparts? Answer:** The Web3 job market is rapidly expanding, offering roles that often didn't exist in Web2.
   - **Blockchain Developer:** Responsible for building decentralized applications (dApps) using blockchain technologies. Skills include programming languages like Solidity (for Ethereum), Rust (for Solana), and understanding of blockchain architecture. Unlike Web2 developers focused on centralized systems, they work on creating transparent and immutable applications.
   - **NFT Creator/Strategist:** Involved in designing, creating, and marketing Non-Fungible Token (NFT) collections. Skills include artistic creation (if applicable), understanding of NFT marketplaces, community building, and marketing strategies. This role is unique to Web3, focusing on tokenizing digital assets and building value around them.
   - **DAO Contributor:** Actively participates in the operation and governance of Decentralized Autonomous Organizations (DAOs). Skills vary widely depending on the DAO's focus but can include writing, design, moderation, research, and community engagement. Unlike traditional organizational roles, DAO contributors often work autonomously and are rewarded in cryptocurrency based on their contributions.

2. **Explain how Web3 empowers innovation and creativity compared to Web2. Provide examples of how creators can leverage Web3 technologies to express their creativity and potentially generate income in novel ways. Answer:** Web3 empowers innovation and creativity by granting creators ownership and control over their work, fostering direct interaction with audiences, and enabling new monetization models.
   - **Ownership via NFTs:** Artists can tokenize their digital art as NFTs, proving authenticity and scarcity, and sell directly to collectors without relying on traditional galleries. They can also program royalties into the NFT smart contract, earning a percentage of future sales.
   - **Decentralized Publishing:** Platforms like Mirror.xyz allow writers to publish their work directly to readers and monetize through cryptocurrency payments, NFT sales of their articles, and community support, bypassing traditional publishing gatekeepers.
   - **Interactive Experiences in the Metaverse:** Designers and developers can create immersive experiences and virtual assets within metaverse platforms like Decentraland or The Sandbox, allowing users to own virtual land and items as NFTs, and potentially earn by creating and selling these assets or offering services within these virtual worlds.

3. **Analyze the income potential within the Web3 ecosystem for individuals with various skills (e.g., coding, design, writing, community management). How does this potential compare to similar roles in Web2, and what factors contribute to these differences? Answer:** The income potential in Web3 can often be significantly higher than in Web2 for skilled individuals, especially for remote and freelance work. Factors contributing to this include:
   - **Global Demand:** The Web3 talent pool is still relatively small compared to the global demand, driving up compensation.
   - **Remote Nature:** Many Web3 roles are remote, allowing individuals to tap into a global market with potentially higher rates.
   - **Direct Monetization:** Web3 enables direct monetization through crypto payments, NFT sales, and DAO rewards, bypassing traditional intermediaries.
   - **Early Adopter Advantage:** Individuals who acquire Web3 skills early are positioned to capitalize on the growth of this nascent industry. However, income can also be volatile and project-dependent. While a Web3 coder might earn $1500-$5000 monthly remotely, a local Web2 coder in a developing region might earn $500-$800. Similarly, community managers in Web3 DAOs, often starting as volunteers in Web2, can earn $500-$1500 monthly in crypto.

4. **Discuss how Web3 is shifting the control and ownership of data compared to Web2. Explain the implications of this shift for individuals and the broader economy. Answer:** Web3 shifts data control and ownership from centralized platforms to

individual users. Through cryptographic wallets and decentralized applications, users have greater autonomy over their digital assets and information. Implications include:

- o **Enhanced Privacy:** Users can interact with services without constantly surrendering personal data to large corporations.
- o **Data Monetization:** Individuals may have the potential to control and even monetize their own data in the future.
- o **Reduced Censorship:** Decentralized platforms are less susceptible to censorship by single entities.
- o **New Business Models:** The economy may see the emergence of business models that directly reward users for their data and participation, rather than solely extracting value from them.

5. **Explain the role of Decentralized Autonomous Organizations (DAOs) in the future economy. How do they differ from traditional organizations, and what opportunities do they offer for individuals seeking work and participation? Answer:** DAOs are community-led organizations governed by rules encoded on a blockchain. They differ from traditional organizations by their decentralized decision-making processes (through token voting) and often transparent operations. DAOs offer opportunities for individuals to contribute their skills (writing, coding, design, etc.) and earn cryptocurrency rewards based on their participation, without the need for traditional resumes or hierarchical structures. This fosters a more meritocratic and globally accessible work environment.

6. **Analyze how Web3 technologies like blockchain and NFTs are impacting traditional industries beyond technology, such as art, finance, and supply chain management. Provide specific examples. Answer:** Web3 technologies are disrupting traditional industries:

- o **Art:** NFTs provide artists with a new way to sell and authenticate digital art, reaching a global audience directly and earning royalties on secondary sales (e.g., Beeple's NFT sale).
- o **Finance (DeFi):** Decentralized Finance (DeFi) platforms offer alternative financial services like lending, borrowing, and trading without traditional intermediaries,[1] potentially increasing accessibility and reducing fees (e.g., Uniswap, Aave).
- o **Supply Chain Management:** Blockchain can create transparent and immutable records of product origins and movements, improving traceability and accountability (e.g., using blockchain to track the journey of ethically sourced coffee beans).

7. **Discuss the potential of Web3 to foster student-driven innovation and entrepreneurship. Highlight examples of successful Web3 startups founded by**

students and explain why the Web3 environment is conducive to such ventures.
Answer: Web3 provides a fertile ground for student-driven innovation due to lower barriers to entry (less reliance on traditional funding), global reach from inception, and the ability to build communities around shared values and tokens. Examples like Lens Protocol (decentralized social media), Mirror.xyz (Web3 writing platform), and Buildspace (Web3 education) were started by young, often student-aged individuals. The "just skills and a wallet" ethos resonates with students who may lack extensive capital but possess technical or creative talents.

8. **Explain the concept of "earning while you learn" in the context of Web3. Provide concrete examples of how students can start generating income while still acquiring Web3 skills and knowledge. Answer:** Web3 offers various avenues for students to earn while learning:
    - **Contributing to DAOs:** Many DAOs reward active community members for tasks like writing, moderation, graphic design, or research with their native tokens.
    - **Freelancing for Web3 Projects:** Platforms and communities often have needs for basic coding tasks, content creation, or social media management that students can fulfill for crypto payment.
    - **Creating and Selling NFTs:** Students with artistic or creative skills can create and sell their digital work as NFTs on various marketplaces.
    - **Participating in Bug Bounties:** Some Web3 projects offer rewards (in crypto) for identifying and reporting security vulnerabilities in their code.

9. **Analyze the potential impact of Web3 on the future of digital identity and online interactions. How might owning your digital identity through wallets change the way we interact with online services and platforms? Answer:** Owning your digital identity through Web3 wallets like MetaMask has the potential to revolutionize online interactions by eliminating the need for repetitive account creation and centralizing personal data with individual platforms. This could lead to:
    - **Greater Privacy:** Users can selectively share information directly from their wallet, reducing the data footprint on individual platforms.
    - **Seamless Interoperability:** Your identity can be used across various decentralized applications without the need for separate logins.
    - **Self-Sovereign Identity:** Individuals have more control over their digital persona and the data associated with it.
    - **New Forms of Authentication:** Proof of ownership of certain digital assets in your wallet could serve as a form of authentication or access to specific communities or services.

10. **Discuss the challenges and opportunities associated with the transition to a Web3-driven economy. What are some potential hurdles that need to be addressed, and what are the most promising aspects for future economic growth and individual empowerment? Answer:** The transition to a Web3 economy presents both challenges and significant opportunities.

   o **Challenges:** Scalability of blockchain networks, regulatory uncertainty, user experience complexities, security risks (smart contract vulnerabilities, scams), and the need for widespread education and adoption are key hurdles.

   o **Opportunities:** Increased transparency and trust, new forms of digital ownership and monetization, democratized access to financial and creative opportunities, the potential for more equitable distribution of wealth, and the creation of entirely new industries and job roles are promising aspects for future economic growth and individual empowerment. Overcoming the challenges will be crucial to realizing the full potential of Web3.

CHAPTER 4: CRYPTOCURRENCY 101 – UNDERSTANDING DIGITAL MONEY

💰 What is Cryptocurrency? A Deep Dive into Digital Money

Core Definition:

At its heart, **cryptocurrency** is a **digital or virtual form of money** that utilizes **cryptography** for security. Unlike traditional fiat currencies (like INR, USD, EUR) issued and regulated by central banks, cryptocurrencies operate on a **decentralized** system, typically based on **blockchain technology**. This means no single entity, like a government or bank, controls or manages them.

Unpacking the Key Components:

1. **Digital Form of Money:** Cryptocurrencies exist purely in the digital realm. There are no physical coins or banknotes associated with them (although some projects might issue physical representations for novelty or marketing). All transactions and holdings are recorded electronically on a distributed ledger.
   - **Example:** When Rahul sends Bitcoin to the artist in France, no physical currency changes hands. The transaction is a digital record of Bitcoin moving from Rahul's digital wallet address to the artist's digital wallet address on the Bitcoin blockchain.
2. **Works Without a Central Bank:** This is a fundamental differentiator. Traditional currencies rely on central banks to issue, regulate, and manage their supply and value. Cryptocurrencies, being decentralized, operate independently of these institutions. Their supply is often predetermined by their underlying code, and transactions are verified by a distributed network of participants.
   - **Example:** The supply of Bitcoin is capped at 21 million coins, a rule written into its original protocol. No central authority can unilaterally decide to print more Bitcoin. Transaction verification is done by a network of miners who compete to solve complex cryptographic puzzles.
3. **Runs on Blockchain Technology:** Blockchain is the underlying infrastructure that makes most cryptocurrencies secure, transparent, and decentralized. It's essentially a distributed, immutable ledger that records every transaction in blocks that are cryptographically linked together.
   - **Example:** Every Bitcoin transaction, including Rahul's payment to the artist, is grouped with other transactions into a "block." This block is then added to the existing "chain" of blocks, with each new block containing a cryptographic "hash" (a unique digital fingerprint) of the previous block. This linking makes it incredibly difficult to tamper with past transactions.
4. **Secure (Encrypted Using Advanced Cryptography):** Cryptography is the backbone of cryptocurrency security. It involves using complex mathematical algorithms to secure transactions and control the creation of new units.
   - **Example:** When Rahul initiates the Bitcoin transaction, it's secured using digital signatures derived from his private key. This ensures that only he can authorize

the transfer of his Bitcoin. The blockchain itself uses hashing algorithms to secure the integrity of the blocks.

5. **Global (Can Be Sent/Received Across Borders):** Cryptocurrencies transcend geographical boundaries. Transactions can be sent and received anywhere in the world where there's internet access, often with lower fees and faster processing times compared to traditional international money transfers.
   - **Example (Revisited):** Rahul's Bitcoin payment reaches the artist in France within minutes, without being subject to the complexities and fees associated with traditional international bank transfers involving currency conversions and intermediary banks.

6. **Peer-to-Peer (No Middleman Like a Bank):** Cryptocurrency transactions typically occur directly between users (peers) without the need for intermediaries like banks or payment processors. The blockchain network itself verifies and records these transactions.
   - **Example:** Rahul's Bitcoin transaction is verified by the Bitcoin network's miners, not by a bank that needs to approve and process the payment. This peer-to-peer nature can reduce transaction fees and increase efficiency.

7. **Transparent (All Transactions Are Public on the Blockchain):** While the identities of cryptocurrency users are often pseudonymous (linked to wallet addresses rather than real names), all transactions recorded on a public blockchain are transparent and publicly viewable. Anyone can access the transaction history and balances of public addresses through a blockchain explorer.
   - **Example:** Anyone with Rahul's or the artist's Bitcoin wallet address could, in theory, view the transaction on a Bitcoin blockchain explorer, seeing the amount of Bitcoin sent and the time it was confirmed. However, they wouldn't necessarily know the real-world identities behind those addresses.

8. **Irreversible (Once Done, a Transaction Cannot Be Undone):** Once a cryptocurrency transaction is confirmed on the blockchain, it is extremely difficult, practically impossible, to reverse it without the recipient's consent. This is due to the distributed and immutable nature of the blockchain.
   - **Cautionary Example:** If Rahul mistakenly sends Bitcoin to the wrong address, there's no central authority he can appeal to for a reversal. He would need to rely on the honesty of the unintended recipient to return the funds. This highlights the importance of double-checking transaction details.

Beyond Basic Transactions:

The initial definition also touches upon the broader applications of cryptocurrencies:

- **Buying Goods and Services:** Increasingly, businesses are accepting cryptocurrencies as a form of payment for goods and services, both online and in some physical locations.
  - **Example:** An online retailer might accept Bitcoin or Ethereum for electronics, or a local coffee shop might accept cryptocurrency payments via a mobile app.
- **Trading and Investing:** Cryptocurrencies have become a popular asset class for trading and investment. Their volatile nature can offer opportunities for significant gains (and losses).

- **Example:** Individuals can buy and sell various cryptocurrencies on exchanges like Binance, Coinbase, or local Indian exchanges, hoping to profit from price fluctuations.
- **Smart Contracts and Decentralized Apps:** Many cryptocurrencies, particularly Ethereum, support the creation and execution of **smart contracts** – self-executing contracts with the terms of the agreement directly written into code. These smart contracts form the backbone of **decentralized applications (dApps)**, which offer a wide range of services without central intermediaries.
  - **Example:** A decentralized lending platform built on Ethereum uses smart contracts to automatically match lenders and borrowers, manage collateral, and execute loan terms without a traditional financial institution.

⬛ Types of Cryptocurrencies: Navigating the Digital Asset Landscape

The world of cryptocurrency is vast and ever-evolving, with thousands of different digital currencies in existence. While Bitcoin holds the crown as the first and most well-known, numerous other cryptocurrencies, collectively known as **altcoins** (alternative coins), serve various purposes and utilize different technologies. Let's explore some of the most important categories and examples:

1. Bitcoin (BTC) – The First and the King 👑

- **Launched in 2009 by Satoshi Nakamoto:** Bitcoin holds the distinction of being the original cryptocurrency, introduced by the pseudonymous entity Satoshi Nakamoto. Its whitepaper, published in 2008, laid the groundwork for a decentralized digital currency system.
- **Known as "Digital Gold":** Bitcoin has often been compared to gold due to its limited supply and its potential as a long-term store of value. Many investors see it as a hedge against inflation and economic uncertainty, similar to how gold has historically been used.
- **Maximum Supply is 21 Million (Scarcity = Value):** A fundamental aspect of Bitcoin's design is its fixed maximum supply. Once all 21 million bitcoins are mined (estimated to occur around the year 2140), no more will ever be created. This scarcity is a key factor contributing to its perceived value proposition. Basic economic principles suggest that limited supply coupled with increasing demand can drive up price.
- **Used as a Store of Value and for Long-Term Investment:** While Bitcoin can be used for transactions, its primary use case has evolved towards being a store of value – an asset held with the expectation that it will maintain or increase its value over time. Many investors "hodl" (a deliberate misspelling of "hold" that became a popular term in the crypto community) Bitcoin for the long term.
  - 🔍 **Example:** You correctly pointed out the significant appreciation of Bitcoin's value. If an investor had purchased 1 BTC in 2013 for around $100, its value peaked at over $69,000 in 2021 (and remains significantly higher than the initial investment today). This dramatic increase illustrates its potential as a long-term

investment, although it's crucial to remember the inherent volatility of the cryptocurrency market.

2. Ethereum (ETH) – The Smart Contract Platform ☐

- **Launched in 2015:** Ethereum emerged as a second-generation cryptocurrency, building upon the foundational principles of Bitcoin but with a significantly broader vision. It was conceived by Vitalik Buterin and others.
- **Ethereum is Not Just Money — It's a Platform for Building Decentralized Apps (dApps):** This is the key differentiator of Ethereum. While its native cryptocurrency, Ether (ETH), is used to pay for transactions on the network (known as "gas"), the Ethereum blockchain is primarily designed as a platform for developers to build and deploy decentralized applications (dApps). These dApps can offer a wide range of services, from decentralized finance (DeFi) to social media and gaming, all running on the transparent and secure Ethereum network.
- **Supports NFTs, DeFi (Decentralized Finance), DAOs, and Smart Contracts:** Ethereum's architecture is particularly well-suited for these innovative applications:
    - **NFTs (Non-Fungible Tokens):** Ethereum became the dominant platform for the creation and trading of NFTs, which represent ownership of unique digital or even physical assets.
    - **DeFi (Decentralized Finance):** A vast ecosystem of financial applications has been built on Ethereum, offering services like lending, borrowing, trading, and yield farming without traditional intermediaries.
    - **DAOs (Decentralized Autonomous Organizations):** Ethereum's smart contract capabilities enable the creation of DAOs, which are community-governed organizations with rules and decision-making processes encoded on the blockchain.
    - **Smart Contracts:** These are self-executing contracts with the terms of the agreement directly written into code. They automatically enforce the terms of an agreement when predefined conditions are met, without the need for intermediaries.
    - **🔍 Example:** Your crowdfunding dApp example perfectly illustrates the power of Ethereum's smart contracts. When someone donates Ether to the project through the dApp (which is essentially a user interface interacting with the smart contract), the smart contract automatically triggers the pre-programmed action of sending thank-you tokens to the donor's Ethereum wallet. This process is transparent, automated, and doesn't rely on a central authority to manage the rewards.

3. Altcoins (Alternative Coins) – The Rest of the Gang 🚀

The term "altcoins" encompasses all cryptocurrencies other than Bitcoin. This is a massive and diverse category, with each altcoin often having its own unique purpose, technology, and community. Here are some major examples and their general aims:

| Coin | Purpose | Detailed Explanation (Binance Coin) | Binance ecosystem, low-fee trading | BNB is the native cryptocurrency of the Binance ecosystem, one of the largest cryptocurrency exchanges globally. It is used to pay for transaction fees on the Binance exchange at a discounted rate and also powers various utilities within the Binance ecosystem, including Binance Chain and Binance Smart Chain (now BNB Chain). Its adoption within the extensive Binance platform gives it significant utility and demand.

💼 Use Cases of Cryptocurrency: Beyond Speculation and into Real-World Application

☐ 1. Payments: Transacting in the Digital Age

Cryptocurrencies are increasingly being adopted as a medium of exchange for goods and services, both online and in the physical world. While widespread adoption is still underway, the infrastructure and acceptance are steadily growing.

- **Buying Everyday Items:** You can now use cryptocurrencies like Bitcoin (BTC) and Ethereum (ETH) to purchase a diverse range of products and services, from your daily coffee to electronic gadgets and software subscriptions. The key is finding businesses that accept crypto as a form of payment.
- **Payment Gateways:** Platforms like **BitPay** and **Coinbase Commerce** act as intermediaries, simplifying the process for businesses to accept cryptocurrency payments. These platforms handle the complexities of crypto transactions, often converting the crypto received into fiat currency for the merchant, mitigating price volatility risks.
- **Accessibility and Convenience:** For consumers, using crypto for payments can offer benefits like potentially lower transaction fees compared to traditional credit card processing, and in some cases, enhanced privacy.
  - **Example:** As you mentioned, a student in Germany could pay for online coding classes offered by a platform that integrates with Coinbase Commerce using their Ethereum (ETH). The transaction is direct, potentially faster than a traditional bank transfer, and avoids the need for the student to have a specific credit card or go through a lengthy payment process.

☐ 2. Smart Contracts: Automating Agreements on the Blockchain

Smart contracts are one of the most revolutionary aspects enabled by blockchain technology, particularly on platforms like Ethereum. They are self-executing contracts where the terms of the agreement between buyer and seller are directly written into code.

- **No Need for Intermediaries:** Once deployed on the blockchain, smart contracts operate autonomously without the need for intermediaries like lawyers, escrow services, or traditional contract enforcement mechanisms.
- **Transparency and Immutability:** The terms of a smart contract are transparent and publicly viewable on the blockchain. Once the contract is created, it cannot be altered, ensuring trust and accountability among the involved parties.

- **Automated Execution:** The contract automatically executes the agreed-upon actions when the predefined conditions are met. This eliminates the risk of human error, delays, and potential manipulation.
  - **Example:** The scenario you provided with the online teacher and student perfectly illustrates a practical application of smart contracts.
    - **Condition:** The student submits the assignment.
    - **Action:** The smart contract automatically releases 0.01 ETH from the student's (or a pre-funded escrow) wallet to the teacher's wallet.
    - **Benefits:** This system ensures that the teacher gets paid promptly upon fulfilling their part of the agreement (grading the assignment, for instance, if that was also a condition) and the student knows their payment will be released once they complete the work. It eliminates the need for trust between the parties and reduces the potential for fraud or payment delays.

3. Decentralized Finance (DeFi): Reimagining Financial Services

Decentralized Finance (DeFi) is an umbrella term for a range of financial applications built on decentralized blockchain networks, primarily Ethereum. DeFi aims to recreate traditional financial services in a more open, transparent, and accessible manner, without relying on traditional intermediaries like banks.

- **Earning Interest (Lending):** You can lend your cryptocurrencies on DeFi platforms and earn interest, similar to depositing money in a savings account. The interest rates can sometimes be significantly higher than those offered by traditional banks, although they also come with their own set of risks.
- **Borrowing Against Crypto:** DeFi allows you to borrow funds by using your cryptocurrency holdings as collateral, often without the need for extensive paperwork or credit checks associated with traditional loans.
- **Decentralized Exchanges (DEXs):** DEXs enable you to trade cryptocurrencies directly with other users from your own wallet, without the need for a centralized exchange to hold your funds. This provides greater control and transparency over your trading activities.
  - **Example:** As you described, Ravi using **Aave**, a popular DeFi lending and borrowing protocol, to lend 100 USDC (a stablecoin pegged to the US dollar) and earn 5% annual interest demonstrates the potential of DeFi. Ravi maintains custody of his USDC in his own wallet and earns passive income without needing to deposit funds in a traditional bank account. The interest rates are determined by market supply and demand on the Aave platform, governed by smart contracts.

4. NFTs and Gaming: Tokenizing Digital Ownership and Rewards

Non-Fungible Tokens (NFTs) have opened up new avenues for digital ownership and have significant applications in the art, collectibles, and gaming industries.

- **Digital Art and Collectibles:** NFTs allow artists and creators to tokenize their digital creations, proving ownership and scarcity. This enables them to sell their work directly to collectors and potentially earn royalties on future sales.
- **Gaming:** Play-to-earn (P2E) games integrate cryptocurrencies and NFTs to reward players for their time and effort. In-game assets like characters, items, and virtual land are often tokenized as NFTs, giving players true ownership that they can trade or sell outside the game's ecosystem.
  - **Example:** The student creating a digital poster and selling it as an NFT on **OpenSea**, a prominent NFT marketplace, for 0.02 ETH (~$40) showcases the direct monetization of digital art enabled by NFTs. The student retains ownership of the copyright but transfers ownership of that specific tokenized version to the buyer. Similarly, a gaming app built on Polygon (MATIC) rewarding users with in-game tokens that can be traded for real items or other cryptocurrencies demonstrates the P2E model, where players earn tangible value for their engagement.

☐ 5. Global Remittances: Streamlining International Money Transfers

Traditional international money transfers through banks and services like PayPal can often be slow, expensive, and involve complex processes, especially for individuals sending smaller amounts or to regions with less developed financial infrastructure.

- **Faster and Cheaper Transfers:** Cryptocurrencies offer the potential for faster and significantly cheaper international money transfers, as they bypass the network of intermediary banks and currency exchange fees associated with traditional methods.
- **Accessibility for the Unbanked:** In regions with a high percentage of unbanked individuals, cryptocurrencies can provide a more accessible means of receiving and sending money internationally, provided they have access to a smartphone and internet connectivity.
- **Stablecoins for Reduced Volatility:** The use of stablecoins, cryptocurrencies pegged to the value of fiat currencies like the US dollar (e.g., USDT, USDC), can mitigate the price volatility associated with other cryptocurrencies, making them more suitable for remittances.
  - **Example:** The student in the Philippines receiving $300 in USDT (a stablecoin) from their US-based client instantly and with minimal fees highlights the efficiency of cryptocurrency for global remittances. The transaction bypasses traditional banking fees and currency conversion costs, allowing the student to receive the full value of the payment much faster.

📚 Summary – Why This Chapter Matters

Concept	What You Learn
✓ Cryptocurrency	Digital money, not controlled by governments
⊙ Blockchain use	Store, verify, and send money transparently
☐ Coins vs Tokens	Understand different types of crypto assets
☐ Real-world impact	Gaming, payments, smart contracts, finance

💡 Final Thought:

"Crypto is like the internet in 1999 — it's early, messy, exciting, and full of opportunities. Learning it today means building tomorrow."

30 multiple-choice questions with answers covering the basics of cryptocurrency, Bitcoin, Ethereum, altcoins, and their use cases:

What is Cryptocurrency?

1. What is the fundamental characteristic of cryptocurrency? a) It is a physical form of currency. b) It operates with a central bank's control. c) It is a digital form of money secured by cryptography. d) It is primarily used for government transactions. **Answer: c)**
2. Cryptocurrencies primarily rely on which technology for their operation? a) Traditional banking systems. b) Centralized databases. c) Blockchain technology. d) Government-issued ledgers. **Answer: c)**
3. A key feature of cryptocurrency is its: a) Centralized control. b) Lack of transparency. c) Decentralized nature. d) Easy reversibility of transactions. **Answer: c)**
4. How are new units of most cryptocurrencies typically created? a) Printed by a central authority. b) Minted through government decree. c) Mined or created through computer algorithms. d) Issued based on population growth. **Answer: c)**
5. Which of the following is NOT a typical use case for cryptocurrency? a) Buying goods and services. b) Trading and investing. c) Physical cash withdrawals from ATMs. d) Smart contracts and decentralized apps. **Answer: c)**
6. What does the "secure" feature of cryptocurrency primarily rely on? a) Physical vaults and guards. b) Advanced cryptography. c) Government regulations. d) The reputation of the issuing company. **Answer: b)**
7. The "global" nature of cryptocurrency means it can be: a) Only used within specific countries. b) Subject to strict international banking fees. c) Sent and received across borders. d) Controlled by international monetary funds. **Answer: c)**
8. What does the "peer-to-peer" feature of cryptocurrency imply? a) Transactions require approval from a central authority. b) Transactions occur directly between users without

intermediaries. c) All users must know each other personally. d) Transactions are always anonymous and untraceable. **Answer: b)**

9. The "transparent" nature of many cryptocurrencies refers to: a) The real identities of users being publicly visible. b) All transactions being publicly recorded on the blockchain. c) The ease with which transactions can be altered. d) The lack of any transaction history. **Answer: b)**

10. Once a cryptocurrency transaction is confirmed on the blockchain, it is generally: a) Easily reversible by the sender. b) Subject to modification by network administrators. c) Irreversible without the recipient's consent. d) Guaranteed to increase in value. **Answer: c)**

Bitcoin, Ethereum, Altcoins

11. Who is credited with launching Bitcoin in 2009? a) Vitalik Buterin. b) Satoshi Nakamoto. c) Charles Hoskinson. d) Changpeng Zhao. **Answer: b)**

12. Bitcoin is often referred to as: a) Digital Silver. b) Digital Oil. c) Digital Gold. d) Digital Currency 2.0. **Answer: c)**

13. What is the maximum supply of Bitcoin ever to be mined? a) 21 billion. b) 21 million. c) An unlimited amount. d) Determined by government regulations. **Answer: b)**

14. Ethereum was launched in which year? a) 2009. b) 2012. c) 2015. d) 2018. **Answer: c)**

15. What is the primary distinguishing feature of Ethereum compared to Bitcoin? a) It has a larger maximum supply. b) It is solely used as a store of value. c) It is a platform for building decentralized applications (dApps). d) Its transactions are always faster and cheaper. **Answer: c)**

16. Ethereum's blockchain technology enables the use of: a) Physical currency printing. b) Centralized banking operations. c) Smart contracts and decentralized finance (DeFi). d) Traditional stock market trading. **Answer: c)**

17. What term is used to describe all cryptocurrencies other than Bitcoin? a) Stablecoins. b) Tokens. c) Altcoins. d) Shitcoins. **Answer: c)**

18. What is the primary purpose of BNB (Binance Coin)? a) To function as a stablecoin. b) To power the Solana blockchain. c) To be used within the Binance ecosystem and for low-fee trading. d) To serve as a meme-based fun token. **Answer: c)**

19. Which altcoin is known for its focus on high-speed decentralized applications (dApps)? a) Cardano (ADA). b) Polygon (MATIC). c) Solana (SOL). d) Dogecoin (DOGE). **Answer: c)**

20. What is a key characteristic often associated with meme coins like Dogecoin (DOGE) and Shiba Inu (SHIB)? a) Strong fundamental technology. b) Primarily driven by community interest and online trends. c) Stable and predictable price movements. d) Wide adoption for real-world payments. **Answer: b)**

Use Cases: From Payments to Smart Contracts

21. Platforms like BitPay and Coinbase Commerce enable businesses to: a) Mine new cryptocurrencies. b) Develop their own blockchain. c) Accept cryptocurrency payments. d) Regulate cryptocurrency transactions. **Answer: c)**

22. What is a key benefit of using cryptocurrency for payments? a) Guaranteed price stability. b) Transactions are always free. c) Potential for lower fees and faster processing, especially internationally. d) Complete anonymity and untraceability. **Answer: c)**
23. Smart contracts are self-executing agreements where the terms are written in: a) Legal documents. b) Traditional databases. c) Blockchain code. d) Government regulations. **Answer: c)**
24. A primary advantage of using smart contracts is the reduction of: a) Transaction speed. b) Network security. c) The need for intermediaries. d) The transparency of transactions. **Answer: c)**
25. In a smart contract-based payment system, funds are typically released when: a) The payer manually confirms the transaction. b) A central authority approves the payment. c) Predefined conditions written in the code are met. d) The recipient requests the payment. **Answer: c)**
26. Decentralized Finance (DeFi) aims to: a) Centralize financial services under government control. b) Recreate traditional financial services on decentralized blockchain networks. c) Eliminate the use of any form of currency. d) Strictly regulate all cryptocurrency trading activities. **Answer: b)**
27. On DeFi platforms like Aave, users can earn interest by: a) Mining new cryptocurrency tokens. b) Lending their cryptocurrency holdings. c) Staking traditional fiat currencies. d) Operating centralized cryptocurrency exchanges. **Answer: b)**
28. Decentralized Exchanges (DEXs) allow users to trade cryptocurrencies: a) Through traditional brokerage accounts. b) Directly with other users from their own wallets. c) With the explicit permission of a central authority. d) Only for government-issued fiat currencies. **Answer: b)**
29. Non-Fungible Tokens (NFTs) are primarily bought and sold using which cryptocurrencies? a) Primarily fiat currencies like USD and EUR. b) Primarily Bitcoin (BTC) and stablecoins. c) Often Ethereum (ETH) and Solana (SOL). d) Only meme coins like Dogecoin and Shiba Inu. **Answer: c)**
30. Play-to-earn (P2E) games reward users with: a) Traditional in-game points with no real-world value. b) In-game cryptocurrencies and NFTs that can have real value. c) Physical prizes and merchandise. d) Discounts on future game purchases. **Answer: b)**

10 mid-size questions with answers covering the fundamentals of cryptocurrency, Bitcoin, Ethereum, altcoins, and their use cases:

1. **Explain the core concept of cryptocurrency and differentiate it from traditional fiat currency. Highlight at least three key characteristics that set cryptocurrencies apart. Answer:** Cryptocurrency is a digital or virtual form of money that utilizes cryptography for security and operates on a decentralized system, typically a blockchain. Unlike traditional fiat currencies issued and regulated by central banks, cryptocurrencies are not physically tangible, lack central authority control, and often offer features like global transferability, peer-to-peer transactions, and transparent, immutable records on the blockchain. Key characteristics include decentralization, cryptographic security, and transparency.

2. **Describe the significance of Bitcoin as the first cryptocurrency. What is its primary use case today, and what fundamental design principle contributes to its perceived value as "digital gold"? Answer:** Bitcoin, launched in 2009, holds immense significance as the pioneering cryptocurrency that introduced the world to decentralized digital money. While it can be used for payments, its primary use case has evolved towards being a store of value and a long-term investment, often referred to as "digital gold." Its fundamental design principle of a fixed maximum supply of 21 million coins creates scarcity, which, according to basic economics, can drive up value if demand increases.

3. **Explain the unique functionality of Ethereum beyond being just a cryptocurrency. What is the role of "smart contracts" on the Ethereum network, and provide a simple example of their application. Answer:** Ethereum, launched in 2015, is more than just a cryptocurrency; it's a platform for building decentralized applications (dApps). Its key innovation is the implementation of "smart contracts" – self-executing contracts with the terms of the agreement directly written into code [1] and stored on the blockchain. For example, a simple smart contract could automatically release cryptocurrency payment to a freelancer once a pre-defined deliverable is cryptographically verified as submitted.

4. **What are "altcoins," and why did they emerge after Bitcoin? Provide two examples of major altcoins and briefly explain their primary purpose or distinguishing feature. Answer:** "Altcoins" is the collective term for all cryptocurrencies other than Bitcoin. They emerged to address perceived limitations of Bitcoin or to introduce new features and functionalities.
   - **Solana (SOL):** Known for its high-speed transaction processing capabilities and its focus on building scalable decentralized applications (dApps).
   - **Cardano (ADA):** A blockchain platform that emphasizes peer-reviewed academic research and a layered architecture for scalability and sustainability.

5. **Discuss the use case of cryptocurrency for everyday payments. What are the current challenges hindering widespread adoption for this purpose, and what solutions are being developed to overcome these hurdles? Answer:** While cryptocurrencies can be used for everyday payments, widespread adoption faces challenges such as price volatility, transaction fees (depending on the network), and the complexity of using crypto wallets for the average consumer. Solutions being developed include stablecoins (cryptocurrencies pegged to fiat currencies to reduce volatility), layer-2 scaling solutions

to lower transaction fees and increase speed, and user-friendly payment gateways that simplify the process for both consumers and merchants.

6. **Explain the concept of "Decentralized Finance (DeFi)" and provide a concrete example of how individuals can utilize DeFi platforms to access financial services without traditional intermediaries. Answer:** Decentralized Finance (DeFi) refers to a range of financial applications built on decentralized blockchain networks, aiming to recreate traditional financial services in a more open and transparent manner. For example, platforms like Aave allow users to lend their stablecoins (like USDC) to borrowers and earn interest, all governed by smart contracts without the need for a traditional bank to act as an intermediary.

7. **Describe the role of cryptocurrencies in the realm of Non-Fungible Tokens (NFTs) and blockchain gaming. How do these technologies intersect to create new forms of digital ownership and economic models? Answer:** Cryptocurrencies, particularly Ethereum (ETH) and Solana (SOL), serve as the primary currencies for buying and selling NFTs, which represent ownership of unique digital assets. In blockchain gaming, cryptocurrencies and NFTs are often integrated to reward players with in-game tokens and allow them to own and trade unique in-game items as NFTs, creating "play-to-earn" economic models where players can earn real value for their participation.

8. **Analyze the potential of cryptocurrencies to revolutionize global remittances. What advantages do they offer over traditional methods for international money transfers, and what are some of the obstacles to widespread use in this area? Answer:** Cryptocurrencies offer the potential for faster and cheaper global remittances compared to traditional methods like banks and services like Western Union, as they can bypass intermediary fees and currency exchange costs. However, obstacles to widespread use include price volatility (for non-stablecoins), regulatory uncertainties in different jurisdictions, and the need for both senders and recipients to have access to and understanding of cryptocurrency wallets and exchanges.

9. **Discuss the security aspects of cryptocurrency transactions and the underlying blockchain. What cryptographic principles ensure the integrity and immutability of these systems, and what are some potential security risks users should be aware of? Answer:** Cryptocurrency transactions and blockchains rely heavily on cryptographic principles like hashing and digital signatures to ensure integrity and immutability. Hashing creates unique fingerprints of data blocks, and linking these hashes creates a tamper-evident chain. Digital signatures verify the authenticity of transactions. However,

users should be aware of risks like private key theft, phishing scams, and vulnerabilities in cryptocurrency exchanges or smart contracts.

10. **Considering the diverse landscape of cryptocurrencies and their various use cases, what are some of the key factors that contribute to the value and adoption of a particular cryptocurrency? Answer:** Several factors contribute to the value and adoption of a cryptocurrency, including its underlying technology and innovation, its utility and real-world use cases (e.g., payments, DeFi, NFTs), the strength and activity of its community and developer ecosystem, its scarcity (if supply is limited), its security and reliability, regulatory clarity (or lack thereof), and market sentiment and speculation. Strong fundamentals and increasing adoption for practical applications tend to drive long-term value.

CHAPTER 5: WALLETS & EXCHANGES – HOW TO HANDLE CRYPTO SAFELY

⚷ Public Key: Your Digital Address for Receiving Funds

Think of your **public key** as your **cryptocurrency address**. It's a string of alphanumeric characters that you can **safely share with anyone** who wants to send you cryptocurrency. Just like your email address allows people to send you emails, your public key allows others to send you crypto.

- **What it Does:**
  - **Receiving Funds:** Its primary function is to serve as the destination address for incoming cryptocurrency transactions. When someone wants to send you crypto, they will need your public key.
  - **Identification (Pseudonymous):** While you share your public key, it's not directly linked to your real-world identity unless you explicitly choose to connect them (e.g., when buying from an exchange that requires KYC - Know Your Customer verification). This provides a degree of pseudonymity.
  - **Derivation from the Private Key:** Your public key is mathematically derived from your private key using complex cryptographic algorithms. However, it is computationally infeasible to reverse this process – meaning someone with your public key cannot easily figure out your private key. This one-way relationship is essential for security.
- **Analogy: The Locker Number:** As you correctly pointed out, the public key is like the **locker number at a train station**. Anyone can see the number of a specific locker, and they know that if they want to put something *into* that locker, they need to use that number as the destination.
- 📌 **Example (Meera):**
  - Meera's public key: `0xAB34...9F2C`
  - When her friend Arjun wants to send her 0.01 ETH, he uses this public key as the "recipient address" in his crypto wallet or exchange interface. The transaction is then broadcast to the Ethereum network, indicating that 0.01 ETH is being sent to the address `0xAB34...9F2C`.

⚷ Private Key: Your Secret Key to Access and Control Funds

Your **private key** is the **secret and highly sensitive piece of information** that grants you the ability to **access and spend the cryptocurrency associated with your public key (address)**. It's like the unique digital signature that proves you are the rightful owner of the funds at that address.

- **What it Does:**
  - **Authorizing Transactions:** When you want to send cryptocurrency *from* your wallet, your private key is used to digitally sign the transaction. This signature acts as proof to the network that you, the owner of the funds at the associated public key, have authorized the transfer.

- **Accessing Your Wallet:** In many cryptocurrency wallets, your private key (or a seed phrase from which it can be derived) is required to access and manage your funds. Losing your private key is akin to losing the key to your bank account – you will likely lose access to your cryptocurrency.
- **Irreversible Loss if Lost:** Unlike a password that can often be reset, **if you lose your private key, there is generally no way to recover your funds**. Because of the decentralized nature of cryptocurrencies, there is no central authority to help you regain access.
- **Absolute Secrecy is Crucial: You should NEVER share your private key with anyone, for any reason.** Anyone who has access to your private key has full control over the cryptocurrency associated with that public key.

- **Analogy: The Unique Key to the Locker:** Your private key is like **your unique key to open that locker**. Only the person holding this key can open the locker and take out what's inside. If someone else gets hold of your key, they can also open the locker and take your belongings.

- 📌 **Example (Meera):**
  - Meera's private key is a long, complex string of characters that she keeps stored securely (e.g., written down offline and stored in a safe place, or secured by a robust password in a reputable crypto wallet).
  - When Meera wants to send some of her ETH to someone else, her crypto wallet software uses her private key in the background to create a digital signature for the transaction. This signature proves to the Ethereum network that the transaction is legitimate and authorized by the owner of the ETH at her public address (`0xAB34...9F2C`).

The Relationship Between Public and Private Keys:

The magic of cryptocurrency security lies in the mathematical relationship between public and private keys:

1. **One-Way Derivation:** The public key is derived from the private key, but the private key cannot be easily derived from the public key.
2. **Digital Signatures:** The private key is used to create digital signatures for transactions. These signatures can be verified by anyone using the corresponding public key, proving the transaction's authenticity and that it was authorized by the owner of the funds at that address.

Key Takeaways for Security:

- **Treat Your Private Key Like Cash:** Never store it online in easily accessible places. Consider offline storage methods (cold storage).
- **Be Wary of Sharing ANY Information Related to Your Wallet:** Phishing scams often try to trick users into revealing their private keys or seed phrases.
- **Understand the Irreversibility:** Once a transaction is signed with your private key and confirmed on the blockchain, it cannot be easily undone. Always double-check recipient addresses.

- **Use Reputable Wallets:** Choose cryptocurrency wallets with strong security features.

Understanding the distinction and the crucial roles of public and private keys is fundamental to using cryptocurrencies safely and effectively. Your public key is for sharing to receive funds, while your private key is the secret that grants you control over those funds and must be protected at all costs.

⬚ Hot Wallets vs. Cold Wallets: Balancing Convenience and Security in Cryptocurrency Storage

You've accurately described the two primary categories of cryptocurrency wallets: **hot wallets** and **cold wallets**. The fundamental difference lies in their connection to the internet, which directly impacts their convenience and security levels. Let's delve deeper into each type with more detailed explanations and examples:

🔥 Hot Wallets – Online & Easy to Access: Convenience at Your Fingertips

Hot wallets are cryptocurrency wallets that are **connected to the internet** in some way. This constant online connection makes them **convenient for frequent transactions, trading, and everyday use.** They are typically software-based and can take various forms:

- **Desktop Wallets:** Software applications installed on your computer (e.g., Exodus, Electrum).
- **Mobile Wallets:** Applications on your smartphone (e.g., Trust Wallet, Coinbase Wallet, Metamask mobile app).
- **Web Wallets:** Wallets accessible through a web browser (e.g., MetaMask browser extension, wallet interfaces on cryptocurrency exchanges).

✅ Pros of Hot Wallets:

- **Fast Access:** Being online allows for quick and easy access to your funds whenever you need them, making them suitable for active trading or making frequent small payments.
- **Ease of Use for Beginners:** Many hot wallets have user-friendly interfaces, making them relatively easy for newcomers to the cryptocurrency space to understand and use. They often integrate seamlessly with exchanges and dApps.
- **Good for Small Amounts:** Due to the inherent online vulnerability, hot wallets are generally recommended for storing smaller amounts of cryptocurrency that you intend to use regularly.
- **Often Free:** Most hot wallet software and apps are free to download and use, although some services integrated within them might have fees.

⚠️ Cons of Hot Wallets:

- **Hackable if Not Secured Properly:** The online connection makes hot wallets potentially vulnerable to hacking attempts, malware, and other online threats if not secured diligently. This includes ensuring your device is free from malware, using strong passwords, and enabling extra security features.
- **Vulnerable to Phishing and Scams:** Users of hot wallets are also susceptible to phishing attacks and social engineering scams that aim to trick them into revealing their private keys or seed phrases.
- **Reliance on the Security of the Device/Platform:** The security of your hot wallet is also dependent on the security of the device (computer or phone) it's installed on and the security practices of the wallet provider.

🔍 Example (Student Using MetaMask):

As you described, a student using **MetaMask** as a browser extension to interact with a Web3 game and collect NFTs benefits from its **fast access and seamless integration** with decentralized applications. They can quickly approve transactions and manage their in-game assets. However, the student wisely **enables 2FA (Two-Factor Authentication)** on their associated accounts (like their email and potentially their operating system) as an **extra layer of security** to protect their browser and wallet from unauthorized access. This helps mitigate some of the inherent risks of an online wallet.

❄ Cold Wallets – Offline & Extra Secure: Fort Knox for Your Crypto

Cold wallets are cryptocurrency wallets that are **not connected to the internet**. This offline nature significantly reduces their exposure to online threats, making them **ideal for the long-term storage of large amounts of cryptocurrency**. They typically come in two main forms:

- **Hardware Wallets:** Physical devices that store your private keys offline (e.g., Ledger Nano S/X, Trezor One/Model T, KeepKey). These devices are designed with security in mind and often require physical confirmation for transactions.
- **Paper Wallets:** Physical documents containing your public and private keys printed on them. While offering offline storage, they can be less convenient to use and carry risks of physical damage or loss.

✅ Pros of Cold Wallets:

- **Ultra-Secure:** Being offline makes cold wallets virtually immune to online hacking attempts, malware, and phishing scams. Your private keys are stored in a secure, offline environment.
- **Immune to Online Attacks:** As long as your private keys remain offline and secure, attackers cannot directly access your funds through the internet.

⚠ Cons of Cold Wallets:

- **Slightly Expensive:** Hardware wallets typically require a one-time purchase cost, ranging from around $50 to $200 or more, depending on the model and features.

- **Less Convenient for Frequent Transactions:** Using a cold wallet to make transactions involves connecting it to a computer, entering your PIN, and manually confirming the transaction, which is less convenient than using a hot wallet for frequent trading or small payments.
- **Potential for Physical Loss or Damage:** Paper wallets are susceptible to physical damage (water, fire) or loss if not stored securely. Hardware wallets can also be lost or damaged.
- **Slightly Technical for Initial Setup:** Setting up a hardware wallet for the first time might involve a slightly more technical process compared to downloading a simple hot wallet app.

🔍 **Example (Investor Holding Bitcoin):**

The example of an investor holding **2 BTC in a Ledger cold wallet** and storing it in a locker for years perfectly illustrates the use case for long-term, secure storage. Even if the investor's computer is compromised by malware or they fall victim to a phishing scam, their private keys and the associated Bitcoin remain **untouched and secure** within the offline Ledger device. To access and move these funds, the investor would need physical access to the Ledger, know the PIN, and manually authorize any transactions.

▢ **Hot vs Cold: Quick Comparison**

Feature	Hot Wallets	Cold Wallets
Internet Access	✅ Yes	✖ No
Security	⚠▢ Lower	🔐 Very High
Ease of Use	✅ Beginner-friendly	✖ Slightly technical
Cost	Mostly free	$50–$150 (one-time)
Ideal For	Daily use, trading	Long-term holding

Export to Sheets

Choosing the Right Wallet:

The best type of wallet for you depends on your individual needs and how you intend to use your cryptocurrency:

- **For small amounts you use regularly or for trading:** A reputable and well-secured hot wallet (with 2FA enabled) is often sufficient and more convenient.
- **For large amounts you intend to hold for the long term:** A cold wallet provides a significantly higher level of security and is the recommended option.

Many cryptocurrency users even adopt a combination of both types: using a hot wallet for smaller, everyday transactions and a cold wallet for the bulk of their holdings. This approach aims to balance convenience with optimal security.

💱 Popular Crypto Exchanges: Your Gateway to the World of Digital Assets

You're spot on! Cryptocurrency exchanges are the essential online platforms that facilitate the buying, selling, and trading of various cryptocurrencies. They act as marketplaces connecting buyers and sellers, and as you mentioned, they can operate under different models: centralized and decentralized. Let's explore each type in detail with examples:

🏦 Centralized Exchanges (CEX): The Traditional Marketplace Model

Centralized Exchanges (CEX) are operated by specific companies or organizations. They function similarly to traditional stock exchanges, providing a platform for users to trade cryptocurrencies against other cryptocurrencies or fiat currencies (like INR, USD, EUR). A key characteristic of CEXs is that they typically **require users to undergo identity verification**, a process known as **KYC (Know Your Customer)**, before they can deposit, withdraw, or trade significant amounts.

- **How They Work:**
    1. **Account Creation and KYC:** Users register an account on the exchange and provide personal identification documents to comply with regulatory requirements.
    2. **Depositing Funds:** Users deposit fiat currency or cryptocurrencies into their exchange accounts.
    3. **Trading:** Users can then place buy or sell orders for various cryptocurrency pairs (e.g., BTC/USD, ETH/BTC). The exchange matches these orders in an order book.
    4. **Withdrawals:** Users can withdraw their fiat currency or cryptocurrencies back to their bank accounts or crypto wallets.
- **Key Examples and Why They're Popular:**

    - **Coinbase:** Popular for its **beginner-friendly interface**, strong focus on compliance, and being based in the **USA**, making it a trusted option for many in that region. It offers a relatively limited selection of cryptocurrencies compared to some other exchanges.
    - **Binance:** The **largest cryptocurrency exchange globally** in terms of trading volume. It's known for its **low fees** and a **wide selection of cryptocurrencies** and trading pairs. Binance offers a comprehensive suite of features, including spot trading, futures, options, and more.
    - **Kraken:** Known for its **strong security reputation** and is often favored by **more experienced traders** due to its advanced trading features and margin trading options. It also has a strong focus on regulatory compliance.
    - **WazirX:** A **popular exchange in India** that supports trading in **Indian Rupees (INR)**. It offers a user-friendly interface tailored to the Indian market and supports a good selection of cryptocurrencies.
- ✅ **Pros of Centralized Exchanges:**

- o **Easy to Use:** CEXs generally have user-friendly interfaces that are relatively straightforward for beginners to navigate.
- o **Fast Trading:** Their centralized infrastructure often allows for quick order execution and high trading volumes.
- o **Customer Support:** CEXs typically offer customer support channels to assist users with any issues they may encounter.
- ⚠️ **Cons of Centralized Exchanges:**
  - o **They Control Your Private Keys:** When you deposit cryptocurrency on a CEX, the exchange holds the private keys to those funds. This means you don't have direct control over your assets; you are essentially trusting the exchange to safeguard them.
  - o **Can Be Hacked (Though Rare with Top Exchanges):** Although major exchanges invest heavily in security, they are still potential targets for hackers. While successful large-scale hacks of reputable exchanges are less frequent now, they have occurred in the past, resulting in users losing their funds.
- 🔍 **Example (Ravi on Binance):**
  - o Ravi creates an account on **Binance** and completes the KYC process.
  - o He deposits ⬜**10,000** into his Binance account using a supported payment method.
  - o He uses the Binance trading interface to buy **0.001 BTC** using his deposited INR.
  - o A week later, he trades his 0.001 BTC for a certain amount of **ETH** on the Binance exchange.
  - o Finally, he **withdraws** the ETH from his Binance account to his personal **crypto wallet**, where he controls the private keys.

🜚 Decentralized Exchanges (DEX): Trading on the Blockchain

Decentralized Exchanges (DEX) operate without a central authority or intermediary. Instead, they facilitate peer-to-peer trading directly between users' wallets using **smart contracts** deployed on a blockchain (most commonly Ethereum). Users connect their own non-custodial wallets (where they control their private keys) directly to the DEX to trade.

- **How They Work:**
  1. **Wallet Connection:** Users connect their crypto wallets (e.g., MetaMask, Trust Wallet) to the DEX interface.
  2. **Trading via Smart Contracts:** Trades are executed directly between users' wallets through automated smart contracts. These contracts hold the assets being traded in a secure escrow until the conditions of the trade are met.
  3. **Liquidity Pools:** Many DEXs utilize **liquidity pools**, where users deposit pairs of cryptocurrencies to provide trading liquidity. Traders then swap between these tokens within the pools, with prices determined by algorithms based on the pool's composition.
- **Key Examples and Unique Features:**

  - o **Uniswap:** One of the **most popular DEXs**, built on the **Ethereum** blockchain. It pioneered the automated market maker (AMM) model using liquidity pools.

- o **PancakeSwap:** A prominent DEX operating on the **Binance Smart Chain** (now BNB Chain). It offers similar functionality to Uniswap but with lower transaction fees compared to Ethereum in many cases.
  - o **1inch:** A **DEX aggregator** that doesn't hold user funds or execute trades itself. Instead, it scans multiple DEXs to find the **best exchange rates** for a user's desired trade and routes the trade through the most efficient platform.
- • ✅ **Pros of Decentralized Exchanges:**
  - o **You Control Your Funds:** You always maintain control of your private keys as you trade directly from your own wallet.
  - o **No KYC Needed (Generally):** Most DEXs do not require users to go through KYC verification, offering a more private trading experience.
  - o **No Downtime:** Because they are based on decentralized blockchain networks, DEXs are less susceptible to single points of failure and server downtime.
- • ⚠️ **Cons of Decentralized Exchanges:**
  - o **Less Beginner-Friendly:** DEX interfaces and the concept of connecting wallets and understanding liquidity pools can be more complex for beginners.
  - o **Higher Gas Fees on Ethereum (Potentially):** Transactions on Ethereum-based DEXs can incur significant "gas" fees (transaction fees on the Ethereum network), especially during times of high network congestion. This can make smaller trades uneconomical.
  - o **Potential for Impermanent Loss (in Liquidity Pools):** Users who provide liquidity to pools can experience "impermanent loss," where the value of their deposited assets changes compared to simply holding them.
- • 🔍 **Example (Anika on Uniswap):**
  - o Anika wants to swap her **100 USDT** (a stablecoin) for **MATIC** (Polygon's native token).
  - o She navigates to the **Uniswap** platform in her web browser.
  - o She clicks the "Connect Wallet" button and selects **MetaMask,** her non-custodial Ethereum wallet. She approves the connection request.
  - o Within the Uniswap interface, she selects USDT as the token she wants to swap and MATIC as the token she wants to receive.
  - o She enters the amount of USDT she wants to swap (100). Uniswap displays the estimated amount of MATIC she will receive and the associated transaction fees (gas fees on Ethereum).
  - o She reviews the details and clicks "Swap." MetaMask prompts her to confirm the transaction on the Ethereum network, and she pays the required gas fees.
  - o Once the transaction is confirmed on the Ethereum blockchain (which usually takes a few minutes), the 100 USDT is deducted from her wallet, and the corresponding amount of MATIC is deposited into her wallet – all **without creating an account or providing any personal identification to Uniswap.**

Choosing Between CEXs and DEXs:

The choice between a centralized and a decentralized exchange often comes down to a trade-off between convenience and control:

- **Centralized Exchanges:** Offer ease of use, fast trading, and customer support, but require trust in the exchange to safeguard your funds and comply with KYC regulations. They are often the entry point for new cryptocurrency users.
- **Decentralized Exchanges:** Provide greater control over your funds and often offer more privacy (no KYC), but can be more complex to use and may incur higher transaction fees on certain blockchains. They are favored by users who prioritize self-custody and decentralization.

Many experienced cryptocurrency users utilize both types of exchanges depending on their specific needs and trading strategies.

⚠️ Crypto Safety Tips for Students: Navigating the Web3 World Responsibly 🌐

You've hit on a crucial point! Just like with any powerful technology, engaging with Web3 and cryptocurrencies requires a strong sense of responsibility, especially when it comes to safeguarding your digital assets. The decentralized nature of crypto means that there's often no central authority to recover lost funds if you make a mistake or fall victim to a scam. Therefore, adopting robust security practices is paramount. Let's break down each of your vital safety tips with detailed explanations and examples tailored for students:

🔑 1. Never Share Your Private Key or Seed Phrase: Your Ultimate Crypto Secret

- **Explanation:** Your **private key** is the unique cryptographic code that grants you complete control over the cryptocurrency associated with your public address. Your **seed phrase** (also known as a recovery phrase) is a set of 12-24 words that can be used to regenerate your private keys and access your entire wallet. Sharing either of these is like giving someone the keys to your bank account – they can do anything they want with your funds.
- **Why it's Critical:** Anyone who possesses your private key or seed phrase can:
    - Send all your cryptocurrency to their own wallet.
    - Access and control any NFTs or other digital assets associated with that wallet.
    - Potentially compromise your entire digital identity within the Web3 ecosystem.
- **Real-World Analogy:** Think of your private key as the PIN to your debit card *and* the password to your online banking, all rolled into one. You would never share that with anyone. Your seed phrase is like the master key that can unlock all your bank accounts if you ever forget your PIN and password – it's even more critical to protect.
- **Student Example:** Imagine a classmate asks you for help with a crypto transaction and requests your "wallet password." Be extremely cautious! While some wallets have a separate password for accessing the interface, your *seed phrase* is the truly sensitive information. Never enter your seed phrase into any website or application unless you are explicitly restoring your wallet on a trusted device. Legitimate support will NEVER ask for your private key or seed phrase.

🔲 2. Double-Check Website URLs: Beware of Imposter Sites

- **Explanation:** The cryptocurrency space is rife with **phishing scams** where malicious actors create fake websites that look identical to legitimate exchanges, wallets, or DeFi platforms. Their goal is to trick you into entering your login credentials, private keys, or seed phrases, which they can then use to steal your funds.
- **Why it's Critical:** A single character difference in a website URL can lead you to a fraudulent site. Always meticulously verify the web address before entering any sensitive information.
- **How to Stay Safe:**
  - **Bookmark Official Links:** Save the correct URLs of your frequently used exchanges, wallets, and platforms in your browser's bookmarks and always access them from your bookmarks.
  - **Be Wary of Links in Emails or Messages:** Never click on links to crypto platforms sent via email, social media direct messages, or other untrusted sources. Always navigate to the site directly through your bookmark or by manually typing the URL.
  - **Look for the Padlock Icon:** Ensure the website has a valid SSL certificate, indicated by a padlock icon in the address bar and the "https://" prefix in the URL. However, even some fake sites can have this, so it's not the only indicator of legitimacy.
  - **Cross-Reference Information:** If you see a promotion or announcement on social media, verify it on the official website of the platform.
- **Student Example:** You see a tweet from what looks like your favorite crypto exchange announcing a special airdrop. The link in the tweet is `binance.promotion.com` (notice the extra ".promotion"). This is likely a fake site designed to steal your login credentials. Always go directly to the official `binance.com` to check for legitimate promotions.

🔒 3. Enable 2FA (Two-Factor Authentication) on All Accounts: Adding an Extra Layer of Security

- **Explanation: Two-Factor Authentication (2FA)** adds an extra layer of security to your accounts by requiring a second verification step in addition to your password. This usually involves a time-sensitive code generated by an authenticator app (like Google Authenticator, Authy), sent via SMS (less secure), or a physical security key.
- **Why it's Critical:** Even if a hacker manages to obtain your password, they will still need access to your second factor (your phone or security key) to log in or perform sensitive actions like withdrawals.
- **How to Implement:** Most reputable cryptocurrency exchanges, wallets, and email providers offer 2FA. Enable it on every account that handles your crypto or sensitive information. Authenticator apps are generally more secure than SMS-based 2FA, which can be intercepted.
- **Student Example:** You use Coinbase to trade crypto. Make sure you enable 2FA using an authenticator app. If someone tries to log into your Coinbase account with your password from a new device, they will also need the unique, time-sensitive code generated by your authenticator app on your phone, which they won't have access to.

☐ 4. Use a Hardware Wallet for Large Holdings: The Gold Standard for Security

- **Explanation: Hardware wallets** are physical devices specifically designed to store your private keys offline. They are considered the most secure way to hold significant amounts of cryptocurrency because your private keys are never exposed to the internet, significantly reducing the risk of online attacks.
- **Why it's Critical for Large Amounts:** If you are holding a substantial amount of cryptocurrency, the added security of a hardware wallet is well worth the investment. It acts like a secure vault for your digital assets.
- **How They Work:** To conduct a transaction with a hardware wallet, you need to physically connect it to your computer and confirm the transaction on the device itself, even if your computer is compromised by malware.
- **Student Example:** If the student in the MetaMask example starts accumulating a significant amount of ETH or valuable NFTs, it would be wise for them to consider transferring those large holdings to a hardware wallet like a Ledger Nano S or Trezor. They would then only connect the hardware wallet when they need to make a transaction, keeping their main stash offline and secure.

⚠️ 5. Be Cautious of "Too Good to Be True" Offers: Recognizing Scams

- **Explanation:** The cryptocurrency space is unfortunately plagued by scams that promise unrealistic returns or free crypto. Common examples include "send us 1 ETH and we'll send you back 2 ETH" schemes, fake airdrops that require you to send a small amount of crypto to receive a larger amount, and Ponzi schemes disguised as legitimate investments.
- **Why it's Critical:** These scams prey on greed and inexperience. Remember the adage: "If it sounds too good to be true, it probably is."
- **How to Identify Scams:**
  - **Unrealistic Promises:** Be skeptical of offers guaranteeing extremely high or risk-free returns.
  - **Pressure to Act Quickly:** Scammers often create a sense of urgency to prevent you from thinking critically.
  - **Requests for Upfront Payments:** Legitimate airdrops or giveaways usually don't require you to send crypto to receive free tokens.
  - **Poor Grammar and Spelling:** Scam messages and websites often contain grammatical errors and typos.
  - **Unofficial Channels:** Be wary of offers promoted through unofficial social media accounts or direct messages. Always verify information on official channels.
- **Student Example:** You see a message on Telegram claiming that a new cryptocurrency is giving away free tokens worth hundreds of dollars, but you need to send a small amount of ETH to verify your wallet. This is a classic example of a scam. Legitimate projects usually conduct airdrops without requiring participants to send them funds.

Additional Important Safety Tips for Students:

- **Educate Yourself Continuously:** The crypto space is constantly evolving. Stay informed about the latest security threats and best practices.

- **Use Strong, Unique Passwords:** For all your crypto-related accounts (exchanges, wallets, email), use strong passwords that are unique and difficult to guess. Consider using a password manager.
- **Be Careful on Public Wi-Fi:** Avoid accessing your crypto wallets or conducting sensitive transactions on public Wi-Fi networks, as they can be less secure. Consider using a VPN.
- **Keep Your Software Updated:** Regularly update your operating system, browser, and crypto wallet software to patch any known security vulnerabilities.
- **Back Up Your Wallet:** Understand how to back up your wallet (usually via the seed phrase) and store this backup securely offline in multiple safe locations.
- **Start Small:** When you're new to crypto, start with small amounts to get comfortable with the technology and security practices before handling larger sums.
- **Trust Your Gut:** If something feels off or too risky, it probably is. Don't let FOMO (Fear Of Missing Out) cloud your judgment.

By understanding and implementing these crypto safety tips, students can navigate the exciting world of Web3 with greater confidence and protect their valuable digital assets. Remember, in the decentralized world of cryptocurrency, you are your own bank, and safeguarding your funds is your primary responsibility.

📖 Summary: What You've Learned

Concept	Key Takeaway
🔐 Public/Private Key	Access and ownership of crypto
🔥 Hot Wallets	Fast, online, convenient
❄️ Cold Wallets	Offline, ultra-secure
💱 Exchanges	Where crypto is bought/sold/traded
⚠️ Safety	Always secure your keys & wallet

💡 Final Thought:

"Owning crypto is like being your own bank. That's power. But also responsibility."

30 multiple-choice questions with answers covering public/private keys, hot/cold wallets, and popular cryptocurrency exchanges:

Public & Private Keys Explained

1. What is the primary purpose of a public key in cryptocurrency? a) To authorize transactions. b) To keep your funds secret. c) To receive cryptocurrency. d) To recover your lost wallet. **Answer: c)**
2. Your public key is like your: a) Bank account password. b) Email address. c) Debit card PIN. d) Social Security number. **Answer: b)**
3. What is the primary purpose of a private key in cryptocurrency? a) To share with others to receive funds. b) To publicly display your balance. c) To access and send funds. d) To verify blockchain transactions for everyone. **Answer: c)**
4. Your private key should be: a) Shared with trusted friends. b) Stored online for easy access. c) Kept secret and never shared. d) Used as your wallet password. **Answer: c)**
5. Your private key is most like your: a) Mailing address. b) Publicly listed phone number. c) Bank account password and PIN combined. d) Username for a website. **Answer: c)**
6. How is a public key typically derived from a private key? a) Through a simple copy-paste. b) Using a complex, one-way cryptographic algorithm. c) By randomly generating a different key each time. d) It is not derived; they are created independently. **Answer: b)**
7. If someone gains access to your private key, they can: a) Only view your transaction history. b) Request funds from others. c) Control and spend your cryptocurrency. d) Freeze your account. **Answer: c)**
8. What is a seed phrase (recovery phrase) used for? a) To publicly identify your wallet. b) To temporarily access your funds. c) To regenerate your private keys and access your wallet. d) To speed up transaction confirmations. **Answer: c)**
9. Sharing your seed phrase is equivalent to: a) Telling someone your public address. b) Showing someone a transaction on the blockchain. c) Giving someone complete control over your wallet. d) Enabling two-factor authentication. **Answer: c)**
10. Can a private key be easily derived from a public key? a) Yes, with the right software. b) Yes, it's a simple mathematical calculation. c) No, it is computationally infeasible due to the cryptography involved. d) Only by the developers of the cryptocurrency. **Answer: c)**

Hot Wallets vs. Cold Wallets

11. What is the primary characteristic of a hot wallet? a) It is a physical device. b) It is not connected to the internet. c) It is connected to the internet. d) It stores your private keys on paper. **Answer: c)**
12. Which of the following is an example of a hot wallet? a) Ledger Nano S. b) Trezor. c) MetaMask. d) Paper wallet stored offline. **Answer: c)**
13. What is a key advantage of using a hot wallet? a) Highest level of security. b) Ideal for long-term storage. c) Fast access and convenience for transactions. d) Immune to online attacks. **Answer: c)**
14. What is a primary security risk associated with hot wallets? a) Susceptibility to physical damage. b) Vulnerability to online hacking and scams. c) Difficulty in accessing funds quickly. d) Higher transaction fees. **Answer: b)**

15. What is the defining characteristic of a cold wallet? a) It is always connected to the internet. b) It stores private keys offline. c) It is primarily used for frequent trading. d) It is usually free to use. **Answer: b)**
16. Which of the following is an example of a cold wallet? a) Trust Wallet. b) Coinbase Wallet. c) Ledger Nano X. d) A browser extension wallet. **Answer: c)**
17. What is a major advantage of using a cold wallet? a) Convenience for daily transactions. b) Immunity to online attacks. c) Typically free of charge. d) Easy recovery if the device is lost. **Answer: b)**
18. What is a potential disadvantage of using a cold wallet? a) Lower security compared to hot wallets. b) Greater vulnerability to phishing scams. c) Less convenient for frequent transactions. d) Usually requires sharing your private keys with a third party. **Answer: c)**
19. For storing large amounts of cryptocurrency long-term, which type of wallet is generally recommended? a) Hot wallet. b) Exchange wallet. c) Cold wallet. d) Custodial wallet. **Answer: c)**
20. A paper wallet is a type of: a) Hot wallet. b) Exchange wallet. c) Cold wallet. d) Multi-signature wallet. **Answer: c)**

Popular Crypto Exchanges

21. What is the primary function of a cryptocurrency exchange? a) To store private keys securely for users. b) To facilitate the buying, selling, and trading of cryptocurrencies. c) To create new cryptocurrencies through mining. d) To regulate cryptocurrency transactions globally. **Answer: b)**
22. Which of the following is a popular centralized cryptocurrency exchange known for its beginner-friendly interface and US-based operations? a) Binance. b) Kraken. c) Coinbase. d) Uniswap. **Answer: c)**
23. Which centralized exchange is known for being the largest globally by trading volume and offering a wide selection of coins? a) Coinbase. b) Kraken. c) Binance. d) WazirX. **Answer: c)**
24. Which centralized exchange is recognized for its strong security measures and appeal to more experienced traders? a) Binance. b) Coinbase. c) Kraken. d) PancakeSwap. **Answer: c)**
25. Which popular centralized exchange is based in India and supports trading in INR? a) Binance. b) Kraken. c) Coinbase. d) WazirX. **Answer: d)**
26. A key characteristic of centralized exchanges is that they typically: a) Do not require any form of user identification. b) Give users full control over their private keys. c) Require KYC (Know Your Customer) verification. d) Operate entirely on smart contracts. **Answer: c)**
27. What is a potential disadvantage of using a centralized exchange? a) Slow transaction speeds. b) Limited selection of cryptocurrencies. c) The exchange controls your private keys. d) High transaction fees for basic trades. **Answer: c)**
28. What is a defining feature of a decentralized exchange (DEX)? a) Operated by a central company. b) Requires users to deposit funds into the exchange's wallet. c) Allows users to trade directly from their own wallets using smart contracts. d) Typically requires extensive KYC procedures. **Answer: c)**

29. Which of the following is a popular decentralized exchange built on the Ethereum blockchain? a) Binance. b) Kraken. c) PancakeSwap. d) Uniswap. **Answer: d)**

30. A potential drawback of using a DEX like Uniswap can be: a) Lower security of user funds. b) The need to trust a central authority. c) Potentially higher gas fees on the Ethereum network. d) Limited trading pairs available. **Answer: c)**

10 mid-size questions with answers covering public/private keys, hot/cold wallets, and popular cryptocurrency exchanges:

1. **Explain the fundamental relationship between public and private keys in cryptocurrency wallets. How do these keys enable secure transactions without relying on traditional intermediaries? Answer:** Public and private keys are a mathematically linked pair. The public key serves as your cryptocurrency address, which you can share to receive funds. The private key is a secret code that allows you to authorize transactions and access the funds associated with that public key. This system enables secure, peer-to-peer transactions because only the owner of the private key can sign and initiate the transfer of funds, and this signature can be verified by anyone using the corresponding public key, all without the need for a central authority to validate each transaction.

2. **Describe the key differences between custodial and non-custodial cryptocurrency wallets. In the context of public and private keys, explain which type of wallet gives users more control over their assets and why. Answer:** Custodial wallets are those where a third party (like a cryptocurrency exchange) holds your private keys on your behalf, similar to a bank holding your money. Non-custodial wallets, on the other hand, give you full control over your private keys, typically through a seed phrase. Non-custodial wallets offer users more control over their assets because they, and only they, possess the private keys necessary to access and move their cryptocurrency, eliminating the risk of the third-party custodian being hacked or going insolvent.

3. **Compare and contrast the security characteristics of hot wallets and cold wallets. Under what circumstances would you recommend using each type of wallet, and what are the primary security considerations for each? Answer:** Hot wallets are connected to the internet, offering convenience for frequent transactions but posing a higher security risk [1] due to potential online vulnerabilities. Security considerations include enabling 2FA, using strong passwords, and being wary of phishing scams. Cold wallets store private keys offline, providing superior security for long-term holdings. Security considerations involve safeguarding the physical device or paper backup and protecting the recovery phrase. Hot wallets are suitable for smaller amounts and regular use, while cold wallets are recommended for securing larger amounts for extended periods.

4. **Explain the process of setting up and using a hardware wallet. How does it enhance the security of your cryptocurrency holdings compared to a software-based hot wallet? Answer:** Setting up a hardware wallet typically involves initializing the device, creating and securely storing a recovery seed phrase, and setting a PIN. To use it, you connect it to a computer, use the associated software to initiate a transaction, and then physically confirm the transaction on the device itself. This significantly enhances security because your private keys remain offline within the hardware device and are never directly exposed to your potentially compromised computer during transaction signing.

5. **Describe the role of KYC (Know Your Customer) procedures on centralized cryptocurrency exchanges like Coinbase and Binance. What are the benefits and drawbacks of these procedures from a user's perspective? Answer:** KYC procedures on centralized exchanges require users to verify their identity by providing personal information and documentation. Benefits include increased security and regulatory compliance for the exchange, potentially making it a more trustworthy platform and facilitating fiat currency transactions. Drawbacks include privacy concerns due to sharing personal data and the potential for account freezes or complications if the verification process is not smooth.

6. **Compare and contrast the trading experience on a centralized exchange (CEX) versus a decentralized exchange (DEX). Consider factors such as user interface, transaction speed, fees, and control over funds. Answer:** CEXs typically offer user-friendly interfaces, faster transaction speeds (due to their centralized infrastructure), and often lower gas fees (though they charge their own trading fees). However, users relinquish control of their private keys. DEXs, on the other hand, allow users to trade directly from their own wallets, maintaining control over their funds and often offering more privacy (no KYC). However, they can have less intuitive interfaces, potentially slower transaction speeds (depending on the underlying blockchain), and higher gas fees (especially on Ethereum).

7. **Explain the concept of "gas fees" on the Ethereum network and how they impact transactions on decentralized exchanges like Uniswap. What are some layer-2 scaling solutions aiming to address this issue? Answer:** Gas fees on Ethereum are the transaction fees required to execute operations on the network, including trades on DEXs. These fees fluctuate based on network congestion and can become quite high, making smaller trades on DEXs uneconomical. Layer-2 scaling solutions like Polygon, Optimism, and Arbitrum aim to address this by processing transactions off the main Ethereum chain, significantly reducing gas fees and increasing transaction throughput while still inheriting Ethereum's security.

8. **Discuss the security measures that users should implement when using both hot and cold wallets to protect their cryptocurrency holdings. Provide specific examples for each type of wallet. Answer:** For hot wallets, users should enable two-factor authentication (2FA), use strong and unique passwords, be vigilant against phishing scams, and only interact with trusted decentralized applications. For cold wallets, users should securely store their recovery seed phrase offline in multiple locations, protect their PIN, and be cautious when connecting their hardware wallet to potentially compromised devices.

9. **Describe the potential risks associated with keeping large amounts of cryptocurrency on a centralized exchange. What historical events illustrate these risks, and what strategies can users employ to mitigate them? Answer:** Keeping large amounts of cryptocurrency on a centralized exchange exposes users to risks like hacking of the exchange, regulatory actions leading to fund freezes, and the exchange potentially becoming insolvent. Historical events like the Mt. Gox and FTX collapses illustrate these dangers. Mitigation strategies include withdrawing large holdings to non-custodial wallets (preferably cold storage) and only keeping the necessary amount for trading on the exchange.

10. **Explain the importance of understanding the difference between a public key, a private key, and a wallet address. How are these three related, and why is it crucial for cryptocurrency users to manage them correctly for security and usability? Answer:** The private key is the master secret that controls your funds. The public key is derived from the private key and serves as the basis for your wallet address, which is the specific string you share to receive funds. Understanding this hierarchy is crucial because you can freely share your public address, but your private key must remain absolutely secret. Mismanaging these keys, such as sharing your private key or losing your recovery phrase, can lead to the permanent loss of your cryptocurrency. Correct management ensures both the security and accessibility of your digital assets.

CHAPTER 6: HOW TO BUY, SELL, AND TRADE CRYPTO

□□ **1. Setting Up a Wallet – Your First Step into the Web3 World**

◆ **Types of Wallets You Can Use: Choosing the Right Fit for Your Needs**

Just like traditional financial accounts come in different forms (savings, checking), cryptocurrency wallets also have various types, each offering different levels of convenience, security, and features. Here's a detailed look at the wallet types you mentioned:

- **Mobile Wallets: Convenience on the Go (e.g., Trust Wallet, Coinbase Wallet)**
  - ○ **Description:** Mobile wallets are smartphone applications that allow you to manage your cryptocurrencies directly from your mobile device. They offer a good balance of convenience and security for everyday use.
  - ○ **Pros:**
    - ▪ **Easy to Use:** Designed with user-friendliness in mind, often featuring intuitive interfaces.
    - ▪ **Convenient for Transactions:** Ideal for making quick payments, interacting with mobile dApps, and checking your balance on the go.
    - ▪ **Integration with Mobile Apps:** Seamlessly connect with decentralized applications (dApps) on your phone.
  - ○ **Cons:**
    - ▪ **Security Risk:** Your phone can be vulnerable to malware, loss, or theft, potentially compromising your wallet if not secured properly (strong screen lock, backups).
    - ▪ **Online Connection:** Being connected to the internet makes them a "hot wallet," which carries inherent online security risks.
  - ○ **Examples:**
    - ▪ **Trust Wallet:** A popular mobile wallet supporting a wide range of blockchains and cryptocurrencies. It also has a built-in dApp browser for interacting with Web3 applications.
    - ▪ **Coinbase Wallet:** A self-custody mobile wallet from Coinbase (separate from the Coinbase exchange app), giving you control over your private keys. It supports multiple cryptocurrencies and NFTs.
- **Browser Wallets: Your Gateway to Web3 on Desktop (e.g., MetaMask)**
  - ○ **Description:** Browser wallets are extensions that you install on your web browser (like Chrome, Firefox, Brave). They act as a bridge between your browser and the blockchain, enabling you to interact with Web3 websites and decentralized applications directly from your computer.
  - ○ **Pros:**
    - ▪ **Seamless Web3 Interaction:** Essential for using dApps, DeFi platforms, and NFT marketplaces on your desktop.
    - ▪ **Relatively Easy to Use:** Once installed, they are generally straightforward to interact with.

- **Support for Multiple Networks:** Many browser wallets, like MetaMask, can be configured to connect to various blockchain networks (e.g., Ethereum, Binance Smart Chain, Polygon).
  - **Cons:**
    - **Security Risk:** Your computer can be vulnerable to malware and online attacks. If your computer is compromised, your browser wallet could be at risk.
    - **Hot Wallet:** Being connected to the internet makes them a hot wallet.
  - **Example (as you provided): MetaMask** is the most popular browser wallet for interacting with the Ethereum ecosystem and many other EVM-compatible blockchains. Its browser extension allows you to manage your Ethereum addresses, send and receive Ether and other tokens, and connect to decentralized applications directly within your web browser.
- **Desktop Wallets: Software for Your Computer (e.g., Exodus, Atomic Wallet)**
  - **Description:** Desktop wallets are software applications that you download and install directly onto your computer. They offer a balance between the convenience of online access and a slightly higher level of security compared to purely mobile or browser-based wallets, as they are not constantly running in a browser.
  - **Pros:**
    - **More Control:** You have more direct control over the wallet software and your private keys compared to exchange-hosted wallets.
    - **Often Multi-Currency Support:** Many desktop wallets support a wide range of cryptocurrencies in one interface.
    - **Enhanced Security Compared to Browser Wallets:** Being a dedicated application can offer some security advantages over browser extensions.
  - **Cons:**
    - **Security Risk:** Your computer is still connected to the internet and can be vulnerable to malware if not properly secured.
    - **Hot Wallet:** They are still considered hot wallets due to their internet connectivity.
  - **Examples:**
    - **Exodus:** A user-friendly desktop wallet with a focus on design and supporting a wide variety of cryptocurrencies. It also has built-in exchange functionality.
    - **Atomic Wallet:** Another multi-currency desktop wallet that allows you to store, manage, and exchange various cryptocurrencies.
- **Hardware Wallets: The Gold Standard for Long-Term Security (e.g., Ledger, Trezor)**
  - **Description:** Hardware wallets are physical devices specifically designed to store your private keys offline. They are considered the most secure way to hold significant amounts of cryptocurrency because your private keys are never exposed to the internet.
  - **Pros:**
    - **Ultra-Secure (Cold Storage):** By keeping your private keys offline, they are virtually immune to online hacking attempts and malware.

- **Transaction Signing:** Transactions are signed on the physical device itself, requiring your manual confirmation and preventing unauthorized access even if your computer is compromised.
- **Recovery Phrase:** They provide a recovery seed phrase that allows you to restore your funds if the device is lost or damaged.
  - **Cons:**
    - **Less Convenient for Frequent Transactions:** Using them requires physically connecting the device to your computer and manually confirming transactions.
    - **Cost:** Hardware wallets require a one-time purchase cost.
    - **Slight Learning Curve:** Initial setup and usage might be slightly more technical for beginners.
  - **Examples:**
    - **Ledger Nano S and Nano X:** Popular hardware wallets known for their security features and wide cryptocurrency support.
    - **Trezor One and Model T:** Another leading hardware wallet brand with a strong focus on open-source security.

🔧 Example: Setting Up MetaMask (Browser Wallet) – A Step-by-Step Guide

Your step-by-step guide for setting up MetaMask is accurate and highlights the critical aspects:

1. **Go to https://metamask.io:** Always ensure you are on the legitimate MetaMask website. Be wary of lookalike domains that could be phishing attempts. Bookmark the correct URL for future access.
2. **Click "Download" and install the browser extension:** Follow the prompts to download and add the MetaMask extension to your chosen browser (Chrome, Firefox, Brave, Edge).
3. **Click "Create a Wallet":** Upon opening the extension for the first time, you will be given the option to create a new wallet or import an existing one. Choose "Create a Wallet."
4. **Set a strong password:** You will be prompted to create a password to protect your MetaMask wallet on your current browser. This password is necessary to access your wallet locally on this device. Choose a strong, unique password that you don't use for other accounts.
5. **Save your Secret Recovery Phrase (12 words) offline – very important!** This is the **most crucial step**. MetaMask will provide you with a 12-word (or sometimes 24-word) **Secret Recovery Phrase** (also known as a seed phrase). This phrase is the master key to your wallet. If you lose access to your device, you can use this phrase to restore your wallet on a new device.
   - **Best Practices for Your Secret Recovery Phrase:**
     - **Write it down on physical paper.** Do not copy and paste it or store it digitally on your computer, phone, or in the cloud (where it could be compromised).
     - **Store it in a secure, offline location.** Consider multiple secure locations to protect against loss or damage.

- **Never share it with anyone, for any reason.** Legitimate support will NEVER ask for your seed phrase.
- **Understand the implications of losing it.** If you lose your seed phrase and lose access to your wallet, your funds will be irretrievable.

6. **You now have a wallet address like: 0xA12B...89CD:** Once you have securely saved your Secret Recovery Phrase and confirmed it, MetaMask will generate your first Ethereum address (which starts with "0x"). This is your **public address** – the one you can share with others to receive Ether (ETH) or other Ethereum-based tokens.

You're now ready to receive, hold, or send crypto!

Congratulations! By setting up your first cryptocurrency wallet, you've taken a significant step into the world of Web3. Remember to prioritize the security of your private keys and seed phrase, as they are the keys to your digital assets. As you become more familiar with the ecosystem, you might explore different types of wallets to best suit your needs and the amount of cryptocurrency you are managing.

📈 2. Understanding Market Trends

🔲 **Key Concepts to Know:**

- **Bull Market: Prices are Going Up** 🚀
  - **Meaning:** A bull market is characterized by a sustained period of increasing prices across the cryptocurrency market or for a specific asset. Investor confidence is generally high, and there's a positive sentiment driving buying activity.
  - **Indicators:** Consecutive periods of price increases, growing trading volume, positive news and adoption announcements, and increased mainstream interest often signal a bull market.
  - **Student Example:** Imagine Bitcoin's price steadily climbing from $30,000 to $45,000 over a few months, with other major cryptocurrencies also showing significant gains. News outlets are reporting increased institutional investment and wider acceptance of Bitcoin. This scenario would likely be considered a bull market for Bitcoin and potentially the broader crypto market.
- **Bear Market: Prices are Going Down** 🐻
  - **Meaning:** Conversely, a bear market is defined by a prolonged period of declining prices. Investor sentiment is typically negative, leading to increased selling pressure and a decrease in overall market confidence.
  - **Indicators:** Consistent price drops, declining trading volume, negative news or regulatory concerns, and a general feeling of pessimism often characterize a bear market.
  - **Student Example:** Following the bull market example, if Bitcoin's price starts to fall sharply from $45,000 down to $28,000 over a few months, accompanied by

negative news about increased regulation or security concerns, and other cryptocurrencies follow a similar downward trend, this would likely be considered a bear market.

- **ATH (All-Time High): The Highest Price a Crypto Has Ever Reached**
  - **Meaning:** The All-Time High (ATH) represents the highest price a particular cryptocurrency has ever traded at since its inception. It's a significant historical price point that investors often watch. Breaking the ATH can sometimes signal further bullish momentum, while failing to reach it can indicate resistance.
  - **Student Example:** If Bitcoin's price previously peaked at $69,000 in 2021, then $69,000 is its ATH. If the price starts approaching and then surpasses this level, it could generate significant excitement and further buying pressure as it enters uncharted territory.

- **Market Cap: Total Value of a Crypto Asset (Price × Circulating Supply)**
  - **Meaning:** Market capitalization (market cap) is a crucial metric that represents the total value of a cryptocurrency. It's calculated by multiplying the current price of one unit of the cryptocurrency by its circulating supply (the number of coins or tokens currently in public hands). Market cap provides an idea of the size and overall value of a cryptocurrency. Larger market caps generally indicate more established and (potentially) less volatile assets.
  - **Student Example:** If Bitcoin is trading at $30,000 and there are 19 million BTC in circulation, its market cap would be $30,000 * 19,000,000 = $570,000,000,000 (570 Billion). Comparing the market caps of different cryptocurrencies can help understand their relative size and dominance in the market.

- **Volume: How Much of a Crypto is Being Bought/Sold**
  - **Meaning:** Trading volume refers to the total amount of a specific cryptocurrency that has been traded (bought and sold) over a specific period, usually 24 hours. High trading volume suggests strong interest and liquidity in the market for that asset, while low volume might indicate a lack of interest or that price movements could be more easily influenced.
  - **Student Example:** If Bitcoin has a 24-hour trading volume of $20 Billion, it means that $20 Billion worth of Bitcoin has been exchanged between buyers and sellers in the last 24 hours across all exchanges. A significant increase in volume often accompanies significant price movements, confirming the strength of the trend.

- **Support & Resistance: Price Levels Where Buying/Selling Pressure is High**
  - **Meaning:** These are key price levels that technical analysts often watch.
    - **Support Level:** A price level where buying pressure is expected to be strong enough to prevent the price from falling further. It's often a level where the price has previously bottomed out or where there's a concentration of buy orders.
    - **Resistance Level:** A price level where selling pressure is expected to be strong enough to prevent the price from rising further. It's often a level where the price has previously peaked or where there's a concentration of sell orders.

- **Breakouts and Breakdowns:** When the price breaks through a support level, it can signal further downward movement. When it breaks through a resistance level, it can suggest further upward momentum.
- **Student Example:** If Bitcoin's price has repeatedly bounced back up whenever it reaches $28,000, then $28,000 might be considered a support level. Conversely, if the price has struggled to break above $32,000 multiple times, then $32,000 could be a resistance level. A break above $32,000 with high volume could indicate a potential bullish trend.

🔍 Example Breakdown:

Your example provides a snapshot of Bitcoin's market data:

- **Bitcoin (BTC) is at $30,000:** This is the current trading price.
- **Last week it was $25,000:** This shows a significant price increase over the past week, indicating potential bullish momentum.
- **Market cap: $600 Billion:** This indicates a large and relatively established cryptocurrency.
- **Volume (24hr): $20 Billion:** This suggests a high level of trading activity and strong interest in Bitcoin.

→ **Your Conclusion:** The combination of a significant price increase and high trading volume suggests **strong buying momentum**. The potential reason you provided – positive news like a country accepting BTC or a major company investing – could indeed be a catalyst for such bullish movement. Fundamental news often plays a significant role in driving market trends.

Tools for Analyzing Trends:

The websites and apps you mentioned are invaluable resources for anyone looking to understand cryptocurrency market trends:

- **CoinMarketCap.com:** Provides comprehensive data on thousands of cryptocurrencies, including price charts, market cap, volume, circulating supply, historical data, and news. It's a great starting point for getting an overview of the market.
- **TradingView.com:** A powerful charting and social networking platform for traders and investors. It offers advanced charting tools, technical indicators, and the ability to share and discuss trading ideas.
- **CoinGecko.com:** Similar to CoinMarketCap, it provides detailed cryptocurrency data, price charts, market analysis, and information on exchanges. It's often seen as a more data-centric alternative.

Analyzing Trends and Using Technical Indicators:

Beyond the basic concepts, analyzing market trends often involves:

- **Reading Charts:** Understanding different types of charts (e.g., line charts, candlestick charts) and identifying patterns (e.g., trend lines, chart formations) that can suggest potential future price movements.
- **Using Technical Indicators:** These are mathematical calculations based on historical price and volume data that can provide insights into trend strength, momentum, volatility, and potential buy/sell signals. Some popular technical indicators include:
  - **Moving Averages (MA):** Smooth out price data to identify trends.
  - **Relative Strength Index (RSI):** Measures the speed and change of price movements to identify overbought or oversold conditions.
  - **Moving Average Convergence Divergence (MACD):** A momentum indicator that shows the relationship between two moving averages.
  - **Bollinger Bands:** Measure volatility and identify potential price extremes.
- **Fundamental Analysis:** Evaluating the intrinsic value of a cryptocurrency based on its technology, adoption rate, use cases, team, and overall ecosystem. Positive fundamental developments can often drive bullish trends.
- **Sentiment Analysis:** Gauging the overall mood and opinions of the market participants towards a particular cryptocurrency or the market as a whole. Social media, news sentiment, and investor surveys can be used for this.

Important Considerations for Students:

- **Start with Education:** Before making any trading or investment decisions, take the time to learn about these key concepts and how to use analytical tools.
- **Practice with Paper Trading:** Many platforms offer "paper trading" accounts where you can simulate trades with virtual money to practice your analysis without risking real capital.
- **Be Aware of Volatility:** The cryptocurrency market is highly volatile. Even with careful analysis, prices can move unexpectedly.
- **Manage Risk:** Never invest more than you can afford to lose. Understand the risks involved before putting your money into cryptocurrencies.
- **Don't Rely Solely on Hype:** Be wary of "pump and dump" schemes and make your own informed decisions based on your research.

Understanding market trends is an ongoing learning process. By familiarizing yourself with these key concepts and utilizing the available analytical tools, you can navigate the cryptocurrency market with more knowledge and make more informed decisions.

3. Real-World Trading Demo (Step-by-Step)

Goal: Buy ETH and Sell it for Profit

This is a common and understandable goal for someone starting in crypto trading. The idea is to purchase an asset at a lower price and sell it at a higher price to realize a profit.

Platform: Binance (Centralized Exchange)

Choosing Binance as the initial platform is sensible due to its relatively user-friendly interface, wide range of supported cryptocurrencies, and generally lower fees compared to some other exchanges. It's a popular choice for both beginners and experienced traders.

Budget: $100

Starting with a small, manageable budget like $100 is highly recommended for students or anyone new to crypto trading. This allows you to learn the process and experience the market's volatility without risking a significant amount of capital. Remember the golden rule: **only invest what you can afford to lose.**

Asset: Ethereum (ETH)

Ethereum (ETH) is the second-largest cryptocurrency by market capitalization and has numerous use cases beyond just being a digital currency (as discussed earlier with smart contracts and dApps). It's a popular trading asset with relatively high liquidity, making it a reasonable choice for a demo.

✅ Step-by-Step: Your Trading Journey

Step 1: Create an Exchange Account

- **Go to Binance.com:** Emphasize the importance of ensuring the URL is correct to avoid phishing scams. Look for the padlock icon in the address bar indicating a secure connection (HTTPS).
- **Sign up with your email & verify identity (KYC):** Centralized exchanges like Binance are regulated and require **Know Your Customer (KYC)** verification. This typically involves providing personal information (name, address, date of birth) and uploading identification documents (passport, driver's license, national ID). The verification process can take some time. It's important to use accurate information.

Step 2: Deposit Fiat Currency

- **Add $100 using bank card / UPI / PayPal:** Binance offers various methods for depositing fiat currency (like USD in this example). The availability of these methods can vary depending on your location.
  - **Bank Card (Debit/Credit):** Often the quickest way but may involve higher fees.
  - **UPI (Unified Payments Interface - relevant for India):** A popular and generally low-cost method in India.
  - **PayPal:** Another widely used online payment platform, fees may apply.
  - **Bank Transfer:** Can have lower fees but may take longer to process.
  - **Students should be aware of potential transaction fees associated with each deposit method.**

Step 3: Buy Ethereum (ETH)

- **Search "ETH":** Binance has a search bar where you can easily find the trading pair you're interested in. You'll likely want to trade ETH against your deposited fiat currency (e.g., ETH/USD).
- **Click "Buy" → Enter $100 → Confirm:** You'll be taken to the ETH trading interface. Ensure you are on the "Buy" tab. You can choose different order types (market order for immediate purchase at the current price, limit order to set a specific price). For simplicity, a market order is usually used for a quick buy. Enter the amount you want to spend in USD ($100 in this case) and click "Buy ETH." Binance will calculate the approximate amount of ETH you will receive based on the current market price and any associated fees. **Always review the details before confirming.**
- **Congrats! You now hold ETH in your Binance wallet:** The purchased ETH will be credited to your Binance "Spot Wallet." You can view your balance in the "Wallet" section of the Binance platform.

Step 4: Wait & Monitor the Market

- **Let's say ETH goes from $2,000 to $2,200:** This illustrates a positive price movement. The time it takes for this to happen can vary greatly – it could be hours, days, weeks, or even longer. Cryptocurrency markets are volatile.
- **You now decide to sell to take profit:** This is a key decision in trading – knowing when to take profits. It depends on your trading strategy and risk tolerance.

Step 5: Sell ETH

- **Go to "Trade" → "ETH/USD":** Navigate back to the ETH trading interface on Binance. This time, ensure you are on the "Sell" tab.
- **Enter amount (e.g., 0.05 ETH):** You can choose to sell a specific amount of ETH (like 0.05 ETH as in the example – the actual amount you can sell will depend on how much you bought with your $100 and the price at the time of purchase) or a percentage of your total ETH holdings.
- **Click "Sell" → Done:** Similar to buying, you can choose a market order for an immediate sale at the current price or a limit order to sell at a specific target price. Review the details (amount of ETH, selling price, estimated USD you will receive, fees) before confirming the sale. The resulting USD will be credited to your Binance fiat balance.

Step 6: Withdraw to Your Wallet

- **If long-term holding: transfer your ETH to MetaMask or Trust Wallet:** This step highlights the difference between keeping your crypto on an exchange (custodial) and having self-custody in your own wallet (non-custodial). For longer-term storage and greater control, transferring your ETH to a wallet where you own the private keys (like MetaMask or Trust Wallet, as discussed earlier) is generally recommended. Be aware of potential withdrawal fees when transferring crypto off an exchange. Ensure you are sending to the correct network address (e.g., Ethereum Mainnet for ETH).

- **If you want fiat back: withdraw $110 to your bank → Done ✅:** If your goal was to make a profit in fiat currency, you can withdraw the USD from your Binance account to your linked bank account or other supported withdrawal methods. Again, be aware of potential withdrawal fees and processing times.

🔥 Bonus: Using a DEX like Uniswap

This section introduces the concept of Decentralized Exchanges (DEXs), which operate differently from CEXs.

- **Go to uniswap.org:** Again, verify the URL to avoid phishing.
- **Connect your MetaMask wallet:** Uniswap doesn't require account creation. You connect your non-custodial wallet (like MetaMask) directly to the platform. This gives you full control over your funds.
- **Choose a token to swap (e.g., USDC to MATIC):** DEXs allow you to swap directly between different cryptocurrencies. You select the token you want to give (e.g., USDC, a stablecoin pegged to the US dollar) and the token you want to receive (e.g., MATIC, the native token of the Polygon network).
- **Confirm gas fee & transaction:** Transactions on blockchains like Ethereum (where Uniswap primarily operates) require "gas fees" to pay for the computational cost of processing the transaction. These fees can fluctuate based on network congestion. MetaMask will show you the estimated gas fee before you confirm the swap.
- **Tokens are instantly swapped in your wallet!:** Once the transaction is confirmed on the blockchain, the swapped tokens will appear directly in your connected MetaMask wallet.

☐ Pro Tips for Student Traders:

These are excellent pieces of advice for anyone starting in crypto trading, especially students:

- **✓☐ Start small – only what you can afford to lose:** This cannot be stressed enough. The cryptocurrency market is highly volatile, and you could lose your initial investment. Treat it as a learning experience with a small amount of risk capital.
- **✓☐ Always double-check token symbols (some fake tokens look like real ones):** Scammers often create fake tokens with symbols that look very similar to legitimate ones. Always verify the full token contract address (especially on DEXs) to ensure you are trading the correct asset. Reliable sources like CoinMarketCap or CoinGecko can provide the correct contract addresses.
- **✓☐ Never invest based on FOMO (Fear Of Missing Out):** Don't make impulsive decisions based on hype or the fear of missing out on potential gains. Do your own research (DYOR) and have a well-thought-out strategy.
- **✓☐ Don't fall for YouTube "gurus" promising fast returns:** Be extremely skeptical of anyone guaranteeing unrealistic profits or providing "secret" trading strategies. Many of these are scams or based on luck rather than skill. Learn from reputable sources.

- ✓☐ **Stay updated with legit news: CoinDesk, Decrypt, Binance Academy:** Staying informed about the cryptocurrency market through reliable news sources and educational platforms is crucial for understanding market movements and potential risks. Binance Academy itself offers a wealth of educational resources.

This step-by-step demo provides a solid foundation for understanding the basic process of cryptocurrency trading on both centralized and decentralized exchanges. However, it's essential to remember that this is a simplified example, and real-world trading involves more complexities, risks, and the need for continuous learning and adaptation.

📚 Summary: What You've Learned

Concept	Key Takeaway
Wallet Setup	MetaMask, Trust Wallet, Ledger
Market Trends	Bull/Bear, market cap, volume
Trading Steps	Deposit → Buy → Monitor → Sell/Withdraw
Exchanges	Binance, Coinbase, Uniswap
Safety	Never share private keys, use 2FA

⬚ Real Impact for Students: Empowering the Next Generation in the Decentralized Digital Economy

Engaging with cryptocurrencies and the underlying Web3 technologies can have a profound and multifaceted impact on students, extending far beyond just potential financial gains. It offers a unique opportunity to develop crucial skills and knowledge that are increasingly relevant in our rapidly evolving world. Let's explore each of these areas in detail with examples relevant to a student's life:

💼 Learn Practical Finance Skills: Beyond Traditional Banking

- **Detailed Explanation:** Traditionally, financial literacy taught to students often revolves around concepts like budgeting, saving in traditional bank accounts, understanding loans, and perhaps basic stock market principles. However, the rise of cryptocurrencies introduces a new paradigm of finance that requires a different set of practical skills. By interacting with crypto, students can gain firsthand experience in managing digital assets, understanding decentralized financial systems, and navigating a global, borderless financial landscape.
- **Examples:**
    - **Wallet Management:** Setting up and managing a cryptocurrency wallet (hot or cold) teaches students about the importance of security, private keys, and responsible asset storage – crucial skills in the digital age.

- o **Transaction Management:** Sending and receiving cryptocurrencies demonstrates how digital transactions work, the concept of network fees (gas fees), and the immutability of blockchain records – providing a deeper understanding of digital value transfer.
- o **Decentralized Finance (DeFi):** Exploring DeFi platforms (even on a small scale) can introduce students to concepts like lending, borrowing, and earning interest without traditional banks, fostering an understanding of alternative financial models.
- o **Risk Assessment:** The volatility of the cryptocurrency market necessitates learning about risk assessment and diversification – essential skills for any form of investment. Students learn to weigh potential rewards against the possibility of losses.
- o **Budgeting in Crypto:** Tracking the value of their crypto holdings and managing transaction costs encourages budgeting and financial planning in a digital context.

☐ Think Analytically Using Charts & Trends: Developing Critical Thinking

- **Detailed Explanation:** The cryptocurrency market is driven by supply and demand, news events, technological advancements, and overall market sentiment. Understanding and interpreting price charts and market trends requires analytical thinking, pattern recognition, and the ability to synthesize information from various sources. This skill set is transferable to many other areas of study and future careers.
- **Examples:**
  - o **Technical Analysis:** Learning to read candlestick charts, identify support and resistance levels, and understand basic technical indicators (like moving averages) helps students develop analytical skills in interpreting visual data and making data-driven inferences.
  - o **Fundamental Analysis:** Researching the underlying technology, use cases, team, and adoption rate of different cryptocurrencies requires critical evaluation of information and the ability to form informed opinions based on evidence.
  - o **Market Sentiment Analysis:** Understanding how news, social media, and community discussions influence price movements encourages students to think about the psychological and social factors that drive markets.
  - o **Identifying Correlations:** Observing how different cryptocurrencies move in relation to each other (e.g., Bitcoin's influence on altcoins) helps students understand market dynamics and interdependencies.
  - o **Evaluating Information Sources:** Navigating the vast amount of information (and misinformation) online about cryptocurrencies teaches students to critically evaluate sources and distinguish credible information from hype or scams.

☐ Potential to Grow Small Investments: The Power of Early Exposure (with Caution)

- **Detailed Explanation:** While it's crucial to emphasize the risks and volatility involved, cryptocurrencies offer the potential for significant growth, even with small initial investments. For students with limited capital, early exposure (with funds they can afford to lose) can provide a valuable learning experience and the possibility of seeing their investments grow over time. However, this must always be approached with caution and a long-term perspective.

- **Examples:**
    - **Dollar-Cost Averaging (DCA):** Investing a small, fixed amount regularly (e.g., $10 per week) can help mitigate the risk of buying at a market peak and allows students to gradually accumulate assets over time.
    - **Early Adoption of Promising Projects:** With thorough research, students might identify promising smaller projects with growth potential (though this also carries higher risk).
    - **Learning about Staking and Yield Farming (Advanced):** As they become more knowledgeable, students might explore low-risk ways to earn passive income on their holdings through staking or participating in carefully vetted DeFi protocols (again, with a strong understanding of the risks involved).
    - **Understanding Long-Term Growth Potential:** Learning about the potential future applications of blockchain technology and cryptocurrencies can provide a long-term perspective on their investment potential (though this is speculative).
- **Crucial Caveat:** It's vital to reiterate that cryptocurrency investments are highly speculative and students should only invest what they can absolutely afford to lose without impacting their essential needs or education. The focus should be on learning and gaining experience, not on get-rich-quick schemes.

☐ Stay Ahead in a Decentralized Digital Economy: Preparing for the Future

- **Detailed Explanation:** The world is increasingly moving towards a more decentralized and digital economy, with blockchain technology and cryptocurrencies playing a significant role. Students who gain an understanding of these technologies now will be better equipped to navigate and contribute to this future landscape. This knowledge can provide a competitive edge in various fields.
- **Examples:**
    - **Understanding Web3:** Learning about cryptocurrencies is a gateway to understanding the broader Web3 ecosystem, including decentralized applications (dApps), NFTs, and DAOs, which are likely to shape the future of the internet and many industries.
    - **Career Opportunities:** The blockchain and cryptocurrency industries are rapidly growing, creating new job opportunities in software development, cybersecurity, finance, law, marketing, and more. Early exposure can spark interest and provide foundational knowledge for these future careers.
    - **Entrepreneurial Ventures:** Understanding decentralized technologies can inspire students to develop innovative solutions and build their own projects in the Web3 space.
    - **Adapting to Technological Change:** Learning about a disruptive technology like blockchain fosters adaptability and a mindset of continuous learning, which is essential in a rapidly changing technological landscape.
    - **Informed Participation in the Digital Society:** As digital currencies and decentralized systems become more mainstream, students with a foundational

understanding will be better equipped to participate in these new economic and social structures in an informed and responsible manner.

30 multiple-choice questions with answers covering setting up a wallet, understanding market trends, and a real-world trading demo:

Setting Up a Wallet

1. What is the primary purpose of a cryptocurrency wallet? a) To mine new cryptocurrencies. b) To track the price of cryptocurrencies. c) To store, manage, send, and receive cryptocurrencies. d) To facilitate fiat currency deposits on exchanges. **Answer: c)**
2. Which type of wallet is a software application on your smartphone? a) Desktop wallet. b) Hardware wallet. c) Mobile wallet. d) Paper wallet. **Answer: c)**
3. MetaMask is an example of a: a) Hardware wallet. b) Mobile wallet. c) Browser wallet. d) Desktop wallet. **Answer: c)**
4. Ledger and Trezor are examples of: a) Hot wallets. b) Cold wallets. c) Exchange wallets. d) Web wallets. **Answer: b)**
5. What is the most crucial piece of information to securely save when setting up a new cryptocurrency wallet? a) Your public address. b) Your username and password. c) Your Secret Recovery Phrase (seed phrase). d) The wallet's customer support number. **Answer: c)**
6. Where should you ideally store your Secret Recovery Phrase? a) In a text file on your computer. b) Backed up in the cloud. c) Written down offline in a secure location. d) Shared with a trusted friend for safekeeping. **Answer: c)**
7. A hardware wallet stores your private keys: a) Online on a secure server. b) Directly on your computer's hard drive. c) Offline on a physical device. d) Encrypted in a mobile app. **Answer: c)**
8. Which type of wallet is generally considered the most convenient for frequent trading? a) Hardware wallet. b) Paper wallet. c) Hot wallet. d) Cold storage. **Answer: c)**
9. Losing access to your private key or seed phrase typically results in: a) A temporary lock on your account. b) The ability to reset it through customer support. c) The permanent loss of your cryptocurrency. d) Automatic recovery by the blockchain network. **Answer: c)**
10. What is a public address used for? a) To authorize transactions. b) To keep your wallet secure. c) To receive cryptocurrency. d) To recover your seed phrase. **Answer: c)**

Understanding Market Trends

11. A sustained period of increasing prices in the cryptocurrency market is known as a: a) Bear market. b) Sideways trend. c) Bull market. d) Correction phase. **Answer: c)**
12. What does ATH stand for in the context of cryptocurrency? a) Average Trading Hour. b) All-Time High. c) Automated Trading Hub. d) Asset Transaction History. **Answer: b)**
13. How is the market capitalization of a cryptocurrency calculated? a) Total supply × Transaction volume. b) Current price × Total supply. c) Current price × Circulating supply. d) Highest price × Lowest price. **Answer: c)**

14. What does trading volume indicate? a) The total number of transactions on the blockchain. b) The average price of a cryptocurrency over a period. c) How much of a cryptocurrency has been bought and sold. d) The market dominance of a particular cryptocurrency. **Answer: c)**
15. A price level where buying pressure is expected to be strong enough to prevent the price from falling further is called: a) Resistance level. b) Support level. c) Breakout point. d) Consolidation zone. **Answer: b)**
16. A price level where selling pressure is expected to be strong enough to prevent the price from rising further is called: a) Support level. b) Accumulation phase. c) Resistance level. d) Distribution phase. **Answer: c)**
17. Websites like CoinMarketCap and CoinGecko are primarily used for: a) Trading cryptocurrencies directly. b) Storing private keys securely. c) Analyzing market trends and viewing cryptocurrency data. d) Mining new cryptocurrency coins. **Answer: c)**
18. What might high trading volume accompanying a price increase suggest? a) Weakening bullish momentum. b) Strong confirmation of the upward trend. c) An impending price reversal. d) A lack of interest in the asset. **Answer: b)**
19. A prolonged period of declining prices in the cryptocurrency market is known as a: a) Bull run. b) Consolidation. c) Bear market. d) Recovery phase. **Answer: c)**
20. Technical indicators are based on: a) Future predictions by analysts. b) Social media sentiment. c) Historical price and volume data. d) Insider information. **Answer: c)**

Real-World Trading Demo (Step-by-Step)

21. What is the first step in the real-world trading demo on Binance? a) Buying Ethereum. b) Depositing fiat currency. c) Creating an exchange account and verifying identity (KYC). d) Withdrawing cryptocurrency to a personal wallet. **Answer: c)**
22. KYC (Know Your Customer) typically involves: a) Sharing your private key with the exchange. b) Providing personal information and identification documents. c) Depositing a large sum of cryptocurrency initially. d) Enabling two-factor authentication. **Answer: b)**
23. On Binance, where would you typically deposit fiat currency to start trading? a) Directly to a trading pair. b) To your exchange wallet. c) To a decentralized wallet connected to Binance. d) To a mining pool. **Answer: b)**
24. To buy Ethereum (ETH) on Binance, you would typically search for which trading pair against your deposited fiat currency (e.g., USD)? a) BTC/ETH. b) ETH/BTC. c) ETH/USD. d) USD/ETH. **Answer: c)**
25. What is a "market order" used for when buying or selling cryptocurrency? a) To set a specific price you are willing to trade at. b) To execute the trade immediately at the current market price. c) To automatically buy or sell when the price reaches a certain level. d) To cancel an existing order. **Answer: b)**
26. If you intend to hold your purchased ETH for a long term, it is generally recommended to: a) Keep it on the Binance exchange for easy trading. b) Transfer it to a secure, non-custodial wallet like MetaMask or Trust Wallet. c) Stake it on the exchange for passive income. d) Trade it frequently to maximize potential gains. **Answer: b)**
27. What are "gas fees" associated with when using a DEX like Uniswap? a) Transaction fees charged by the centralized exchange. b) Fees for converting fiat currency to crypto. c)

Transaction fees on the underlying blockchain network (e.g., Ethereum). d) Fees for withdrawing funds from the DEX. **Answer: c)**

28. When using a DEX like Uniswap, you typically connect your: a) Bank account directly. b) Centralized exchange account. c) Non-custodial cryptocurrency wallet (e.g., MetaMask). d) Government-issued digital ID. **Answer: c)**

29. What is a crucial tip for student traders regarding the amount they should invest? a) Invest as much as possible to maximize potential returns. b) Borrow money to capitalize on promising opportunities. c) Only invest what they can afford to lose. d) Follow the investment advice of online "gurus." **Answer: c)**

30. Why is it important to double-check token symbols when trading on cryptocurrency exchanges? a) To ensure faster transaction speeds. b) To verify the legitimacy of the exchange platform. c) To avoid trading fake tokens that look like real ones. d) To understand the market capitalization of the token. **Answer: c)**

10 mid-size questions with answers covering setting up a wallet, understanding market trends, and a real-world trading demo:

1. **Explain the difference between a custodial and a non-custodial cryptocurrency wallet. When setting up your first wallet, which type is recommended for beginners who prioritize ease of use, and which is better for those prioritizing full control and security of their private keys? Answer:** A custodial wallet is where a third party (like an exchange) holds your private keys for you, offering convenience but less control. A non-custodial wallet gives you full control over your private keys. For beginners prioritizing ease of use, a reputable mobile or browser-based non-custodial wallet (where they still manage their keys but with a user-friendly interface) is often a good starting point. For those prioritizing full control and security, especially for larger amounts, a hardware wallet (a type of cold, non-custodial storage) is generally recommended, although it might have a slightly steeper learning curve.

2. **Describe the process of setting up a browser-based wallet like MetaMask. What is the significance of the Secret Recovery Phrase (seed phrase) during this process, and what are three critical security measures a new user should take to protect this phrase? Answer:** Setting up MetaMask involves downloading the browser extension, creating a password, and then being presented with a Secret Recovery Phrase (typically 12 words). This phrase is a master backup key to your wallet. Critical security measures include: 1) Writing it down on physical paper and storing it offline in a secure location. 2) Never sharing it with anyone or entering it on any website other than when restoring your wallet on a trusted device. 3) Considering storing it in multiple secure, separate locations to prevent loss.

3. **Explain the concepts of a "bull market" and a "bear market" in the context of cryptocurrency trading. What are some common indicators that might suggest the**

market is entering either of these phases? Answer: A bull market is a sustained period of rising prices and positive investor sentiment, often indicated by consecutive price increases, growing trading volumes, and positive news. A bear market is a prolonged period of declining prices and negative sentiment, often characterized by consistent price drops, decreasing trading volumes, and negative news.

4. **Describe how market capitalization and trading volume can provide insights into the strength and liquidity of a cryptocurrency. Provide an example of how a trader might use these metrics in their analysis. Answer:** Market capitalization (price × circulating supply) indicates the overall size and value of a cryptocurrency. A larger market cap often suggests a more established and potentially less volatile asset. Trading volume shows how much of a cryptocurrency is being bought and sold over a period. High volume often accompanies significant price movements, indicating strong interest and liquidity. A trader might look for a breakout above a resistance level accompanied by a significant increase in volume as a potential buy signal, suggesting strong conviction behind the price increase.

5. **Explain the difference between a "market order" and a "limit order" when buying or selling cryptocurrency on a centralized exchange like Binance. When might a beginner trader choose to use each type of order? Answer:** A market order executes immediately at the best available current price, prioritizing speed. A limit order allows you to set a specific price at which you want to buy or sell, and the order will only execute if the market reaches that price, prioritizing price control. A beginner might use a market order for a quick and simple purchase or sale at the current price. They might use a limit order to try and buy at a slightly lower price or sell at a slightly higher price than the current market value, but it carries the risk of not being filled if the market doesn't reach their target.

6. **Describe the process of withdrawing cryptocurrency from a centralized exchange (like Binance) to a personal, non-custodial wallet (like MetaMask). What are some important considerations and potential risks involved in this process? Answer:** Withdrawing crypto involves navigating to the "Withdraw" section of the exchange, selecting the cryptocurrency and the withdrawal network, and entering the recipient address (your public address from MetaMask). Important considerations include: ensuring you select the correct withdrawal network (e.g., Ethereum Mainnet for ETH to MetaMask), double-checking the recipient address for accuracy (as transactions are irreversible), and being aware of any withdrawal fees charged by the exchange. A key risk is sending funds to the wrong address, which can result in permanent loss.

7. **Explain the role of "gas fees" on decentralized exchanges (DEXs) like Uniswap. Why can these fees sometimes be significantly higher than transaction fees on centralized exchanges, and what is their purpose? Answer:** Gas fees on DEXs like Uniswap are transaction fees paid to the underlying blockchain network (like Ethereum) to compensate miners or validators for processing transactions. These fees can be higher than on CEXs because they reflect the real-time demand for block space on the decentralized network. Their purpose is to incentivize the network to process transactions and maintain its security. High network congestion leads to higher gas fees.

8. **In a real-world trading scenario, what are some psychological biases that beginner traders should be aware of and actively try to avoid? Provide two specific examples. Answer:** Beginner traders should be aware of psychological biases like:
   - **FOMO (Fear Of Missing Out):** This can lead to impulsive buying at inflated prices based on hype, without proper research, often resulting in losses when the hype subsides.
   - **Loss Aversion:** This can cause traders to hold onto losing positions for too long, hoping they will recover, rather than cutting their losses and preserving capital. They might also sell winning positions too early out of fear of losing their profits.

9. **Discuss the importance of "doing your own research" (DYOR) before investing in any cryptocurrency. What are at least three key areas a student should investigate when researching a potential crypto investment? Answer:** Doing your own research is crucial to make informed decisions and avoid scams or poorly understood projects. Key areas to investigate include: 1) The project's fundamentals: What problem does it solve? What is the underlying technology? What is the use case? 2) The team and community: Who are the developers and advisors? Is there an active and engaged community supporting the project? 3) Tokenomics: What is the token supply and distribution? What are the token's utility and potential for value accrual?

10. **Beyond just buying and selling, what are some other ways students can engage with the cryptocurrency and Web3 ecosystem (even with limited capital) to learn and potentially benefit in the long term? Answer:** Besides trading, students can engage by: 1) Exploring and interacting with decentralized applications (dApps) to understand their functionality. 2) Learning about and potentially participating in decentralized autonomous organizations (DAOs) to understand governance. 3) Creating and managing a non-fungible token (NFT) to understand digital ownership. 4) Following reputable educational resources and communities to stay informed about the evolving landscape. 5) Exploring opportunities to earn small amounts of crypto through activities like participating in testnets or contributing to open-source projects (with caution and proper research).

CHAPTER 7: CRYPTO EARNING FOR STUDENTS – LEARN & EARN

Imagine earning real money (yes, real crypto!) by learning, playing games, or doing simple online tasks — without a boss or office. Sounds cool? This is the new economy of **Web3**, and it's open to students like YOU.

This chapter introduces legit and beginner-friendly ways students can **earn crypto online** — even without investing any money upfront.

🎮 1. Play-to-Earn (P2E) Games – Earn While You Game

What Is It? The Core Concept of P2E

At its heart, a P2E game is a video game that incorporates blockchain technology to create a player-driven economy. Unlike traditional games where in-game items and currencies have no value outside the game's ecosystem, P2E games empower players to earn digital assets that can be traded, sold, or exchanged for other cryptocurrencies or even fiat money on external marketplaces and exchanges.

- **Rewards Mechanisms:** Players can earn these rewards through various in-game activities, such as:
    - **Completing Missions and Quests:** Achieving specific objectives or storylines within the game.
    - **Winning Battles and Competitions:** Engaging in player-versus-player (PvP) or player-versus-environment (PvE) combat and emerging victorious.
    - **Participating in In-Game Economies:** Engaging in activities like crafting items, owning virtual land, providing services to other players, or contributing to the game's ecosystem.
    - **Collecting Rare Items and NFTs:** Discovering or earning unique digital assets that have inherent scarcity and value.
    - **Staking and Governance:** In some P2E games with their own cryptocurrencies, players can earn rewards by staking their tokens or participating in the game's governance decisions.
- **Real-World Value:** The key differentiator of P2E games is that the earned cryptocurrencies and NFTs are often tradeable on cryptocurrency exchanges and NFT marketplaces. This allows players to convert their in-game earnings into real money, creating a potential income stream.

🔥 Real Example: Axie Infinity – Pioneering the P2E Revolution

Axie Infinity is a prime example of a successful P2E game that gained significant traction, particularly in regions like the Philippines.

- **Gameplay:** Players collect, breed, raise, battle, and trade adorable digital creatures called **Axies**. Each Axie is a unique **NFT** with different attributes, strengths, and weaknesses.
- **Earning Mechanism:** Players primarily earn the in-game cryptocurrency called **Smooth Love Potion (SLP)** by:
    - **Winning Battles:** Competing against other players' Axie teams in the Arena mode.
    - **Completing Daily Quests:** Fulfilling specific tasks within the game.
    - **Adventure Mode:** Progressing through the game's story mode and defeating monsters.
- **Real-World Trading:** The **SLP tokens** earned by players are **traded on major cryptocurrency exchanges like Binance**. This allows players to sell their earned SLP for other cryptocurrencies (like ETH or USDT) and eventually convert them into fiat currency. Additionally, the **Axie NFTs themselves can be bought and sold on NFT marketplaces** for varying prices depending on their rarity, attributes, and demand.

How Students Earn: The Scholarship Model

The example of the "Scholarship Program" in Axie Infinity highlights an innovative way for students and others with limited upfront capital to participate in P2E games:

- **Borrowing Axies:** More established players ("Managers") who own multiple Axie teams can "lend" or "delegate" Axies to new players ("Scholars") through a profit-sharing agreement. The Scholar can play the game using the borrowed Axies without having to invest the initial cost of purchasing their own team (which can be significant).
- **Daily Play:** Scholars then play the game daily, engaging in battles and completing quests to earn SLP tokens.
- **Earning SLP:** As mentioned, players can earn between **50–100 SLP per day**, which, at the example price point, translates to approximately **$1–$2 per day**. This value can fluctuate based on the market price of SLP.
- **Cashing Out:** The earned SLP is typically tracked and then distributed between the Manager and the Scholar according to their agreed-upon percentage split. The Scholar then receives their share in their in-game wallet, which they can eventually withdraw to their own cryptocurrency wallet and trade on exchanges for other cryptocurrencies or fiat money.

⚡ Other Popular P2E Games: Expanding the Earning Opportunities

The P2E gaming landscape is constantly evolving, with new games emerging and existing ones developing further. Here are some other popular examples with different earning mechanisms and platforms:

- **Gods Unchained:**
    - **What You Earn:** Players earn **GODS tokens** by winning ranked matches and through participation in weekly reward pools based on their rank. They also earn **NFT cards** which can be traded.
    - **Platform:** PC (primarily).

- o **Earning Mechanism:** Skill-based card battles where strategic gameplay and deck building are key to earning rewards.
- **The Sandbox:**
  - o **What You Earn:** Players can earn **LAND NFTs** (representing virtual real estate) and **SAND tokens** by creating and monetizing experiences on their LAND, participating in events, and staking SAND.
  - o **Platform:** PC.
  - o **Earning Mechanism:** Focuses on user-generated content, creativity, and virtual land ownership. Players can build games, create assets, and host events on their LAND to earn.
- **Zed Run:**
  - o **What You Earn:** Players own, breed, and race digital racehorses, which are **NFTs**. They earn rewards in cryptocurrency (often ETH or stablecoins) by winning races and can also earn by breeding and selling valuable horses.
  - o **Platform:** Web-based.
  - o **Earning Mechanism:** Combines horse racing with NFT ownership and breeding mechanics. Rarity, breed type, and racing performance influence the value and earning potential of the horses.

💡 Real-World Impact: Earning Potential for Students

The example of students in the Philippines earning **$100–$300 per month** just by playing P2E games highlights the real economic impact these games can have, particularly in regions with lower average incomes. While the earning potential can vary greatly depending on the game, the player's skill, the market value of the earned assets, and the time invested, P2E games offer a unique opportunity for students to supplement their income or even contribute significantly to their household finances.

Important Considerations for Students Engaging in P2E:

- **Time Investment:** Earning significant amounts in P2E games often requires a substantial time commitment. Students need to balance gaming with their studies and other responsibilities.
- **Market Volatility:** The value of the cryptocurrencies and NFTs earned in P2E games can be highly volatile. Earnings in one month might be significantly different in the next.
- **Initial Investment (Sometimes Required):** While scholarship programs exist, some P2E games require an initial investment to purchase the necessary NFTs or in-game assets to start earning.
- **Game Economics:** The earning potential within a P2E game can change over time based on the game's economy, the influx of new players, and updates to the reward structure.
- **Scams and Risks:** The P2E space is not immune to scams and rug pulls (where developers abandon a project after raising funds). Students should thoroughly research games before investing time or money.
- **Tax Implications:** Earnings from P2E games may be subject to taxation depending on the jurisdiction. Students should be aware of their local tax laws.

Despite these considerations, P2E games represent an exciting evolution in the gaming industry, offering students and others a novel way to potentially earn income while engaging in a popular form of entertainment. As the technology matures and the ecosystem develops, P2E games could become an increasingly significant part of the digital economy.

---

2. Airdrops, Staking, and DeFi (Passive Income): Exploring Ways to Earn in the Crypto Space

Beyond active trading and play-to-earn games, the cryptocurrency world offers several avenues for generating **passive income**. These methods allow you to potentially earn rewards on your existing cryptocurrency holdings or by participating in the growth of new projects. Let's delve into airdrops, staking, and Decentralized Finance (DeFi) with detailed explanations and student-friendly examples:

Airdrops – Free Crypto for Early Users: Rewarding Early Adoption

- **What Is It?** Airdrops are a marketing strategy used by cryptocurrency projects to distribute free tokens to a large number of people, [1] typically early users, testers, or holders of a specific cryptocurrency. Think of it as a promotional giveaway or a loyalty bonus for being among the first to engage with a new platform or technology. The goal is to increase awareness, adoption, and decentralization of the project.
- **How They Work:** To be eligible for an airdrop, you usually need to perform certain actions, such as:
    - **Using/Testing the Platform:** Interacting with a new decentralized application (dApp), blockchain network, or wallet during its early stages. This helps the project gather feedback and build an initial user base.
    - **Joining Communities:** Becoming a member of the project's online communities on platforms like Discord, Telegram, or Twitter and actively engaging with the community.
    - **Holding Specific Cryptocurrencies:** Sometimes, projects airdrop new tokens to existing holders of a well-established cryptocurrency (e.g., a new token on the Solana blockchain might airdrop to SOL holders).
    - **Completing Tasks:** Following the project on social media, retweeting announcements, or completing simple tasks.
    - **Participating in DAOs (Decentralized Autonomous Organizations):** Voting on proposals or actively participating in the governance of a decentralized project.
- ✅ **Example: Uniswap Airdrop**
    - **Context:** Uniswap is a leading decentralized exchange (DEX) on the Ethereum blockchain. In September 2020, they launched their own governance token, **UNI**.
    - **Reward:** Uniswap airdropped **400 UNI tokens** to every wallet address that had ever interacted with the Uniswap protocol before a specific date.
    - **Value:** At the time of the airdrop, UNI tokens were trading at around $3 each, making the airdrop worth approximately **$1,200**. The value of UNI has fluctuated significantly since then, reaching much higher prices.

- **Student Impact:** As your example highlights, some students who had simply swapped a small amount of crypto (even just **$5 worth**) on Uniswap in its early days were eligible for this substantial airdrop, receiving a significant windfall simply for being early users.
- **How to Get Airdrops (Strategies for Students):**
  - **Use New Crypto Apps:** Keep an eye out for announcements of new and promising decentralized applications (dApps) and blockchain networks (like **Arbitrum**, **Optimism**, **LayerZero** are mentioned as examples of Layer-2 scaling solutions on Ethereum that have hinted at or conducted airdrops). Early interaction can make you eligible for future token distributions.
  - **Join Communities:** Follow the official social media channels (Twitter) and join community platforms (Discord, Telegram) of new projects you find interesting. Being active and engaging in these communities can sometimes increase your chances of receiving airdrops.
  - **Stay Active:** If you are using a new platform or wallet, try to be an active user. Swap tokens, provide liquidity (if you understand the risks), and explore the platform's features.
  - **Participate in DAOs:** If a project you are involved with has a DAO, consider participating in voting on proposals. Active participation can sometimes be rewarded with airdrops.
  - **Be Patient:** Airdrops often happen retroactively, rewarding early users who may not have even been expecting a reward. Stay engaged with projects you believe in.
- **Important Note:** Be cautious of fake airdrops and scams that require you to send cryptocurrency to receive free tokens. Legitimate airdrops usually involve receiving tokens, not sending them. Always verify the authenticity of an airdrop announcement through official project channels.

☐ Staking – Earn Passive Rewards Like a Crypto Bank: Locking Up Your Assets

- **What Is It?** Staking is the process of "locking up" a certain amount of your cryptocurrency in a blockchain network for a specific period to support the network's operations (like validating transactions in Proof-of-Stake blockchains). In return for your contribution, you earn rewards, similar to earning interest on a fixed deposit in a traditional bank.
- **How It Works:**
  - **Proof-of-Stake (PoS):** Many modern blockchains use a Proof-of-Stake consensus mechanism. In PoS, participants (stakers) are chosen to validate new transactions and add new blocks to the blockchain based on the amount of cryptocurrency they have staked.
  - **Earning Rewards:** Staking rewards are typically distributed in the form of the native cryptocurrency of the blockchain you are staking. The percentage of rewards can vary depending on the blockchain, the amount staked, and the duration of the staking period.

- o **Unstaking:** You can usually "unstake" your cryptocurrency after a certain period (which can vary), at which point it becomes liquid again and you can trade or use it.
- ✅ **Example: Staking ETH (Ethereum)**
  - o **Context:** Ethereum transitioned to a Proof-of-Stake consensus mechanism (Eth2 or The Merge).
  - o **Process:** Users can "stake" their Ether (ETH) to help secure the Ethereum network.
  - o **Reward:** As of the example, staking 1 ETH (worth around $3,000 at that price) could earn you an annual reward of approximately **4%**, which would be **$120 per year** in ETH (the actual amount of ETH earned would be 0.04 ETH). The value of this ETH reward would then fluctuate with the price of ETH.
  - o **Platforms:** Staking ETH (and other cryptocurrencies) can be done through:
    - **Centralized Exchanges (Binance, Coinbase):** These platforms often offer easy-to-use interfaces for staking, handling the technical complexities for you. However, you entrust your staked ETH to the exchange.
    - **Decentralized Platforms (Lido, RocketPool):** These are decentralized protocols that allow you to stake ETH and receive liquid staking tokens (like stETH or rETH) in return, which can be used in other DeFi applications while your ETH remains staked.
    - **Directly on the Ethereum Network (for more tech-savvy users):** Running your own validator node requires a larger amount of ETH (currently 32 ETH) and technical expertise.
- 🏦 **Where to Stake:**
  - o **Centralized (Binance, Coinbase): Pros:** Easy to use, often lower technical barrier. **Cons:** Less control over your assets, potential platform risks.
  - o **Decentralized (Lido, RocketPool, Ethereum Staking Directly): Pros:** More control, often better rewards (though not always guaranteed), contributes to network decentralization. **Cons:** Can be more complex to set up and manage, may involve smart contract risks.

☐ DeFi – Decentralized Finance: Banking Without Banks

- **What Is It?** Decentralized Finance (DeFi) is a revolutionary movement that aims to recreate traditional financial services (like lending, borrowing, trading, and earning interest) in a decentralized and transparent manner, without relying on traditional intermediaries like banks. DeFi protocols are typically built on blockchain networks, primarily Ethereum.
- **How It Works:** DeFi applications (often called dApps) use smart contracts to automate financial services. These contracts are transparent and publicly auditable on the blockchain.
- ✅ **Example: A Student in Nigeria Using Aave**
  - o **Context:** Aave is a popular DeFi lending and borrowing protocol.
  - o **Action:** A student in Nigeria deposits **$100** worth of **USDC** (a stablecoin pegged to the US dollar) into the Aave protocol.

- - **Earning Interest:** The student earns an annual percentage yield (APY) of **6%** on their deposited USDC. This interest is earned passively, and the student can typically withdraw their deposited USDC and accrued interest at any time (subject to market conditions and protocol rules).
  - **Benefits: No bank account is needed**, and there are **no traditional ID requirements** beyond having a cryptocurrency wallet to interact with the Aave protocol. This can provide financial access to individuals who may be unbanked or face barriers with traditional financial systems.
- **Other DeFi Use Cases:**
  - **Lending and Borrowing:** You can lend out your cryptocurrencies to earn interest or borrow cryptocurrencies by providing collateral. Platforms like Compound and Aave facilitate this.
  - **Providing Liquidity:** On decentralized exchanges (DEXs) like Uniswap and PancakeSwap, you can deposit pairs of cryptocurrencies into liquidity pools and earn a share of the trading fees generated by swaps within that pool. This can be lucrative but also carries the risk of "impermanent loss."
  - **Yield Farming:** More advanced strategies involve moving your cryptocurrency between different DeFi protocols to maximize yield. This can be complex and carries higher risks.
- **Important Considerations for DeFi:**
  - **Smart Contract Risks:** DeFi protocols rely on smart contracts, which can have vulnerabilities that could lead to loss of funds.
  - **Impermanent Loss:** Liquidity providers on DEXs can experience impermanent loss, where the value of their deposited assets changes compared to just holding them.
  - **Volatility:** While stablecoins aim to maintain a stable value, other cryptocurrencies used in DeFi can be highly volatile.
  - **Complexity:** Understanding and navigating the various DeFi protocols can be complex, especially for beginners.
  - **Gas Fees:** Transactions on Ethereum-based DeFi protocols can incur significant gas fees.

Passive Income Opportunities for Students:

Airdrops, staking, and DeFi offer potential avenues for students to earn passive income in the cryptocurrency space. However, it's crucial to approach these opportunities with caution, conduct thorough research, understand the risks involved, and start with small amounts if any capital is required. These methods can be a valuable way to learn more about the crypto ecosystem while potentially earning some rewards.

💼 **3. Freelancing in the Crypto Space: Monetizing Your Skills in the Decentralized Web**

🔍 **Freelance Roles in Demand: Your Skills are Valuable in Web3**

The Web3 landscape is constantly evolving and requires a wide range of expertise to build, grow, and maintain projects. Here's a closer look at the in-demand skills you mentioned and where students might find opportunities:

- **Writing:**
  - **Job Example:** Many crypto projects need writers to create various forms of content, including blog posts explaining complex concepts, articles for crypto news outlets, white papers detailing project goals and technology, website copy, social media updates, and technical documentation.
  - **Platform Examples:**
    - **CryptoJobs.com:** A dedicated job board for blockchain and cryptocurrency roles, including freelance writing gigs.
    - **ContentFi:** A platform specifically connecting Web3 projects with content creators.
    - **Medium:** While not exclusively crypto-focused, many individuals and projects in the space publish articles on Medium and may hire writers.
    - **Direct Outreach:** Students can also directly reach out to crypto projects they find interesting and offer their writing services.

- **Design:**
  - **Job Example:** The visual aspect of Web3 is crucial. Designers are needed for creating NFT art collections, user interfaces (UI) and user experiences (UX) for dApps and websites, logos, marketing materials, infographics, and website mockups.
  - **Platform Examples:**
    - **Upwork, Fiverr:** General freelancing platforms with a growing number of Web3-related design gigs.
    - **NFT Marketplaces (e.g., OpenSea, Foundation):** Artists can create and sell their own NFT art. Projects launching NFT collections often hire designers.
    - **Direct Outreach:** Students with design portfolios can directly contact Web3 projects or NFT communities.

- **Marketing:**
  - **Job Example:** Marketing is essential for the growth and adoption of crypto projects. Freelance roles include managing and growing community channels (Discord, Telegram), running social media campaigns (Twitter, Reddit), creating engaging content, influencer marketing, search engine optimization (SEO), and managing email marketing.
  - **Platform Examples:**
    - **Crew3 (now Layer3):** Platforms where Web3 projects offer tasks and quests to community members, often with rewards in crypto and potential for ongoing roles.
    - **Zealy (formerly Crew3):** Similar to Crew3, focusing on community engagement and growth.
    - **Discord and Telegram Communities:** Many projects hire community managers and moderators directly from within their active communities.
    - **Upwork, Fiverr:** General freelancing platforms with marketing roles.

- **Coding:**
  - **Job Example:** Developers with coding skills are in high demand to build smart contracts (especially in Solidity for Ethereum and Rust for Solana), develop decentralized applications (dApps), contribute to blockchain protocols, and build Web3 infrastructure.
  - **Platform Examples:**
    - **Gitcoin:** A platform that funds open-source blockchain projects and often lists bounties for specific coding tasks.
    - **Bounties Network:** Another platform where projects offer rewards for completing specific technical tasks.
    - **LinkedIn:** Increasingly used by Web3 companies to hire developers.
    - **Direct Outreach:** Students with coding portfolios can directly contact Web3 projects or contribute to open-source initiatives.

✅ Example: Paid in Crypto – A Student's Success Story

Your example beautifully illustrates the potential:

- **Skill:** Writing crypto blogs on Medium.
- **Client:** Likely a Web3 startup or a crypto news outlet.
- **Payment: $50 per article in USDT (Tether),** a stablecoin pegged to the US dollar. This provides a degree of price stability compared to more volatile cryptocurrencies.
- **Impact:** The student earns income that can be saved for college expenses, demonstrating that freelancing in crypto can provide a viable alternative to traditional part-time jobs. The fact that it's location-independent also offers flexibility.

✦ Bonus: Learn-to-Earn Programs – Earning While Acquiring Knowledge

These programs are a fantastic way for students to simultaneously learn about the crypto space and earn small amounts of cryptocurrency:

- **Coinbase Earn:**
  - **How it Works:** Coinbase, a major centralized exchange, offers short, educational videos about various cryptocurrencies. After watching the videos, users can take a quiz to test their understanding and earn a small amount of the featured cryptocurrency as a reward.
  - **Benefit for Students:** It's a low-risk way to learn about different crypto projects and earn a bit of crypto to get started.
- **RabbitHole (now defunct, but similar platforms exist):**
  - **How it Worked:** RabbitHole provided "quests" that involved interacting with different Web3 applications (dApps). By completing these quests (e.g., making a swap on a DEX, providing liquidity), users could earn cryptocurrency rewards.
  - **Benefit for Students:** It offered hands-on experience with using Web3 tools while earning crypto, promoting active learning.
  - **Note:** While RabbitHole is no longer active, the concept of learn-to-earn through interacting with dApps is still prevalent on other platforms.

- **Layer3.xyz:**
  - **How it Works:** Layer3 offers daily and ongoing crypto challenges that involve interacting with various Web3 protocols and platforms. Participants who complete these challenges are often rewarded with cryptocurrency prizes or exclusive NFTs.
  - **Benefit for Students:** It provides a gamified way to learn about and engage with different parts of the Web3 ecosystem while having the opportunity to earn rewards.

Key Takeaways for Students Interested in Freelancing in Crypto:

- **Identify Your Skills:** Think about your existing talents and how they might be applicable to the Web3 space.
- **Build a Portfolio:** Showcase your writing samples, design work, coding projects, or social media management experience.
- **Network:** Engage with crypto communities online (Discord, Twitter, Telegram) and let people know about your skills.
- **Be Proactive:** Don't just wait for opportunities to come to you. Reach out to projects you're interested in and offer your services.
- **Be Patient:** Building a freelance career takes time and effort. Don't get discouraged if you don't see results immediately.
- **Learn Continuously:** The Web3 space is constantly evolving, so it's crucial to stay updated on the latest trends and technologies.
- **Be Professional:** Treat your freelance work seriously, meet deadlines, and communicate effectively.
- **Understand Payment Methods:** Be prepared to be paid in various cryptocurrencies or stablecoins. Set up appropriate wallets to receive these payments.

Freelancing in the crypto space offers a unique and potentially lucrative opportunity for students to utilize their skills, gain real-world experience in a cutting-edge industry, and earn income in a decentralized digital economy – all without the traditional barriers of entry. The learn-to-earn programs further provide a low-risk way to acquire knowledge and potentially earn small amounts of crypto while exploring this exciting new frontier.

📚 Summary – Student Earning Checklist

Method	Earnings Potential	Risk	Time
P2E Games	$50–$300/mo	Medium	High
Airdrops	$100–$1,000+	Low	Low
Staking	3–10% APY	Low	Low

Method	Earnings Potential	Risk	Time
DeFi Lending	5–15% APY	Medium	Medium
Freelance	$10–$100/hr	Low	Medium
Learn-to-Earn	$5–$100/task	None	Low

🎯 Final Thoughts: Why Students Should Try This

- ☐ No location limits — work from anywhere
- 🕐 Part-time or full-time flexibility
- 💰 Build **real income** without traditional jobs
- 📚 Learn real-world skills in finance, tech, and business
- 🚀 Gain early exposure to **future careers in Web3**

30 multiple-choice questions with answers covering Play-to-Earn games, Airdrops/Staking/DeFi, and Freelancing in the Crypto Space:

Play-to-Earn (P2E) Games

1. What is the core concept of Play-to-Earn (P2E) games? a) Games that are free to download and play. b) Games where players compete for high scores on leaderboards. c) Blockchain-based games that reward players with crypto or NFTs for in-game activities. d) Traditional games that have integrated cryptocurrency payments for in-game items. **Answer: c)**
2. In P2E games, rewards are typically earned by: a) Watching advertisements. b) Completing missions, winning battles, or participating in economies. c) Sharing the game on social media. d) Referring new players to the game. **Answer: b)**
3. Axie Infinity primarily rewards players with which cryptocurrency? a) Bitcoin (BTC) b) Ethereum (ETH) c) Smooth Love Potion (SLP) d) Axie Infinity Shards (AXS) **Answer: c)**
4. In Axie Infinity, the cute creatures players collect and battle with are: a) Tokens. b) NFTs. c) Avatars. d) Skins. **Answer: b)**
5. What is a "Scholarship Program" in the context of Axie Infinity? a) A program where experienced players teach new players the game for free. b) A system where managers lend Axies to new players to earn SLP under a profit-sharing agreement. c) A university scholarship sponsored by the Axie Infinity developers. d) A program where players can earn extra SLP by referring friends. **Answer: b)**
6. Gods Unchained rewards players primarily with: a) SLP tokens. b) AXS tokens. c) GODS tokens and NFT cards. d) SAND tokens. **Answer: c)**

7. The Sandbox allows players to earn by: a) Only winning battles against other players. b) Mining cryptocurrency within the game world. c) Creating and monetizing experiences on virtual LAND and earning SAND tokens. d) Completing simple daily tasks. **Answer: c)**

8. Zed Run involves earning through: a) Building virtual houses and selling them. b) Racing, breeding, and selling NFT racehorses. c) Trading in-game resources on a marketplace. d) Completing story-driven quests. **Answer: b)**

9. A potential risk associated with P2E games is: a) The games are often not fun to play. b) The value of earned cryptocurrencies and NFTs can be volatile. c) They require a very high-end gaming PC. d) They are not accessible to students. **Answer: b)**

10. What is a key difference between traditional games and P2E games? a) P2E games have better graphics. b) P2E games are always free to play. c) P2E games allow players to earn digital assets with real-world value. d) Traditional games have more complex storylines. **Answer: c)**

Airdrops, Staking, and DeFi

11. What is a cryptocurrency airdrop? a) A sudden drop in the price of a cryptocurrency. b) A marketing strategy to distribute free tokens to early users. c) A secure method of storing cryptocurrency offline. d) A type of decentralized exchange. **Answer: b)**

12. Eligibility for airdrops often involves: a) Holding large amounts of existing cryptocurrency. b) Using or testing new crypto platforms early. c) Predicting the price movements of cryptocurrencies. d) Mining a specific cryptocurrency. **Answer: b)**

13. Uniswap's 2020 airdrop rewarded users who had: a) Held a specific amount of Bitcoin. b) Referred the most new users to Uniswap. c) Previously used the Uniswap protocol. d) Staked their Ethereum on the platform. **Answer: c)**

14. What is cryptocurrency staking? a) Actively trading cryptocurrencies on an exchange. b) Lending cryptocurrency to borrowers for interest. c) Locking up cryptocurrency in a network to earn rewards and support its operations. d) Using cryptocurrency to purchase goods and services. **Answer: c)**

15. Staking rewards are often similar to: a) Stock dividends. b) Lottery winnings. c) Interest earned on a bank fixed deposit. d) Capital gains from trading. **Answer: c)**

16. Where can you typically stake cryptocurrencies? a) Only on decentralized exchanges. b) Only on hardware wallets. c) On centralized exchanges and decentralized platforms. d) Only directly on the blockchain network by running a node. **Answer: c)**

17. What is DeFi (Decentralized Finance)? a) A regulatory body governing cryptocurrency exchanges. b) Traditional banking services offered online. c) Financial services built on decentralized blockchain networks without intermediaries. d) A type of centralized cryptocurrency lending platform. **Answer: c)**

18. Examples of activities you can do in DeFi include: a) Mining Bitcoin and Ethereum. b) Only buying and selling cryptocurrencies. c) Lending crypto for interest, providing liquidity, and borrowing against crypto. d) Storing all your cryptocurrency on a single platform. **Answer: c)**

19. Platforms like Aave allow users to: a) Mine new cryptocurrencies. b) Lend and borrow cryptocurrencies. c) Trade stocks and bonds with crypto. d) Play decentralized games. **Answer: b)**

20. A potential risk associated with participating in DeFi is: a) The lack of user-friendly interfaces. b) The requirement of a college degree. c) Smart contract vulnerabilities and impermanent loss. d) High transaction speeds. **Answer: c)**

Freelancing in the Crypto Space

21. What types of skills are in demand for freelancing in the crypto space? a) Only coding and technical skills. b) Only finance and trading expertise. c) Writing, design, coding, marketing, and community management. d) Only mining and blockchain analysis. **Answer: c)**
22. Platforms like CryptoJobs and ContentFi primarily list freelance jobs related to: a) Graphic design for NFTs. b) Writing content for crypto projects. c) Developing smart contracts. d) Managing social media for Web3 startups. **Answer: b)**
23. Freelance designers in the crypto space might work on: a) Creating blog articles. b) Developing blockchain protocols. c) NFT art and UI/UX design for dApps. d) Managing online communities. **Answer: c)**
24. Managing Discord or Telegram groups for crypto projects is an example of a freelance role in: a) Writing. b) Design. c) Marketing and community management. d) Coding. **Answer: c)**
25. Platforms like Gitcoin and Bounties Network often list freelance tasks for: a) Content creation. b) Graphic design. c) Software development and coding. d) Social media management. **Answer: c)**
26. Payment for freelance work in the crypto space is often done in: a) Traditional fiat currencies only. b) Only in the native token of the project. c) Cryptocurrencies or stablecoins like USDT. d) Through centralized payment processors. **Answer: c)**
27. What is a potential benefit of freelancing in the crypto space for students? a) Guaranteed high income with no effort. b) Opportunity to earn income without traditional job requirements and gain experience in a new field. c) Protection from market volatility. d) Automatic investment advice. **Answer: b)**
28. Coinbase Earn is an example of a: a) Freelancing platform for crypto jobs. b) Play-to-earn game. c) Learn-to-earn program where you earn crypto for watching educational videos. d) Decentralized finance protocol. **Answer: c)**
29. Platforms like Layer3.xyz offer: a) High-yield staking opportunities. b) Airdrops for holding specific tokens. c) Daily crypto challenges with prizes for completing Web3 tasks. d) A decentralized marketplace for freelance services. **Answer: c)**
30. A crucial tip for students looking to freelance in the crypto space is to: a) Only work for established, well-known companies. b) Be willing to learn new skills and adapt to the evolving industry. c) Demand payment only in the most volatile cryptocurrencies for maximum potential gain. d) Overpromise their abilities to secure more gigs. **Answer: b)**

10 mid-size questions with answers covering Play-to-Earn games, Airdrops/Staking/DeFi, and Freelancing in the crypto space:

1. **Explain the fundamental economic model behind Play-to-Earn (P2E) games. How do players generate value, and what mechanisms allow them to convert in-game earnings into real-world income? Answer:** The P2E model revolves around rewarding

players for their time and effort within the game with digital assets like cryptocurrencies and NFTs. Players generate value by participating in gameplay (completing quests, winning battles), contributing to the in-game economy (crafting, land ownership), and acquiring rare or valuable NFTs. These earned assets gain real-world value through their scarcity, utility within the game, and demand from other players or collectors. Conversion to real-world income happens when players trade these assets on cryptocurrency exchanges or NFT marketplaces for other cryptocurrencies or fiat currencies.

2. **Compare and contrast the earning mechanisms in two different P2E games mentioned (e.g., Axie Infinity and The Sandbox). What types of skills or activities are typically rewarded in each, and what are the potential barriers to entry for new players? Answer:** In Axie Infinity, players primarily earn SLP tokens through skill-based card battles and completing daily quests, with the initial barrier being the cost of purchasing an Axie team (though scholarships mitigate this). The Sandbox focuses on rewarding creativity and land ownership, where players earn SAND tokens and potentially monetize their virtual LAND through user-generated content. The barrier here can be the cost of LAND NFTs and the time/skill required to build engaging experiences. Axie emphasizes strategic gameplay, while The Sandbox emphasizes creative development and virtual real estate management.

3. **Describe the concept of a cryptocurrency airdrop and explain the motivations behind projects conducting them. What are some common ways students can increase their chances of being eligible for future airdrops, and what key precautions should they take to avoid scams? Answer:** A cryptocurrency airdrop is the free distribution of tokens to a large number of people, often early adopters or users of a platform. Projects conduct airdrops to increase awareness, adoption, and decentralization. Students can increase their chances by actively using new crypto apps, joining project communities on Discord and Twitter, and engaging with platforms (swapping tokens, using wallets). To avoid scams, they should never send cryptocurrency to receive an airdrop and always verify announcements through official project channels.

4. **Explain the process of staking cryptocurrency. What are the potential benefits and risks involved, and how does the concept of "Proof-of-Stake" relate to staking rewards? Answer:** Staking involves locking up cryptocurrency in a Proof-of-Stake (PoS) network to support its operation and earn rewards. Benefits include earning passive income and contributing to network security. Risks include potential lock-up periods, the fluctuating value of the staked asset, and slashing penalties for network misbehavior. PoS blockchains select validators based on the amount of crypto they stake, incentivizing participation with staking rewards for those who help secure the network.

5. **Describe the fundamental principles of Decentralized Finance (DeFi). How does it differ from traditional finance, and what are two examples of financial services students might access through DeFi platforms? Answer:** DeFi aims to recreate traditional financial services without intermediaries like banks, using decentralized blockchain networks and smart contracts. It differs from traditional finance by being more transparent, permissionless, and globally accessible. Students might access services like lending stablecoins (e.g., USDC) on platforms like Aave to earn interest or swapping different cryptocurrencies on decentralized exchanges (DEXs) like Uniswap.

6. **Discuss the growing demand for freelance skills within the cryptocurrency and Web3 space. What are three specific examples of roles a student with relevant skills could pursue, and what are some platforms they could use to find such opportunities? Answer:** The Web3 space needs diverse skills for content creation, design, community management, and technical development. Three examples include: writing blog posts for crypto projects, designing NFT art collections, and managing Discord communities. Platforms like CryptoJobs, ContentFi, Upwork, Fiverr, Crew3 (Zealy), and Gitcoin can be used to find these opportunities.

7. **Explain the concept and potential benefits of "learn-to-earn" programs like Coinbase Earn and Layer3. How do these platforms incentivize users to learn about different aspects of the cryptocurrency ecosystem? Answer:** Learn-to-earn programs reward users with small amounts of cryptocurrency for completing educational tasks, such as watching videos and taking quizzes (Coinbase Earn) or completing Web3 quests and challenges (Layer3). These platforms incentivize learning by providing tangible rewards, making the process of understanding complex crypto concepts more engaging and financially beneficial for users.

8. **What are some key considerations and potential challenges students might face when trying to earn income through P2E games or freelancing in the crypto space, especially regarding time management, financial risks, and the volatility of the crypto market? Answer:** Students need to balance their studies with the time commitment often required for P2E or freelancing. Financial risks include the volatility of earned cryptocurrencies and the potential for initial investment in P2E games. The fluctuating market can impact the real-world value of their earnings, requiring careful financial planning and risk management.

9. **Compare and contrast the level of risk and potential reward associated with participating in cryptocurrency airdrops versus engaging in DeFi activities like yield**

farming. Which option might be more suitable for a student with limited capital and risk tolerance? Answer: Airdrops generally have lower financial risk (as they are free), but the rewards can be uncertain and often small. Yield farming in DeFi can offer higher potential rewards but also carries significant risks like smart contract vulnerabilities and impermanent loss, often requiring more capital and technical understanding. For a student with limited capital and risk tolerance, focusing on identifying legitimate airdrops that require minimal or no investment might be more suitable as a way to learn and potentially earn small amounts.

10. **Discuss the long-term implications of the Play-to-Earn and Web3 freelancing models for the future of work and education, particularly for students entering the digital economy. How might these models change traditional career paths and learning approaches? Answer:** P2E and Web3 freelancing models suggest a shift towards more decentralized and skill-based earning opportunities, potentially disrupting traditional employment structures. For students, this could mean new pathways to income generation that value specific skills over formal degrees in some cases. Education might need to adapt to focus more on practical digital skills and continuous learning within these rapidly evolving ecosystems, potentially leading to more flexible and globally accessible career paths.

CHAPTER 8: NFTS DEMYSTIFIED – WHAT THEY REALLY ARE

Welcome to the world of **NFTs** – the digital revolution that turned memes into million-dollar art and college students into digital entrepreneurs. This chapter unpacks what NFTs actually are, how they work, and why they're much more than just "JPEGs."

🎨 What Are NFTs and How Do They Work?

🔍 NFT stands for: Non-Fungible Token

- **Non-Fungible = Unique and cannot be replaced.** This is the core characteristic that distinguishes NFTs from cryptocurrencies and many other digital assets. Think of it in terms of physical objects: your car is unique (non-fungible) due to its specific Vehicle Identification Number (VIN), mileage, and history; you can't simply swap it for any other car and expect it to be exactly the same. In contrast, one rupee note is generally interchangeable with any other rupee note of the same denomination (fungible).
- **Token = A digital certificate of ownership stored on the blockchain.** In the context of NFTs, a "token" refers to a digital asset that exists on a blockchain. The blockchain acts as a decentralized and immutable ledger, permanently recording the ownership and history of that token. This digital certificate provides proof of who owns a specific digital item.

🔲 **Unlike cryptocurrency (which is fungible, meaning 1 Bitcoin = 1 Bitcoin), NFTs are unique digital assets. No two NFTs are the same — just like original paintings or trading cards.**

NFTs, however, possess unique characteristics and metadata that make each one distinct. Even if two NFTs depict similar artwork, their underlying token IDs on the blockchain, their history of ownership, or specific attributes embedded in their metadata will differentiate them. This uniqueness is what gives them value as collectibles, digital art, and representations of other unique items.

✅ How NFTs Work (Step-by-Step): From Creation to Ownership

Let's break down the process of how an NFT comes into existence and changes hands:

1. **An artist uploads their digital art to a blockchain (like Ethereum).** This is the initial step where the creator decides to tokenize their digital work. "Digital art" here is a broad term encompassing various forms of digital creations, including images, videos, audio files, 3D models, and more. The artist chooses a blockchain that supports NFTs, with

Ethereum being the most popular, although other blockchains like Solana, Polygon, and Tezos also have thriving NFT ecosystems.

2. **The artwork is minted as an NFT — creating a unique token on the blockchain.** "Minting" is the process of converting a digital file into a unique digital asset on the blockchain. This involves writing the information about the artwork (and a link to the artwork itself) onto the blockchain as a new NFT. This process creates a permanent and verifiable record of the artwork's existence and initial ownership. Each minted NFT has a unique identifier (token ID) within the smart contract that governs the NFT collection.

3. **The NFT contains metadata (owner, description, image link, etc.).** When an NFT is minted, it's associated with metadata – data that provides additional information about the digital asset. This metadata is typically stored on the blockchain or linked to from the blockchain. Common metadata includes:

   o **Owner:** The current address of the wallet that holds the NFT. This is publicly viewable on the blockchain.
   o **Creator:** The address of the wallet that originally minted the NFT.
   o **Description:** A textual description of the artwork or the NFT project.
   o **Image Link (or Link to Other Digital Asset):** A URL pointing to where the actual digital file (the artwork, music, video, etc.) is stored. This is often stored off-chain on platforms like IPFS (InterPlanetary File System) to manage file sizes and costs. The link on the blockchain ensures the NFT is associated with a specific piece of digital content.
   o **Attributes/Properties:** Specific characteristics of the NFT, which can influence its rarity and value (e.g., the color of a character's hat in a digital artwork collection).
   o **Smart Contract Address:** The unique address of the smart contract on the blockchain that governs the NFT collection to which this specific NFT belongs.

4. **The NFT can be bought, sold, or traded on marketplaces like OpenSea.** Once an NFT is minted, the owner can choose to list it for sale on NFT marketplaces. These platforms provide a user-friendly interface for buying, selling, and trading NFTs. When a transaction occurs:

   o The buyer sends cryptocurrency (usually the native currency of the blockchain the NFT is on, like ETH on Ethereum) to the seller's wallet through a smart contract on the marketplace.
   o Upon confirmation of the transaction on the blockchain, the ownership of the NFT is transferred from the seller's wallet address to the buyer's wallet address. This change in ownership is permanently recorded on the blockchain.
   o Marketplaces often charge a fee (a percentage of the sale price) for facilitating the transaction.
   o Creators can also embed "creator royalties" into the NFT's smart contract, ensuring they receive a percentage of the sale price for all future secondary market transactions.

🎁 Think of NFTs Like: Real-World Analogies

- **Real-World: Autographed football jersey**

- **NFT Equivalent: NFT of a moment in sports.** Just as an autographed jersey is a unique collectible item with verifiable authenticity tied to a specific event or player, an NFT representing a significant moment in sports (e.g., a clip of a winning goal, a digital trading card of a star player) is a unique digital asset with its ownership and history recorded on the blockchain. No two NFTs of different moments or even different editions of the same moment would be exactly the same.
- **Real-World: First-edition comic book**
  - **NFT Equivalent: NFT of original digital artwork.** A first-edition comic book is valuable due to its rarity, historical significance, and verifiable authenticity. Similarly, an NFT of original digital artwork represents a unique digital creation with its ownership and provenance (history of ownership) immutably recorded on the blockchain. Later editions or copies of the digital artwork would not have the same verifiable history and uniqueness as the original NFT.
- **Real-World: Concert ticket**
  - **NFT Equivalent: NFT event pass.** A concert ticket is a unique digital or physical item that grants access to a specific event. It has a limited supply and is only valid for that particular event. An NFT event pass serves a similar purpose in the digital realm, providing verifiable proof of ownership and access to online or even physical events. It can also potentially have additional unique attributes or benefits tied to it.

♛ Ownership, Royalties & Metadata: The Pillars of Digital Provenance and Creator Empowerment

Within the burgeoning realm of Non-Fungible Tokens, three core concepts underpin their transformative potential: the immutable ledger of ownership, the enduring mechanism of creator royalties, and the rich tapestry of identifying metadata. These elements, interwoven with the fabric of blockchain technology, are reshaping how digital assets are perceived, valued, and exchanged, offering profound implications for creators and collectors alike.

☐ Ownership (Proven by Blockchain): The Immutable Decree

At the heart of NFT ownership lies the unyielding certainty provided by the blockchain. When an individual acquires an NFT, they are not merely possessing a digital file; rather, they are obtaining a verified and irrefutable record of ownership inscribed upon a distributed and tamper-proof ledger. This digital inscription serves as an indisputable claim, asserting their right to that specific digital item. Unlike traditional digital assets that can be easily copied or whose ownership can be ambiguous, the blockchain provides a transparent and auditable history, tracing the lineage of the NFT back to its very creation.

- **Example:** Consider the instance of a discerning student, a denizen of the burgeoning metaverse, who elects to procure an NFT representing a meticulously crafted digital sneaker for their avatar's digital perambulations within a virtual world such as

Decentraland. Upon the successful transaction, the blockchain irrevocably records this student as the rightful owner of that particular digital sneaker NFT. This ownership is not confined to the confines of a single platform; it is a provable and transferable right, recognized across the interconnected landscape of Web3. Should the student choose, they possess the autonomy to trade this unique digital asset, showcasing its verifiable provenance and inherent digital scarcity. No other entity can legitimately assert ownership unless the student willingly relinquishes it through a subsequent sale or transfer.

♪ Royalties – Artists Earn Forever: A Legacy of Enduring Remuneration

One of the most revolutionary aspects of NFTs lies in their capacity to embed enduring economic rights for creators through the mechanism of royalties. Unlike the traditional art world, where artists often relinquish all future financial interest upon the initial sale of their work, NFTs can be programmed to automatically remit a predetermined percentage of the sale price back to the original creator each time the NFT is subsequently resold on the secondary market. This intrinsic feature fosters a paradigm shift, enabling artists to benefit from the appreciation and ongoing value of their creations throughout their digital lifespan.

- ⬜⬜ **Example:** Imagine a gifted digital artist who mints and sells an original piece of digital artwork as an NFT for an initial price of $100. This NFT, imbued with a smart contract specifying a 10% creator royalty, finds a discerning collector. Years later, as the artist's reputation grows and the demand for their early works increases, this same NFT is resold on a vibrant digital marketplace for the significant sum of $1,000. Through the embedded royalty mechanism, the original artist automatically receives 10% of this secondary sale, amounting to $100, directly into their designated digital wallet. This continuous stream of income, generated from the ongoing appreciation of their work, represents a transformative shift, particularly for emerging artists and students who previously lacked access to the established structures of the traditional art market. NFTs empower them to participate in a global marketplace and reap the rewards of their creative endeavors in perpetuity.

⬜⬜ Metadata – The NFT's Identity Card: Unveiling the Digital Essence

Each NFT is not merely a token representing ownership; it is also accompanied by a rich layer of **metadata**, akin to a digital identity card that provides comprehensive information about the unique digital asset. This metadata is typically stored on the blockchain itself or linked to from the blockchain via a standardized protocol. It is this intricate web of data that imbues each NFT with its distinct characteristics and facilitates its verification and categorization within the vast digital landscape.

- ⬜ **Components of NFT Metadata:**
  - **Name:** A specific identifier given to the NFT, often part of a larger collection.
  - **Creator:** Identifies the original artist or entity that minted the NFT.
  - **Description:** A textual narrative providing context, background, or details about the NFT.

- o **File Link:** A crucial pointer (often a URL or IPFS hash) that directs to the actual digital content associated with the NFT – be it the artwork, a musical composition, a video file, or another form of digital media.
- o **Properties:** Specific attributes or characteristics of the NFT, often denoting rarity, edition number within a series, or unique traits within a generative art collection (e.g., the color of a specific element, the presence of a rare feature).

This meticulously curated metadata is paramount in establishing the uniqueness and verifiability of each individual NFT. It allows marketplaces and collectors to discern one NFT from another, even within the same collection. The properties, in particular, play a significant role in determining the perceived rarity and, consequently, the potential value of an NFT. The immutable nature of the blockchain ensures that this metadata, once recorded, cannot be arbitrarily altered, further solidifying the NFT's identity and provenance.

In essence, ownership, royalties, and metadata form the foundational pillars upon which the value and utility of NFTs are constructed. The blockchain provides the unshakeable proof of ownership, smart contracts enable artists to benefit from the ongoing appreciation of their work, and metadata imbues each token with its unique identity and verifiable characteristics. Together, these elements are fostering a more equitable and transparent digital economy for creators and collectors worldwide.

✿ Popular NFT Examples & Trends: A Kaleidoscope of Digital Innovation

The landscape of Non-Fungible Tokens is a vibrant tapestry woven with threads of artistic expression, community identity, virtual experiences, and novel forms of digital ownership. From groundbreaking digital art auctions to coveted profile picture collections and the tokenization of real-world assets, NFTs are demonstrating a remarkable versatility, captivating creators and collectors across diverse domains. Let us explore some prominent examples and prevailing trends that illuminate the transformative potential of these unique digital identifiers.

🎨 1. Digital Art: Ushering in a New Era of Artistic Ownership

The advent of NFTs has irrevocably altered the paradigm of digital art ownership, providing artists with a mechanism to verifiably authenticate and monetize their creations in a digital realm previously plagued by limitless reproducibility.

- **Example:** The landmark sale of Beeple's "Everydays: The First 5000 Days" serves as a seminal moment in this evolution. This monumental digital artwork, a breathtaking collage comprising 5,000 individual digital drawings meticulously crafted over as many days, was auctioned by the esteemed Christie's for an astounding $69 million. The ownership of this singular digital masterpiece was immutably enshrined as an NFT on the Ethereum blockchain, bestowing upon the buyer not just an image, but a verifiably unique piece of digital history. This event underscored the potential for digital art, authenticated and owned via NFTs, to command prices comparable to traditional physical art.

👹 2. PFPs (Profile Picture NFTs): Emblems of Digital Identity and Community

Beyond singular artworks, NFTs have spawned entire ecosystems centered around Profile Picture (PFP) projects. These collections typically comprise thousands of uniquely generated avatars, often with varying degrees of rarity based on their distinct attributes. Owning a PFP NFT can serve as a form of digital identity and a membership token to an exclusive online community.

- **Example:** The Bored Ape Yacht Club (BAYC) stands as a quintessential example of a highly successful PFP project. Consisting of 10,000 unique ape avatars, each algorithmically generated with a distinct combination of traits, BAYC has transcended mere digital collectibles to become coveted status symbols within the digital sphere. Endorsement and ownership by a constellation of celebrities, including Eminem, Neymar Jr., and Snoop Dogg, have further amplified their cultural significance. Owning a Bored Ape NFT often grants access to exclusive online and real-world events, fostering a strong sense of community and shared digital identity among holders.

⬜⬜ 3. Gaming & Virtual Items: Tokenizing the Metaverse

NFTs are also revolutionizing the gaming industry and the burgeoning metaverse by enabling true ownership of in-game assets and virtual land. This empowers players and creators within these digital realms with unprecedented economic opportunities.

- **Example:** Platforms like Decentraland and The Sandbox exemplify this trend. Within these virtual worlds, parcels of virtual land are represented as NFTs, allowing users to verifiably own, buy, and sell digital real estate. Owners can then develop their LAND by creating virtual buildings, interactive games, hosting virtual events, and populating their spaces with unique digital assets, also often represented as NFTs. This ownership allows for monetization through various means, such as earning rent from other users, charging tickets for access to events or games, or profiting from the resale of developed land or created assets. NFTs thus form the foundational building blocks of these decentralized metaverses, enabling user-driven economies.

🎶 4. Music NFTs: Empowering Artists and Engaging Fans

The music industry, historically grappling with issues of digital ownership and artist compensation, is finding innovative solutions through Music NFTs. These tokens allow musicians to sell unique digital assets directly to their fans, bypassing traditional intermediaries.

- **Example:** Artists like 3LAU and the iconic band Kings of Leon have pioneered the use of Music NFTs. They have sold limited-edition songs, entire albums, and even exclusive experiences like backstage passes as unique digital tokens. This model allows fans to own a verifiable piece of music history, directly supporting their favorite artists and potentially gaining access to exclusive content or experiences not available through traditional music distribution channels. Music NFTs foster a deeper connection between artists and their audience, creating new avenues for engagement and monetization.

□□ 5. Event Tickets, Certificates & Courses: Leveraging NFTs for Authenticity and Utility

Beyond art and entertainment, NFTs are finding practical applications in areas requiring verifiable digital ownership and authenticity.

- **Example:** Consider the scenario of attending a virtual seminar or completing an online blockchain course. Instead of receiving a traditional, easily replicable digital certificate, attendees or graduates can be issued an NFT certificate or course badge. This NFT serves as an immutable and verifiable record of their participation or achievement, stored securely on the blockchain. The inherent properties of NFTs – their uniqueness and tamper-proof nature – make them ideal for combating fraud and duplication in areas like event ticketing and academic credentials. An NFT event ticket can also potentially offer additional benefits, such as exclusive content or future discounts, enhancing its utility beyond mere access.

💡 Why Should Students Care About NFTs? Unlocking Opportunities in the Decentralized Future

In this burgeoning era of digital transformation, where the contours of ownership, creativity, and commerce are being redefined by blockchain technology, Non-Fungible Tokens (NFTs) emerge as a significant and multifaceted phenomenon. For students, the generation poised to inherit and shape this evolving landscape, understanding and engaging with NFTs transcends mere curiosity; it represents an opportunity to cultivate vital skills, explore novel pathways for creative expression and entrepreneurial endeavors, and position themselves at the forefront of a decentralized digital future. Let us delve into the compelling reasons why NFTs should command the attention of today's students.

Reason	Impact
🎨 Creators	Monetize digital art, music, memes, and other digital creations.
💼 Entrepreneurs	Launch innovative NFT collections, build digital brands, and explore new business models.
📈 Investors	Engage in the dynamic NFT marketplace, trading digital assets for potential profit (with inherent risks).
🎓 Learners	Build a demonstrable Web3 resume, showcasing skills and engagement in a cutting-edge field.
💡 Innovators	Explore and implement novel applications of NFTs in diverse sectors like education, healthcare, and digital identity.

Export to Sheets

🎨 Creators: Empowering Digital Expression and Monetization

For students with artistic inclinations, musical talents, a knack for creating viral content, or any form of digital creative output, NFTs offer an unprecedented avenue for direct monetization. By tokenizing their digital creations as unique NFTs, students can bypass traditional gatekeepers and directly connect with a global audience of collectors and enthusiasts.

- **Example:** Consider a student with a talent for digital illustration. Instead of relying solely on commissions or traditional art sales, they can mint their artwork as a limited-edition NFT collection. This allows them to set their own pricing, control the distribution of their work, and even embed creator royalties to earn a percentage of future resales. Similarly, a student musician could tokenize a unique song or album as an NFT, offering fans exclusive ownership and potentially unlocking new forms of engagement and revenue. Even the creator of a popular meme could tokenize their creation, transforming ephemeral internet culture into a collectible digital asset.

💼 Entrepreneurs: Forging New Digital Ventures and Brands

NFTs are not merely limited to individual creations; they provide a fertile ground for entrepreneurial students to launch innovative digital ventures and build distinct brands. The unique properties of NFTs – their verifiability, scarcity, and transferability – lend themselves to novel business models and the creation of engaged online communities.

- **Example:** A student with a keen eye for market trends could conceive and launch an NFT collection centered around a compelling narrative or a unique aesthetic. By strategically marketing their collection and building a strong community around it, they can establish a valuable digital brand. Furthermore, NFTs can be integrated into existing businesses or used to create entirely new models, such as tokenized memberships granting exclusive access to content or services, or fractionalized ownership of high-value assets.

📈 Investors: Navigating the Dynamic Digital Asset Landscape

For students with an interest in finance and investment, the NFT marketplace presents a dynamic and rapidly evolving asset class. While inherently volatile and carrying significant risks, the potential for value appreciation in carefully selected NFTs can be considerable.

- **Example:** A student who diligently researches emerging NFT projects and understands market trends might identify a promising collection early on. By acquiring NFTs from this collection before mainstream adoption, they could potentially see their value increase significantly as demand grows. However, it is crucial for students to approach NFT investing with caution, understanding the illiquid nature of some NFTs and the potential for rapid price declines. Thorough research, risk management, and investing only what one can afford to lose are paramount.

🎓 Learners: Building a Web3-Ready Résumé

In an increasingly digital world powered by blockchain technology, demonstrating practical experience and engagement within the Web3 ecosystem can provide students with a significant competitive edge in the job market. Creating, buying, selling, or even actively participating in NFT communities showcases a proactive engagement with this cutting-edge technology.

- **Example:** As illustrated by the real-world example of Sophie, a design student who created and sold her own pixel-style animal NFTs, engaging with the NFT space can directly contribute to building a compelling Web3 résumé. Sophie's experience not only provided her with a side income but also demonstrated her creative skills, understanding of blockchain technology (by minting on Polygon), and entrepreneurial drive. This tangible experience directly led to an internship opportunity with an NFT game studio, highlighting how NFT engagement can translate into real-world career prospects.

💡 Innovators: Pioneering Novel Applications Beyond Art and Collectibles

The utility of NFTs extends far beyond digital art and collectibles. Their unique properties make them powerful tools for innovation across a diverse range of sectors, offering students with a forward-thinking mindset the opportunity to explore and implement novel applications.

- **Example:** In education, NFTs could serve as verifiable and tamper-proof digital diplomas or certifications, providing a more secure and easily shareable record of academic achievements. In healthcare, NFTs could represent ownership of medical records, granting patients greater control and portability of their health information. Even in the realm of digital identity, NFTs could be used to create self-sovereign identity solutions, empowering individuals with greater control over their personal data. The possibilities for innovative applications of NFTs are vast and ripe for exploration by creative and technically astute students.

30 multiple-choice questions with answers covering what NFTs are and how they work, ownership/royalties/metadata, and popular NFT examples/trends:

What are NFTs and How Do They Work?

1. What does NFT stand for? a) Non-Financial Transaction b) Non-Fungible Token c) New Financial Technology d) Network File Transfer **Answer: b)**
2. What does "non-fungible" mean in the context of NFTs? a) Easily replaceable b) Divisible into smaller units c) Unique and cannot be replaced d) Having a stable value **Answer: c)**
3. An NFT is a digital certificate of ownership stored on: a) A central server b) The cloud c) The blockchain d) A personal computer **Answer: c)**
4. Unlike cryptocurrency, NFTs are: a) Fungible b) Primarily used for payments c) Unique digital assets d) Not stored on the blockchain **Answer: c)**
5. The process of creating a unique token on the blockchain for a digital asset is called: a) Mining b) Staking c) Minting d) Burning **Answer: c)**

6. When an artist uploads their digital art to a blockchain to create an NFT, which blockchain is most commonly used? a) Bitcoin b) Litecoin c) Ethereum d) Dogecoin **Answer: c)**

7. What does the metadata of an NFT typically contain? a) Only the image or file itself b) Only the owner's information c) Owner, description, image link, and other properties d) Only the transaction history **Answer: c)**

8. NFTs can be bought, sold, or traded on: a) Traditional stock exchanges b) Cryptocurrency mining pools c) Online forums d) Marketplaces like OpenSea **Answer: d)**

9. Which real-world item is a good analogy for the non-fungible nature of an NFT? a) A dollar bill b) A share of a company's stock c) An autographed baseball card d) A liter of gasoline **Answer: c)**

10. What is often used to store the actual digital file linked to an NFT? a) Directly on the main blockchain b) In the NFT marketplace's database c) Off-chain storage like IPFS d) Encrypted on the owner's computer **Answer: c)**

Ownership, Royalties, and Metadata

11. When you own an NFT, the verified record of your ownership is stored on: a) Your personal device b) A centralized database c) The blockchain d) The NFT marketplace's server **Answer: c)**

12. Can someone else claim ownership of your NFT if they have a copy of the digital file? a) Yes, as long as they have the file. b) Only if they created the original artwork. c) No, ownership is proven by the blockchain record. d) Only if they list it for sale on a marketplace first. **Answer: c)**

13. What is a significant benefit of NFTs for artists regarding secondary sales? a) They always get the initial sale price. b) They can earn royalties every time their NFT is resold. c) They have to pay a fee for every secondary sale. d) Their work is automatically removed from marketplaces after the first sale. **Answer: b)**

14. The percentage an artist earns on secondary sales is typically: a) Determined by the buyer. b) Fixed by the blockchain network. c) Programmed into the NFT's smart contract by the creator. d) Negotiated with each subsequent buyer. **Answer: c)**

15. The data included within an NFT, such as name, creator, and file link, is called: a) Transaction history b) Smart contract code c) Metadata d) Gas fees **Answer: c)**

16. What aspect of the metadata helps establish the uniqueness and verifiability of an NFT? a) The file size b) The date it was created c) Properties like rarity and edition number d) The current market price **Answer: c)**

17. The link within the metadata typically points to: a) The current owner's wallet address b) The smart contract governing the NFT c) The actual digital art, music, or video file d) A description of the blockchain technology **Answer: c)**

18. Why is the blockchain's role in NFT ownership considered significant? a) It allows for easy duplication of digital assets. b) It provides a decentralized and tamper-proof record of ownership. c) It is controlled by a single authority. d) It makes transactions anonymous and untraceable. **Answer: b)**

19. What prevents someone from forging or duplicating an NFT certificate of ownership? a) Copyright laws b) The security of the blockchain c) Watermarks on the digital file d) Terms of service on NFT marketplaces **Answer: b)**
20. The creator's identity is often permanently recorded within the NFT's: a) Buyer's wallet b) Transaction history c) Metadata d) Marketplace listing **Answer: c)**

Popular NFT Examples and Trends

21. Beeple's "Everydays: The First 5000 Days" is an example of which type of NFT? a) PFP (Profile Picture) b) Gaming virtual item c) Digital art d) Music NFT **Answer: c)**
22. What was notable about the sale of Beeple's "Everydays"? a) It was the first NFT sold on a major cryptocurrency exchange. b) It was sold for a very low price. c) It was sold at a traditional auction house (Christie's) for a significant sum. d) It was a collection of physical artworks. **Answer: c)**
23. Bored Ape Yacht Club (BAYC) is a popular example of: a) Music NFTs b) PFP (Profile Picture) NFTs c) Virtual land NFTs d) Event ticket NFTs **Answer: b)**
24. Owning a Bored Ape NFT often serves as a: a) License to use a specific software. b) Digital identity and membership to an exclusive community. c) Proof of attendance at a virtual event. d) A discount coupon for online marketplaces. **Answer: b)**
25. In virtual worlds like Decentraland and The Sandbox, what are represented as NFTs? a) In-game currencies b) Player avatars c) Virtual land d) Gameplay achievements **Answer: c)**
26. How can owners of virtual land NFTs in Decentraland and The Sandbox potentially earn income? a) By mining cryptocurrency within the virtual world. b) By referring new users to the platform. c) Through rent, ticket sales for events, or resale profits. d) By winning in-game tournaments. **Answer: c)**
27. Musicians are using NFTs to sell: a) Physical instruments. b) Concert merchandise. c) Songs, albums, and backstage passes directly to fans. d) Tickets to traditional concerts. **Answer: c)**
28. What is a benefit of using NFTs as event tickets or certificates? a) They are easily reproducible. b) They guarantee the event will be successful. c) They offer anti-fraud measures due to their uniqueness on the blockchain. d) They are always cheaper than traditional tickets. **Answer: c)**
29. Earning an NFT course badge after completing a blockchain course serves as a: a) Temporary discount on future courses. b) Verifiable digital record of achievement. c) A key to access exclusive online communities. d) A collectible item with no practical use. **Answer: b)**
30. Which trend highlights the use of NFTs for digital identity and community building? a) Digital art auctions b) Music NFTs c) PFP (Profile Picture) NFTs d) Virtual land sales **Answer: c)**

10 mid-size questions with answers covering what NFTs are and how they work, ownership/royalties/metadata, and popular NFT examples/trends:

1. **Explain the fundamental difference between a fungible asset like Bitcoin and a non-fungible asset like an NFT. Provide a real-world analogy for each to illustrate this**

distinction. Answer: Fungible assets are interchangeable and have the same value (e.g., one Bitcoin is equivalent to any other Bitcoin; one rupee is equivalent to any other rupee). Real-world analogy: cash. Non-fungible assets are unique and cannot be replaced by something identical (e.g., a specific piece of digital art, a first-edition book). Real-world analogy: a unique painting signed by the artist.

2. **Describe the process of "minting" an NFT. What key information is typically recorded on the blockchain during this process, and why is this significant for establishing ownership and provenance? Answer:** Minting is the process of creating a new NFT on the blockchain by converting a digital file into a unique token. Key information recorded includes the token ID, the creator's address, a link to the digital asset (often via metadata), and initial ownership. This is significant because it creates an immutable and publicly verifiable record of the asset's origin and ownership history (provenance), establishing its authenticity and uniqueness.

3. **Explain how blockchain technology ensures ownership of an NFT. What makes this form of ownership different from owning a digital file stored on a personal computer or a centralized server? Answer:** Blockchain ensures NFT ownership through its decentralized and distributed ledger system. The record of ownership is transparent, immutable, and cannot be altered or deleted by any single entity. This differs from owning a digital file on a personal computer or server, where ownership is often based on user accounts and can be subject to control or loss due to platform failures or malicious actors. Blockchain-based ownership is direct and verifiable on a public ledger.

4. **Describe the concept of creator royalties in the context of NFTs. Why is this feature considered beneficial for digital artists, and how are these royalties typically enforced during secondary market sales? Answer:** Creator royalties in NFTs allow the original artist to automatically receive a percentage of the sale price every time their NFT is resold on a marketplace. This is beneficial as it provides a continuous income stream for artists from the ongoing value of their work. Royalties are typically enforced through the smart contract code embedded in the NFT, which automatically triggers a payout to the creator's wallet when a secondary sale occurs on a platform that supports these standards.

5. **Explain the role of metadata in defining an NFT. What types of information are commonly included in an NFT's metadata, and how does this data contribute to the NFT's identity and potential value? Answer:** Metadata acts as an NFT's "identity card," providing crucial information about the digital asset. Common information

includes the name, creator, description, a link to the digital file, and properties (e.g., rarity, edition). This data makes each NFT unique and verifiable, allowing for categorization, tracking of rarity, and ultimately influencing its perceived value and desirability among collectors.

6. **Discuss the significance of Beeple's "Everydays: The First 5000 Days" NFT sale. How did this event impact the perception of digital art ownership and the broader NFT market? Answer:** The $69 million sale of Beeple's "Everydays" at Christie's was a watershed moment that brought NFTs into the mainstream art world and demonstrated the potential for digital art, authenticated by blockchain, to command high prices. It significantly increased awareness and credibility of NFTs as a legitimate form of art ownership and spurred a massive influx of interest and investment into the NFT market.

7. **Explain the concept and appeal of PFP (Profile Picture) NFT projects like Bored Ape Yacht Club. What factors contribute to their value beyond just the visual artwork itself? Answer:** PFP NFTs are collections of unique avatar-style images used as online profile pictures. Their appeal often stems from a combination of factors beyond the art, including community membership (granting access to exclusive online and real-world events), status symbol within the digital space, and speculative value based on demand and cultural relevance. The scarcity of the collection (e.g., 10,000 unique apes) also contributes to their perceived value.

8. **Describe how NFTs are being utilized in the gaming and virtual worlds (metaverse) space, using Decentraland or The Sandbox as an example. What benefits does NFT ownership bring to users within these digital environments? Answer:** In platforms like Decentraland and The Sandbox, virtual land and in-game items are represented as NFTs. This allows users to have true ownership of their digital assets, enabling them to buy, sell, trade, and monetize their virtual property and creations. Benefits include the ability to earn income through rent, hosting events, selling virtual goods, and having a portable digital identity and assets across compatible virtual worlds.

9. **Explain how musicians are leveraging Music NFTs to connect with fans and generate revenue. Provide an example of a potential benefit for both the artist and the fan in this model. Answer:** Music NFTs allow artists to sell unique digital assets directly to fans, such as limited-edition songs, albums, or exclusive experiences. A benefit for the artist is a direct revenue stream, potentially bypassing traditional intermediaries and retaining more control over their work and earnings. A benefit for the fan is owning a unique, verifiable piece of music history or a special experience, fostering

a deeper connection with the artist and potentially gaining access to exclusive content or perks.

10. **Discuss the potential applications of NFTs beyond art and collectibles, providing an example of how they could be used for event tickets, certificates, or academic credentials. What advantages do NFTs offer in these contexts compared to traditional methods? Answer:** Beyond art, NFTs can be used for verifiable digital ownership in various sectors. For event tickets, NFTs offer anti-fraud measures due to their unique and non-replicable nature. For certificates or academic credentials, NFTs provide tamper-proof and easily verifiable records of achievement that can be shared digitally. Advantages over traditional methods include enhanced security, reduced fraud, easier verification, and potential for added utility (e.g., access to exclusive alumni networks tied to a certificate NFT).

CHAPTER 9: CREATE YOUR FIRST NFT – A PRACTICAL GUIDE

🔧 Tools & Platforms: Navigating the Digital Emporiums of OpenSea, Rarible, and Beyond

To partake in the burgeoning ecosystem of Non-Fungible Tokens, whether as a creator seeking to unveil digital masterpieces or a collector yearning to acquire unique digital artifacts, access to specialized online marketplaces is paramount. These platforms serve as the central hubs for the creation, acquisition, and exchange of NFTs, functioning akin to digital emporiums where the wares are not physical commodities but rather tokenized representations of digital assets. They provide the essential infrastructure for users to mint their creations into existence, engage in the intricate dance of buying and selling, and curate their digital collections for the world to admire.

◆ OpenSea: The Foremost Digital Marketplace

Eminently recognized as the most widely adopted NFT marketplace, OpenSea commands a significant presence within the digital asset landscape. Its intuitive design and comprehensive feature set render it particularly accessible to newcomers venturing into the realm of NFTs, while its robust infrastructure caters to the needs of seasoned collectors and creators alike. OpenSea extends its reach across prominent blockchain networks, notably supporting the expansive Ethereum network and the increasingly popular Polygon network, known for its lower transaction fees.

- **Example:** Consider a student, endowed with artistic talent, who channels their creative energies into crafting compelling digital art. Seeking to share their vision and potentially monetize their endeavors, they navigate to the user-friendly interface of OpenSea. Through a straightforward process, they upload their digital artwork, imbue it with descriptive metadata, and mint it as a unique NFT upon the chosen blockchain (perhaps Polygon, to minimize initial costs). They then offer this singular digital creation for sale at a price of 0.02 ETH, an amount approximating $30 USD at prevailing exchange rates, thereby entering the global marketplace of digital art.

◆ Rarible: Empowering Creators with Customizable Royalties

Rarible stands as another prominent NFT marketplace, sharing many functionalities with OpenSea in terms of facilitating the minting, buying, and selling of digital assets. However, Rarible distinguishes itself by offering creators a greater degree of control over the crucial aspect of creator royalties. This platform empowers artists to customize the percentage of royalties they wish to receive on all subsequent secondary market sales of their NFTs, fostering a more tailored and potentially rewarding experience for creators. Furthermore, Rarible accommodates the creation of both single, unique edition NFTs and multiple editions of a single digital asset, rendering it particularly well-suited for projects involving collectibles or limited-run digital items.

- **Example:** Imagine a musically gifted student who has meticulously composed and produced an original song. Recognizing the unique nature of their creation, they choose to mint their sonic masterpiece as an NFT on Rarible. Leveraging the platform's features, they opt to release 100 distinct digital editions of their song NFT, each representing a verifiable piece of their musical work. Crucially, they configure the smart contract associated with these NFTs to automatically grant them a 15% royalty on every future resale of any of these 100 editions. This ensures that as their music gains traction and their NFTs are traded among collectors, they will continue to earn a portion of the value generated by their initial creative output.

Beyond these two prominent platforms, a diverse ecosystem of NFT marketplaces exists, each often catering to specific niches or offering unique features. Platforms like SuperRare focus on curated, high-end digital art, while Foundation emphasizes artist exclusivity and auctions. Niche marketplaces dedicated to specific types of NFTs, such as those for gaming assets or music, also abound. The choice of platform often depends on the creator's goals, the type of NFT being offered, the target audience, and the specific features and fee structures of the marketplace. As the NFT landscape continues to evolve, these tools and platforms will undoubtedly play an increasingly vital role in shaping the future of digital ownership and creative economies.

💰 Minting, Gas Fees, and Wallets: The Essential Trinity of NFT Creation

To embark upon the journey of transforming digital creations into enduring Non-Fungible Tokens, a trinity of fundamental concepts must be understood: the transformative process of minting, the transactional cost of gas fees, and the indispensable role of the digital wallet as one's Web3 passport. These elements interlock to facilitate the creation and management of NFTs within the decentralized landscape of blockchain technology.

☐ What is Minting? The Genesis of a Digital Asset

Minting represents the pivotal act of imbuing a digital file – be it a visual artwork, a musical composition, a textual document, or any other form of digital creation – with the indelible characteristics of an NFT upon the blockchain. Visualize this process as the act of "publishing" one's work into the expansive and transparent realm of Web3. Once a digital file undergoes the process of minting, it transcends its former existence as a mere collection of bits and bytes, becoming a permanent, tamper-proof, and publicly verifiable digital asset, its lineage and ownership immutably recorded upon the blockchain's distributed ledger.

👛 Wallets: Your Web3 Passport – The Key to Interaction

Prior to engaging in the act of minting, an indispensable prerequisite is the possession of a cryptocurrency wallet. This digital instrument serves as one's passport to the Web3 ecosystem, fulfilling several critical functions:

- **Payment of Gas Fees:** The execution of transactions on blockchain networks, including the minting of NFTs, typically incurs a cost known as a gas fee. A cryptocurrency wallet is necessary to hold the native cryptocurrency of the chosen blockchain (e.g., ETH for Ethereum, MATIC for Polygon) and facilitate the payment of these fees.

- **Signing Blockchain Transactions:** When initiating an action on the blockchain, such as minting an NFT or transferring ownership, the wallet is used to digitally "sign" the transaction. This signature, cryptographically linked to the wallet's private key, serves as proof of authorization and ensures the integrity of the transaction.
- **Storage of NFTs:** Once an NFT is successfully minted or acquired, it resides within the user's cryptocurrency wallet, securely linked to their unique blockchain address. The wallet acts as a digital vault for these valuable digital assets.

A widely adopted and user-friendly cryptocurrency wallet, particularly for those navigating the Ethereum and Polygon ecosystems, is **MetaMask**.

- **MetaMask:** This versatile tool is available as both a browser extension, seamlessly integrating with Web3 applications on desktop browsers, and a mobile application, providing on-the-go access to the decentralized web. MetaMask supports a multitude of blockchain networks, including the prominent Ethereum and the efficient Polygon, among others. Crucially, the creation and basic usage of a MetaMask wallet are offered free of charge to users.
- **Example:** A prospective NFT creator, eager to tokenize their digital artistry, first undertakes the essential step of downloading and installing the MetaMask browser extension. During the initial setup, they are presented with a crucial **seed phrase** – a series of recovery words that serve as the ultimate key to their wallet. Recognizing its paramount importance, the user diligently records this seed phrase offline in a secure location, safeguarding it against potential digital threats. Subsequently, to prepare for the anticipated gas fees associated with minting their NFT, they fund their newly created MetaMask wallet with $20 worth of Ether (ETH), acquiring the necessary digital currency to cover the transactional costs on the Ethereum network.

⚡ What Are Gas Fees? The Cost of Decentralization

Gas fees represent the cost associated with utilizing the computational resources of a blockchain network. These fees are not arbitrary but rather a mechanism to incentivize the network's participants (e.g., miners or validators) to process and validate transactions, ensuring the security and integrity of the blockchain. The magnitude of gas fees can fluctuate based on several factors, most notably the current level of network traffic and the computational complexity of the action being performed. During periods of high demand, when numerous users are simultaneously interacting with the blockchain, gas fees tend to escalate due to increased competition for limited network resources. Similarly, more intricate smart contract interactions will typically necessitate higher gas fees due to the greater computational power required for their execution.

Network	Typical Gas Fee
Ethereum	$10 – $50 (high but more widely recognized)
Polygon	~$0.01 (cheap and fast)

Export to Sheets

As the table illustrates, different blockchain networks exhibit varying levels of typical gas fees. The Ethereum network, while being the most established and widely recognized ecosystem for NFTs, often experiences higher gas fees due to its high level of activity. In contrast, networks like Polygon, designed as a scaling solution for Ethereum, offer significantly lower and faster transactions, making them an attractive alternative for users seeking to minimize costs.

- **Tip for Beginners:** For individuals new to the world of NFTs and potentially hesitant about incurring substantial gas fees, many platforms, such as OpenSea, offer the option to mint NFTs on the Polygon network with **zero upfront gas fees**. This provides a cost-effective entry point into NFT creation, allowing beginners to tokenize their work without the immediate financial burden associated with the Ethereum network. The gas fees for transactions on Polygon are typically negligible, making it a particularly appealing choice for initial experimentation and smaller-scale NFT projects.

Understanding the interplay between minting, gas fees, and wallets is crucial for anyone venturing into the creation and ownership of Non-Fungible Tokens. The wallet serves as the gateway, minting transforms digital creations into blockchain-secured assets, and an awareness of gas fees allows for informed decision-making regarding the choice of blockchain network and the timing of transactions.

□ □ Embark with us upon a detailed exposition of the process by which one can transmute their digital creations into Non-Fungible Tokens, leveraging the accessible platform of OpenSea and the efficient Polygon network. This step-by-step guide shall illuminate the path for aspiring digital artisans to inscribe their work onto the immutable ledger of the blockchain.

☵ Step 1: Establish Your Digital Vault – Setting Up Your Wallet

The inaugural step in this digital alchemy necessitates the acquisition and configuration of a cryptocurrency wallet, your secure portal to the Web3 ecosystem. MetaMask, a widely embraced and versatile wallet, serves as an exemplary choice for this purpose.

- **Install MetaMask Browser Extension:** Navigate to the official MetaMask website and procure the browser extension compatible with your preferred web navigator.
- **Create a New Wallet:** Upon installation, follow the intuitive prompts to establish a new digital wallet. This process will generate a unique cryptographic address that will serve as your identifier on the blockchain.
- **Store Your Seed Phrase (Of Utmost Importance – Refrain from Disclosure!):** During wallet creation, you will be presented with a **seed phrase**, a sequence of twelve or more words. This phrase is the master key to your wallet and its contents. Exercise the utmost diligence in recording this phrase accurately and storing it offline in a secure and undisclosed location. Its compromise could lead to the irretrievable loss of your digital assets.

- **Switch the Wallet Network to Polygon (Via ChainList.org or Manually):** To avail oneself of the lower transaction fees offered by the Polygon network, it is imperative to configure your MetaMask wallet to interact with this specific blockchain. This can be achieved either through the convenient third-party website ChainList.org, which simplifies the process of adding and switching networks, or through a manual configuration within MetaMask by inputting the specific network parameters for Polygon (Network Name, RPC URL, Chain ID, Currency Symbol, Block Explorer URL).

☐☐ Step 2: Prepare Your Digital Canvas – Create Your NFT Content

The genesis of your NFT lies in the digital file you intend to tokenize. Ensure that your creative work is prepared in a compatible digital format:

- **Visual Art:** PNG, JPG, GIF
- **Auditory Compositions:** MP3
- **Cinematic Works:** MP4
- **Textual Documents:** PDF
- **Example:** Imagine your artistic endeavors culminate in the creation of a captivating digital painting, christened "Dreamscape 2025." This visual narrative of imagined futures is meticulously saved as a high-resolution JPG file, ready for its transformation into a unique digital asset.

☐ Step 3: Establish Connection – Link Your Wallet to OpenSea

With your digital wallet primed and your creative content prepared, the next step involves establishing a secure connection between your wallet and the OpenSea marketplace.

- **Visit https://opensea.io:** Navigate your web browser to the official OpenSea website.
- **Click on the Wallet Icon:** Locate and select the wallet icon, typically situated in the upper right-hand corner of the webpage.
- **Select MetaMask and Connect:** From the list of available wallet providers, choose MetaMask. A prompt will appear within your MetaMask extension, requesting your authorization to connect your wallet to the OpenSea platform. Grant this permission to establish the link.

✍☐ Step 4: The Alchemical Process – Mint the NFT

With your wallet securely connected, you are now poised to transmute your digital file into an NFT.

- **Click "Create" on OpenSea:** On the OpenSea platform, locate and select the "Create" button, usually found in the upper right-hand corner.
- **Upload Your File:** A dialogue box will appear, prompting you to upload the digital file you prepared in Step 2 (e.g., your "Dreamscape 2025" JPG).
- **Add Essential Metadata:** Imbue your NFT with identifying information:
  - **Title:** Assign a distinct name to your NFT (e.g., Dreamscape 2025).

- o **Description:** Provide a concise narrative or context for your NFT (e.g., "A digital artwork depicting the serene landscapes of future metropolises").
- o **Properties (Optional):** Add specific attributes or characteristics that further define your NFT (e.g., Edition: 1/1, Color Type: Vibrant). These properties can enhance the uniqueness and discoverability of your NFT.
- **Select Polygon under Blockchain (To Avoid Gas Fees):** Crucially, under the "Blockchain" section, choose **Polygon**. This selection ensures that the minting process occurs on the Polygon network, thereby circumventing the potentially higher gas fees associated with the Ethereum mainnet.
- **Click "Create":** Once you have uploaded your file and added the necessary metadata, click the "Create" button. A confirmation will appear, signifying the successful minting of your NFT on the Polygon blockchain.

✅ **Your NFT is Minted!** Your digital creation now exists as a unique and verifiable Non-Fungible Token on the blockchain, ready to be shared with the world.

☐☐ **Step 5: Presenting Your Creation – List for Sale**

With your NFT successfully minted, the final step involves making it available for acquisition on the marketplace.

- **Click on the NFT from Your Profile:** Navigate to your profile on OpenSea, where you will find the newly minted NFT. Click on it to view its dedicated page.
- **Hit "Sell":** On the NFT's page, locate and select the "Sell" button.
- **Set Your Terms:** Define the parameters of your sale:
  - o **Price:** Specify the desired price for your NFT. In this example, you might set it at 0.01 ETH, which approximates $15 USD based on the current exchange rate between ETH and USD.
  - o **Duration:** Determine the length of time your listing will remain active on the marketplace (e.g., 7 days).
- **Confirm the Listing Via MetaMask:** After setting your price and duration, click the "Complete listing" button. A prompt will appear in your MetaMask extension, requesting your signature to authorize the listing of your NFT for sale on OpenSea. Confirm this transaction within MetaMask.

🔊 **Your NFT is Now Live on the Marketplace.** Your digital artwork, "Dreamscape 2025," is now publicly listed for sale on the OpenSea marketplace, ready to be discovered by potential collectors within the vast and evolving world of Non-Fungible Tokens.

💡 **Real Student Example: A Case Study in Digital Entrepreneurship**

To illustrate the practical application of NFT technology and the potential it holds for aspiring creators, consider the experience of Nikhil, a 21-year-old animation student from India, whose foray into the digital asset space offers a compelling narrative.

🎓 Nikhil, a 21-year-old animation student from India:

Driven by his artistic pursuits and a keen awareness of emerging digital trends, Nikhil embarked on a project to create a series of ten unique digital animations, each reflecting his distinct creative vision. Opting for the OpenSea platform and leveraging the Polygon network's efficient and cost-effective infrastructure, he took the following steps:

- **Minted 10 NFTs on Polygon using OpenSea:** Employing the established protocols for NFT creation, Nikhil successfully minted each of his ten animations as individual Non-Fungible Tokens on the Polygon blockchain via OpenSea. This strategic choice allowed him to minimize the financial burden associated with transaction fees, a common consideration for creators operating with limited resources.
- **Promoted on Instagram and Twitter:** Recognizing the importance of visibility in the digital marketplace, Nikhil proactively marketed his creations through social media channels. He showcased his animations on Instagram, a platform well-suited for visual content, and engaged with potential collectors and the broader NFT community on Twitter.
- **Sold 3 NFTs in the First Week (~$50):** Nikhil's efforts to promote his work yielded positive results. Within the initial week of listing his NFTs, he successfully sold three pieces, generating approximately $50 USD in revenue. This early success validated his approach and provided a tangible return on his creative investment.
- **Used Profits to Pay for a New Drawing Tablet:** Demonstrating financial prudence and a commitment to his artistic development, Nikhil reinvested his earnings to acquire a new drawing tablet. This acquisition enhanced his ability to create further digital artwork, highlighting the potential for NFTs to facilitate self-funding for creative endeavors.

Nikhil's experience exemplifies how students can harness NFT technology to monetize their creative skills and support their artistic growth. His story underscores the accessibility of the NFT space and its capacity to empower individuals to participate in the digital economy.

🎁 Optional Bonus: Deferred Minting Protocols

Certain platforms offer an alternative approach to NFT creation known as "lazy minting." This method postpones the actual minting process—the inscription of the NFT onto the blockchain—until the point of sale.

- **Availability:** This functionality is available on platforms such as OpenSea (when utilizing the Polygon network) and Rarible. By deferring the minting process, creators can list their NFTs for sale without incurring any upfront costs. The associated gas fees are typically borne by the buyer upon purchase. This approach can significantly reduce the financial barrier to entry for creators, particularly those who wish to gauge market demand for their work before committing resources to the minting process.

30 multiple-choice questions with answers covering OpenSea and Rarible, Minting/Gas Fees/Wallets, and the Step-by-Step Walkthrough:

Tools & Platforms: OpenSea, Rarible

1. OpenSea is best described as: a) A cryptocurrency exchange. b) A blockchain network. c) A popular NFT marketplace. d) A hardware wallet provider. **Answer: c)**
2. Which blockchain networks does OpenSea primarily support? a) Bitcoin and Litecoin. b) Ethereum and Polygon. c) Solana and Cardano. d) Binance Smart Chain and Tron. **Answer: b)**
3. Rarible is similar to OpenSea but offers: a) Lower transaction fees for buyers. b) Built-in cryptocurrency mining capabilities. c) Creator royalties customization. d) Decentralized governance of the platform. **Answer: c)**
4. Rarible allows creators to mint: a) Only single editions of NFTs. b) Only multiple editions of NFTs. c) Both single and multiple editions of NFTs. d) Only fractionalized NFTs. **Answer: c)**
5. For beginners, which NFT marketplace is often considered more user-friendly? a) Rarible b) SuperRare c) Foundation d) OpenSea **Answer: d)**
6. Platforms like OpenSea and Rarible allow users to: a) Mine new cryptocurrencies. b) Stake their existing NFTs. c) Mint, buy, sell, and display NFTs. d) Directly control blockchain network parameters. **Answer: c)**
7. Which platform mentioned is particularly suitable for collectibles with multiple editions? a) OpenSea b) Rarible c) SuperRare d) Nifty Gateway **Answer: b)**
8. SuperRare, mentioned in the broader context, focuses on: a) Affordable NFTs for mass adoption. b) Curated, high-end digital art. c) Gaming-related NFTs. d) Music NFTs. **Answer: b)**
9. Foundation, another NFT platform, emphasizes: a) Low transaction fees. b) Artist exclusivity and auctions. c) Social interaction between buyers and sellers. d) Integration with traditional art galleries. **Answer: b)**
10. Niche NFT marketplaces often cater to: a) Only the most popular NFT collections. b) Specific types of NFTs like gaming assets or music. c) Trading of fractionalized NFTs. d) Cross-chain NFT transfers. **Answer: b)**

Minting, Gas Fees, and Wallets

11. What is the process of converting a digital file into an NFT on the blockchain called? a) Burning b) Mining c) Minting d) Staking **Answer: c)**
12. Once an NFT is minted, it is: a) Easily editable by the creator. b) Stored on a central server. c) Permanent, tamper-proof, and publicly viewable on the blockchain. d) Only visible on the marketplace where it was minted. **Answer: c)**
13. Before minting an NFT, you primarily need a: a) High-speed internet connection. b) Cryptocurrency exchange account. c) Crypto wallet. d) Digital art software subscription. **Answer: c)**
14. What is a popular cryptocurrency wallet used for interacting with NFT marketplaces? a) Coinbase Wallet (the exchange app) b) MetaMask c) Robinhood d) PayPal **Answer: b)**
15. MetaMask is available as a: a) Hardware device only. b) Mobile app only. c) Browser extension and mobile app. d) Desktop application only. **Answer: c)**

16. What are "gas fees" in the context of NFTs? a) The cost of storing the NFT file off-chain. b) The commission charged by the NFT marketplace. c) The cost of using the blockchain for transactions. d) A mandatory donation to the NFT creator. **Answer: c)**
17. Gas fees typically vary based on: a) The size of the NFT file. b) The reputation of the NFT creator. c) Network traffic and the complexity of the action. d) The fiat currency exchange rate. **Answer: c)**
18. Which blockchain network often has higher gas fees? a) Polygon b) Solana c) Ethereum d) Cardano **Answer: c)**
19. Which blockchain network is known for its cheap and fast transactions, often appealing to NFT beginners? a) Ethereum b) Binance Smart Chain c) Polygon d) Avalanche **Answer: c)**
20. What is "lazy minting"? a) Minting NFTs using only free software. b) Minting NFTs on a blockchain with zero gas fees permanently. c) A process where your NFT is only minted when it is sold. d) Minting multiple NFTs at once to save on gas fees. **Answer: c)**

Step-by-Step Walkthrough: Mint Your First NFT on OpenSea (Polygon)

21. The first step in minting on OpenSea (Polygon) is to: a) Create your digital art. b) List your NFT for sale. c) Set up your crypto wallet and switch to the Polygon network. d) Visit the OpenSea website. **Answer: c)**
22. Storing your seed phrase securely is: a) Optional for experienced users. b) Only important if you plan to sell your NFTs. c) Very important – don't share it. d) Handled automatically by OpenSea. **Answer: c)**
23. To avoid high gas fees when minting on OpenSea, you should select which blockchain? a) Ethereum b) Bitcoin c) Polygon d) Binance Smart Chain **Answer: c)**
24. On OpenSea's "Create" page, what is the first thing you need to do? a) Set the price of your NFT. b) Upload your digital file. c) Write a description of your NFT. d) Choose the blockchain. **Answer: b)**
25. What information do you typically add when minting an NFT on OpenSea? a) Only the file and your wallet address. b) Title, description, and optionally properties. c) Your full legal name and address. d) The current market value of similar NFTs. **Answer: b)**
26. Under the "Blockchain" option on OpenSea's create page, you should select: a) Ethereum Mainnet. b) Your hardware wallet. c) Polygon. d) The default option. **Answer: c)**
27. After clicking "Create" on OpenSea, your NFT is: a) Immediately sold to the highest bidder. b) Sent to OpenSea for review. c) Minted on the chosen blockchain. d) Stored as a draft until you list it. **Answer: c)**
28. To list your NFT for sale on OpenSea, you navigate to your profile and click on the NFT, then hit: a) "Transfer" b) "Burn" c) "Sell" d) "Edit" **Answer: c)**
29. When listing your NFT for sale, you need to set the: a) Gas fee you are willing to pay. b) Price and duration of the listing. c) Number of editions you want to sell. d) Royalty percentage for future sales (if applicable). **Answer: b)**
30. Confirming the listing on OpenSea typically involves a transaction through your: a) Bank account. b) Email address. c) Crypto wallet (like MetaMask). d) Social media account. **Answer: c)**

10 mid-size questions with answers covering OpenSea/Rarible, Minting/Gas Fees/Wallets, and the Step-by-Step Walkthrough:

1. **Compare and contrast OpenSea and Rarible as NFT marketplaces. What are the key similarities in their functionality, and what is a notable differentiating feature offered by Rarible to creators? Answer:** Both OpenSea and Rarible serve as platforms for users to mint, buy, sell, and display NFTs, supporting similar blockchain networks like Ethereum and Polygon. A notable differentiating feature of Rarible is its emphasis on creator empowerment through customizable royalty percentages on secondary sales, offering artists more control over their ongoing earnings compared to OpenSea's more standardized royalty options.

2. **Explain the significance of a cryptocurrency wallet, such as MetaMask, in the process of interacting with NFT marketplaces and the broader Web3 ecosystem. What are the three primary functions a wallet serves in this context? Answer:** A cryptocurrency wallet is essential as it acts as a user's digital passport to Web3. Its three primary functions are: 1) Facilitating the payment of gas fees required for blockchain transactions like minting and selling NFTs. 2) Enabling users to sign blockchain transactions, providing authorization for actions taken on the network. 3) Securely storing the user's NFTs and other cryptocurrency assets, linked to their unique blockchain address.

3. **Describe the concept of "gas fees" on blockchain networks like Ethereum and Polygon. What purpose do these fees serve, and why can they vary significantly between different networks and at different times? Answer:** Gas fees are the costs associated with using a blockchain network's computational resources to process and validate transactions. They incentivize network participants (miners or validators) to maintain the blockchain's security and integrity. Gas fees vary based on network traffic (higher demand leads to higher fees) and the computational complexity of the transaction (more complex smart contract interactions require more gas). Polygon generally has significantly lower gas fees than Ethereum due to its design as a scaling solution.

4. **Outline the general steps involved in minting an NFT on a platform like OpenSea. What is the crucial decision a beginner should make regarding the choice of blockchain during this process to potentially avoid high initial costs? Answer:** The general steps include connecting a crypto wallet to the platform, navigating to the "create" section, uploading the digital file, adding metadata (title, description, properties), and then selecting the blockchain. For beginners aiming to avoid high initial costs, choosing the Polygon network (if supported by the platform) for minting is crucial, as it typically involves significantly lower gas fees compared to the Ethereum mainnet.

5. **Explain the purpose and benefits of adding "properties" or "attributes" to an NFT's metadata during the minting process on platforms like OpenSea or Rarible. How can these properties influence the perceived value or rarity of an NFT within a collection? Answer:** Adding properties or attributes to an NFT's metadata allows creators to define specific characteristics of their digital asset (e.g., color, edition number, special features). This detailed information enhances the NFT's identity and can significantly influence its perceived value and rarity within a larger collection. NFTs with rarer or more desirable properties, as defined in the metadata, often command higher prices among collectors.

6. **Describe the process of listing an NFT for sale on OpenSea after it has been successfully minted. What key parameters does the seller need to define when creating a listing, and how is the transaction typically finalized? Answer:** To list an NFT for sale on OpenSea, the seller navigates to their profile, selects the NFT, and clicks "Sell." Key parameters to define include the price (usually in ETH or another supported cryptocurrency) and the duration of the listing. The transaction is finalized when a buyer agrees to the price and completes the purchase, which involves a blockchain transaction confirmed through their connected crypto wallet (like MetaMask), transferring ownership of the NFT and the payment to the seller.

7. **What is "lazy minting," and how does it differ from the traditional NFT minting process in terms of upfront costs for the creator? On which platforms is lazy minting typically available, and what is the primary advantage it offers to new creators? Answer:** Lazy minting is a process where the NFT is not actually minted on the blockchain until it is purchased. In contrast to traditional minting where the creator pays gas fees to tokenize the asset upfront, lazy minting allows creators to list their NFTs for sale with zero upfront gas costs. This feature is typically available on platforms like OpenSea (on Polygon) and Rarible, offering a significant advantage to new creators by removing the initial financial barrier to entry and allowing them to test market demand before incurring minting expenses.

8. **Discuss the importance of securely storing the seed phrase associated with a cryptocurrency wallet like MetaMask. What potential risks arise from the compromise of this seed phrase, and what are some best practices for its safe storage? Answer:** The seed phrase is the master key to a cryptocurrency wallet and all the digital assets it contains, including NFTs. If compromised, malicious actors can gain complete and irreversible access to the wallet and steal all its contents. Best practices for safe storage include writing it down on physical paper (not digitally), storing it offline in a secure and private location, and potentially dividing it into multiple parts stored separately.

9. **Compare the typical gas fees associated with the Ethereum and Polygon networks for NFT-related transactions. What factors contribute to this difference, and when might a user choose one network over the other for minting or trading NFTs?**
   Answer: Ethereum typically has significantly higher gas fees than Polygon due to its higher network congestion and the complexity of its mainnet. Polygon, as a Layer-2 scaling solution, offers much lower fees and faster transaction times. A user might choose Polygon for minting or trading NFTs when cost is a primary concern, especially for beginners or those dealing with lower-value NFTs. Ethereum might be preferred for higher-value NFTs or when interacting with projects exclusively on the Ethereum mainnet due to its broader recognition and established ecosystem.

10. **Beyond OpenSea and Rarible, briefly mention two other types of NFT marketplaces (e.g., curated platforms, niche marketplaces) and describe their general focus or target audience. How do these alternative platforms cater to different segments of the NFT ecosystem? Answer:** Two other types of NFT marketplaces include: 1) **Curated platforms** like SuperRare and Foundation, which focus on showcasing high-quality, often one-of-a-kind digital art selected by an internal team or through a voting process. These platforms target serious collectors willing to pay higher prices for vetted artwork. 2) **Niche marketplaces** that specialize in specific types of NFTs, such as those for gaming assets (e.g., Axie Marketplace), music NFTs (e.g., Catalog), or virtual land (e.g., in specific metaverses). These platforms cater to specific communities and interests within the broader NFT space.

☐ Summary

Creating your first NFT is more than just a tech demo — it's a step into the creator economy of the future. Whether you're an artist, musician, coder, or content creator, this hands-on experience builds your confidence in Web3.

🔗 You are now not just a student — you are a creator on the blockchain.

CHAPTER 10: THE BUSINESS OF NFTS – ART, GAMING & BEYOND

NFTs are no longer limited to digital art. They are reshaping careers, industries, and even the way we think about ownership and value. In this chapter, we'll explore **how NFTs are becoming a career launchpad** for students and creators, and why understanding the risks is as important as seizing the rewards.

🎨 NFT Careers: Forging New Professional Pathways in the Decentralized Age

The burgeoning realm of Non-Fungible Tokens has not only revolutionized digital ownership and creative monetization but has also catalyzed the emergence of entirely novel professional roles, occupations that were hitherto absent from the traditional employment landscape. These are not mere ephemeral side ventures; for a growing number of individuals, they represent full-time vocations, pathways to earning a livelihood that often prioritize creativity, intellectual curiosity, and unwavering commitment over the conventional prerequisites of formal academic degrees. Let us explore some of the key career avenues that are blossoming within the NFT ecosystem.

1. Digital Artists: Direct Engagement with a Global Patronage

NFTs have bestowed upon digital artists an unprecedented level of autonomy, empowering them to directly engage with a global network of discerning buyers, unencumbered by the traditional intermediaries of galleries or agents. Furthermore, the embedded mechanism of royalties ensures that the original creator continues to derive economic benefit from the subsequent appreciation and exchange of their artwork in the secondary market, fostering a sustainable model for artistic endeavors.

- **Example:** Consider a talented digital artist who meticulously crafts a unique, one-of-one artwork and mints it as an NFT, initially offering it for 0.1 Ether (ETH), an equivalent of approximately $300 USD. Over the ensuing year, this singular digital creation garners increasing recognition and is resold on three separate occasions. Each transaction triggers the embedded 10% royalty, yielding the artist earnings of $30, $50, and $70 respectively, demonstrating the potential for ongoing income generation from a single creative act.

2. Smart Contract Developers: Architects of the Decentralized Infrastructure

Underpinning the functionality of every NFT lies the intricate framework of code, specifically smart contracts meticulously written in programming languages such as Solidity. These skilled developers serve as the architects of the decentralized infrastructure, building bespoke NFT projects, constructing the digital marketplaces where these assets are exchanged, and even developing the interactive mechanics of NFT-integrated games.

- **Example:** Imagine a student possessing a strong aptitude for computer programming who hones their skills in Solidity, the primary language for smart contract development on the Ethereum blockchain. Recognizing her expertise, a prominent fashion brand seeks to launch an innovative NFT collection to engage with its digitally savvy clientele. The student, operating as a freelance smart contract developer through platforms like Fiverr, is commissioned to build the underlying smart contracts that govern the creation, ownership, and potential utility of these fashion-related NFTs, earning a substantial fee of $5,000 for her specialized skills.

3. Community Managers: Cultivating the Web3 Agora

Within the decentralized ethos of Web3, the concept of community assumes paramount importance. The vibrant ecosystems surrounding NFT projects thrive on active engagement, meaningful interaction, and a shared sense of belonging. To foster and nurture these digital agorae, the role of the community manager has become indispensable. These individuals are tasked with managing and moderating online spaces such as Discord servers, Telegram groups, and Twitter Spaces, cultivating a welcoming environment, facilitating discussions, addressing inquiries, and strategically growing the project's audience.

- **Example:** Consider a diligent college student with exceptional communication and organizational skills who possesses a genuine enthusiasm for a burgeoning NFT-based game. Recognizing their aptitude for fostering online engagement, the game's developers enlist them as a part-time community manager. In this role, the student earns a monthly stipend of $400 by diligently hosting weekly Twitter Spaces to engage with the player base, moderating discussions within the project's Discord server, and strategically managing the game's social media presence to expand its reach and cultivate a loyal community.

4. NFT Strategists and Marketers: Navigating the Evolving Digital Landscape

As the NFT space continues its rapid evolution, a specialized demand has emerged for individuals possessing a nuanced understanding of its intricate dynamics. NFT strategists and marketers are sought after by both individual creators and established companies seeking to navigate this novel landscape effectively. Their expertise encompasses a wide range of critical areas, including discerning prevailing NFT trends, establishing optimal pricing strategies, orchestrating successful NFT drops (launches), and ethically cultivating anticipation and excitement ("hype") around projects to drive adoption and engagement. These professionals play a crucial role in bridging the gap between creative vision and market success within the burgeoning NFT economy.

⬚ NFT in Music, Fashion, Education & More: Transcending the Realm of Art

The transformative potential of Non-Fungible Tokens extends far beyond the realm of digital art, permeating and reshaping established industries with innovative and practical applications. From revolutionizing how artists connect with their audiences to verifying academic achievements, NFTs are demonstrating a versatility that promises to redefine traditional paradigms.

♪ Music: Tokenizing Sound and Fostering Fan Engagement

The music industry, long navigating the complexities of digital distribution and artist compensation, is embracing NFTs as a novel medium for artists to release their sonic creations, fostering a direct and exclusive relationship with their fanbase.

- **Example:** Consider a visionary singer who chooses to release a limited edition of 100 NFT tracks. Each discerning buyer not only gains exclusive ownership of a unique digital audio file but also unlocks access to a private virtual concert via Zoom, offering an intimate and interactive experience. Furthermore, they might receive exclusive behind-the-scenes content, forging a deeper connection between the artist and their most dedicated supporters.
- 🎧 **The Tokenization of Royalties:** In an even more groundbreaking application, some forward-thinking artists are exploring the tokenization of their music royalties. By offering fans a fractional ownership stake in the earnings generated by their songs through streaming platforms and other channels, artists can cultivate a loyal community of micro-investors who are directly incentivized to support their work and promote its success. This innovative model has the potential to democratize music ownership and create a more equitable ecosystem for both creators and listeners.

👗 Fashion: Weaving Digital Threads into the Tangible World

The vanguard of the fashion industry, including iconic brands such as Gucci, Adidas, and Dolce & Gabbana, has ventured into the metaverse with the launch of wearable NFTs. These digital garments and accessories allow users to adorn their virtual avatars in various online environments. Intriguingly, in certain innovative instances, these digital fashion NFTs are intrinsically linked to their real-world counterparts.

- **Example:** Imagine acquiring a coveted fashion NFT that not only bestows upon your digital avatar in virtual worlds like Decentraland a stylish digital jacket but also includes the tangible benefit of a physical version of the same jacket being meticulously crafted and delivered directly to your physical doorstep. This convergence of the digital and the physical realms blurs the lines between virtual identity and tangible possessions, offering a novel form of brand engagement and exclusivity.

🎓 Education: Certifying Skills and Empowering Learners

The immutable and verifiable nature of NFTs is finding compelling applications within the education sector, offering a secure and transparent method for issuing digital diplomas, certificates of completion, and skill-based badges.

- **Example:** Upon successfully completing a rigorous blockchain course, a student might receive a non-transferable NFT certificate. This digital credential, securely recorded on the blockchain, becomes a permanent and tamper-proof testament to their acquired knowledge and skills. This NFT can be readily displayed on their digital résumé or professional profiles, offering employers an easily verifiable and credible validation of their qualifications, thereby enhancing their employability in an increasingly digital world.

⚠️ Risks and Rewards of the NFT World: Navigating a Nascent Ecosystem

Like any rapidly evolving ecosystem, the NFT landscape presents a duality of potential benefits and inherent risks. Prudent participation necessitates a comprehensive understanding of both the alluring rewards and the potential pitfalls. Vigilant awareness serves as the primary safeguard for those venturing into this dynamic space.

🎁 Rewards: Unlocking New Value and Opportunities

The NFT world offers several compelling advantages:

- **Ownership & Royalties: Empowering Creators:** NFTs have fundamentally altered the traditional model of artistic compensation. Artists are no longer limited to a single sale; instead, they can programmatically secure a percentage of every subsequent resale of their work. This innovative royalty structure provides a sustained income stream, directly aligning the artist's financial interests with the long-term value of their creations.
- **Global Reach: Disintermediation and Direct Access:** NFTs transcend geographical barriers, enabling creators to connect directly with a global audience of buyers, collectors, and enthusiasts. By eliminating intermediaries such as galleries and agents, artists gain greater control over the distribution, pricing, and promotion of their work, fostering a more equitable and efficient marketplace.
- **Innovation Space: A Fertile Ground for Experimentation:** The NFT space is characterized by its openness to novel ideas and unconventional approaches. It is a realm where experimentation is not only encouraged but often rewarded. Even projects initiated by students or emerging creators can achieve widespread recognition and substantial financial success, highlighting the democratizing nature of this technology.

⚠️ Risks: Navigating the Perils of a Developing Frontier

Alongside these enticing rewards, the NFT world is also susceptible to certain risks:

- **Scams and Rug Pulls: Protecting Against Deception:** The rapid growth and decentralized nature of the NFT market have, unfortunately, attracted malicious actors seeking to exploit unsuspecting participants. "Rug pulls" are a particularly insidious form of fraud, wherein creators abandon a project shortly after launch, often after raising significant funds from investors, leaving buyers with worthless assets. It is imperative to exercise extreme caution and conduct thorough due diligence ("Do Your Own Research" - DYOR) before committing any capital.
- **Volatility: Managing Market Fluctuations:** The prices of NFTs, like those of other digital assets, can exhibit extreme volatility, characterized by rapid and unpredictable fluctuations. The value of an NFT that is highly sought after today may decline

significantly or even become negligible tomorrow, reflecting the speculative nature of this emerging market and the ever-shifting tides of consumer interest.

- **Environmental Concerns: Addressing Sustainability:** Early iterations of some blockchain networks, most notably Ethereum, relied on energy-intensive consensus mechanisms (like Proof of Work) that raised concerns about their environmental impact. However, the Ethereum network has since transitioned to a more energy-efficient mechanism known as Proof of Stake. While this transition has drastically reduced energy consumption, it's important to stay informed about the environmental impact of the blockchains used for NFT transactions.
- **Legal Grey Areas: Navigating Regulatory Uncertainty:** The legal and regulatory framework surrounding NFTs, particularly concerning copyright and trademark law, is still in a nascent stage and continues to evolve. The unauthorized minting and sale of copyrighted material as NFTs can lead to legal action, underscoring the importance of respecting intellectual property rights in this space.

☐ **Case Study: From Student to NFTpreneur: A Success Story**

- **Name:** Emily, 22
- **Occupation:** Graphic Design Student
- **Location:** United Kingdom
- **Story:**

Emily, a graphic design student with a passion for digital art, embarked on a creative endeavor to produce a limited NFT series featuring animated characters imbued with a vibrant, neon aesthetic, which she titled "Neon Dreams."

```
* Leveraging the cost-effective Polygon network, Emily minted her NFT
collection on OpenSea, thereby avoiding the substantial upfront gas fees that
would have been incurred on the Ethereum mainnet.
* To generate awareness and cultivate interest in her work, Emily employed a
strategic promotional campaign across social media platforms, notably
Instagram and Reddit, where she showcased the unique visual appeal and
narrative elements of her "Neon Dreams" series.
* Emily's efforts proved fruitful, as she successfully sold 50 NFTs within
the first week of listing her collection. This initial success translated to
earnings of over £1,000, providing a significant boost to her burgeoning
artistic career.
* Emily's talent and innovative use of NFT technology caught the attention of
a gaming startup, which subsequently hired her to design in-game NFT avatars.
This opportunity allowed her to apply her creative skills in a professional
capacity, marking a transition from student artist to sought-after digital
asset designer.
```

✅ Final Thoughts

The business of NFTs is more than just headlines and hype — it's a **gateway to economic freedom**, especially for students. Whether you're an artist, a tech enthusiast, a community builder, or a marketer, there's space for you in the NFT economy.

But like any business, it requires **skills, learning, ethical practices, and caution.** By understanding both the **opportunities and the pitfalls,** you empower yourself to make informed decisions and carve your niche in this future-facing world.

🎯 **Remember:** You don't need permission to start — just passion and a little curiosity. The NFT world is waiting.

30 multiple-choice questions with answers covering NFT careers, applications in music, fashion, and education, and the risks and rewards of the NFT world:

NFT Careers: Artists, Coders, Community Managers

1. Which of the following NFT careers directly involves creating the underlying code for NFT projects? a) Digital Artist b) Community Manager c) Smart Contract Developer d) NFT Strategist Answer: c
2. An NFT artist earns not only from the initial sale but also from: a) Inflation b) Royalties c) Taxes d) Discounts Answer: b
3. Which role is responsible for engaging, moderating, and growing the audience of an NFT project? a) Smart Contract Developer b) NFT Strategist c) Community Manager d) Digital Artist Answer: c
4. Which skill is NOT typically required for a Community Manager in the NFT space? a) Moderation b) Engagement c) Coding in Solidity d) Audience growth Answer: c
5. What is a primary responsibility of an NFT Strategist? a) Writing smart contracts b) Creating digital artwork c) Understanding NFT trends and pricing d) Managing online communities Answer: c
6. A digital artist who sells an NFT for 2 ETH with a 15% royalty, and it's resold for 5 ETH, earns how much in royalty? a) 0.3 ETH b) 0.75 ETH c) 2 ETH d) 5 ETH Answer: b
7. Which career path in the NFT space requires knowledge of languages like Solidity? a) Digital Artist b) Community Manager c) NFT Strategist d) Smart Contract Developer Answer: d
8. True or False: NFT careers often require traditional degrees. a) True b) False Answer: b
9. Which of the following is NOT a typical platform used by NFT community managers? a) Discord b) Telegram c) Twitter Spaces d) Adobe Photoshop Answer: d
10. What is a key aspect that NFTs have enabled for digital artists? a) Reliance on galleries b) Direct sales to global buyers c) Exclusively selling physical art d) Limited edition prints Answer: b

NFT in Music, Fashion, Education

11. In the music industry, NFTs can provide fans with: a) Only digital copies of songs b) Exclusive ownership and access c) Physical CDs d) Streaming service subscriptions Answer: b
12. Some musicians use NFTs to: a) Sell concert tickets b) Tokenize royalties c) Create physical instruments d) Distribute sheet music Answer: b

13. Fashion brands use NFTs to create: a) Only physical clothing b) Wearable NFTs for the metaverse c) Traditional advertisements d) Discount coupons Answer: b
14. An NFT in fashion that comes with a real-life item is an example of: a) A virtual-only asset b) A hybrid physical-digital product c) A traditional garment sale d) A metaverse exclusive Answer: b
15. NFTs are being used in education for: a) Creating physical diplomas b) Digital diplomas and certificates c) Replacing textbooks d) Funding school construction Answer: b
16. How do NFTs help verify credentials in education? a) By storing them on paper b) By making them tamper-proof and verifiable c) By emailing them d) By mailing physical copies Answer: b
17. Which industry is NOT directly mentioned as being transformed by NFTs? a) Music b) Fashion c) Education d) Real Estate Answer: d
18. What is a potential benefit of using NFTs for music artists? a) Increased reliance on record labels b) Direct fan engagement and new revenue streams c) Exclusively selling physical albums d) Limiting music distribution Answer: b
19. In what way are NFTs changing the fashion industry? a) By increasing the production of physical clothing b) By enabling the creation of digital wearables for virtual worlds c) By replacing traditional fashion shows d) By eliminating the need for designers Answer: b
20. How might NFTs be used for educational purposes beyond certificates? a) As virtual textbooks b) For student loan management c) To represent attendance records d) All of the above Answer: d

Risks and Rewards of the NFT World

21. A significant reward of NFTs for artists is: a) Dependence on middlemen b) Ownership and royalties c) Limited reach d) Stable prices Answer: b
22. A key benefit of NFTs for creators is the ability to: a) Sell only in local markets b) Sell directly to buyers worldwide c) Avoid new ideas d) Rely on traditional agents Answer: b
23. Which of the following is a significant risk in the NFT world? a) Guaranteed profits b) Scams and rug pulls c) Stable prices d) Low volatility Answer: b
24. "DYOR" in the NFT space stands for: a) Don't Yield On Research b) Do Your Own Research c) Digital Output of Revenue d) Define Your Own Rules Answer: b
25. NFT prices are known for their: a) Stability b) Volatility c) Predictability d) Gradual increase Answer: b
26. What is a "rug pull" in the NFT world? a) A type of artwork b) A fake project where creators disappear c) A price increase d) A legal contract Answer: b
27. Which is a potential legal issue in the NFT space? a) Clear copyright laws b) Evolving trademark laws c) No legal framework d) Standardized regulations Answer: b
28. What is one way the environmental impact of NFTs has been reduced? a) Increased use of Proof of Work b) The Ethereum merge to Proof of Stake c) Higher gas fees d) Centralized networks Answer: b
29. Emily, in the case study, avoided high upfront costs by: a) Minting on Ethereum b) Minting on Polygon c) Not minting at all d) Using a traditional gallery Answer: b
30. What did Emily NOT do to promote her NFT series? a) Promote on Instagram b) Promote on Reddit c) Hire a marketing agency d) Sell 50 NFTs in the first week Answer: c

10 mid-size questions and answers on NFT careers, applications, and the risks and rewards of the NFT world:

NFT Careers: Artists, Coders, Community Managers

1. **Question:** Describe the role of a Smart Contract Developer in the NFT ecosystem. What specific skills are essential for this career, and how do they contribute to the functionality of NFTs?

   Answer: A Smart Contract Developer is crucial in the NFT ecosystem, as they are responsible for creating and implementing the underlying code (smart contracts) that governs the behavior and functionality of NFTs. These contracts define the rules of ownership, transfer, and usage of NFTs. Essential skills include proficiency in programming languages like Solidity (for Ethereum) and others, a deep understanding of blockchain technology, and knowledge of decentralized applications (dApps). They contribute by building custom NFT projects, marketplaces, and interactive experiences.

2. **Question:** Explain how NFTs have changed the way digital artists monetize their work. What are the advantages of this new model compared to traditional methods like selling through galleries?

   Answer: NFTs have revolutionized how digital artists monetize their work by enabling them to sell their creations directly to a global audience without intermediaries like galleries or agents. This direct-to-consumer model offers several advantages: artists retain a larger share of the profits, they have greater control over pricing and distribution, and they can benefit from resale royalties, ensuring continued income as their artwork appreciates in value.

3. **Question:** What does a Community Manager do in the NFT space, and why is this role considered essential? What are some key responsibilities and the platforms they use?

   Answer: A Community Manager in the NFT space is responsible for building, engaging, and moderating the online community surrounding an NFT project. This role is essential because strong communities drive project success, foster loyalty, and create a sense of belonging among holders. Key responsibilities include managing Discord servers, Telegram groups, and Twitter Spaces, organizing events, addressing inquiries, and promoting the project.

NFT in Music, Fashion, Education

4. **Question:** Discuss how NFTs are being used in the music industry beyond simply selling songs. Provide examples of innovative applications and their potential impact on artists and fans.

   Answer: Beyond selling songs, NFTs in the music industry are used for tokenizing royalties (allowing fans to earn a share when a song is streamed), offering exclusive access to behind-the-scenes content or private events, and creating unique digital collectibles. This can revolutionize artist-fan relationships by fostering direct engagement, providing new revenue streams for artists, and offering fans unique ownership experiences.

5. **Question:** How are NFTs changing the fashion industry, and what are some examples of brands utilizing this technology? What are the potential benefits and challenges for the fashion sector? **Answer:** NFTs are changing the fashion industry by enabling the creation of digital wearables for the metaverse, authenticating ownership of physical items, and creating new forms of brand engagement. Brands like Gucci, Adidas, and Dolce & Gabbana use NFTs to launch virtual collections and offer hybrid physical-digital products. Benefits include new revenue streams, enhanced brand exclusivity, and innovative marketing. Challenges include copyright issues, market volatility, and the environmental impact of certain blockchains.

6. **Question:** Explain how NFTs can be applied in the education sector. Provide specific examples and discuss the potential impact on students and institutions.

   Answer: NFTs in education can be used to issue digital diplomas, certificates, and badges, providing tamper-proof and verifiable credentials. This can streamline verification processes for employers, enhance the value of credentials, and empower students with greater control over their academic records. Institutions can benefit from reduced administrative costs and increased transparency.

Risks and Rewards of the NFT World

7. **Question:** What are the primary rewards for artists in the NFT space, and how do these differ from the traditional art market?

   Answer: The primary rewards for artists in the NFT space include ownership and royalties, allowing them to earn not only from the initial sale but also from subsequent resales. They also gain global reach, enabling them to sell directly to buyers worldwide, bypassing traditional intermediaries. This differs from the traditional art market, which often involves galleries taking a large commission and artists not benefiting from resales.

8. **Question:** Describe the major risks associated with investing in or participating in the NFT market. What steps can individuals take to mitigate these risks? **Answer:** Major risks include scams and rug pulls (where creators abandon projects), price volatility, environmental concerns (though reduced with Ethereum's Proof of Stake), and legal grey areas (like copyright issues). Individuals can mitigate these risks by doing their own research (DYOR), being cautious of suspicious projects, understanding the volatility, staying informed about environmental impacts, and being aware of evolving legal frameworks.

9. **Question:** Discuss the concept of "rug pulls" in the NFT world. How do these scams work, and what can potential buyers do to protect themselves?

Answer: "Rug pulls" are a type of scam where NFT creators generate hype around a project, collect funds from investors, and then abandon the project, leaving buyers with worthless NFTs. These scams work by creating fake marketplaces or projects with promises of high returns or exclusive access. Buyers can protect themselves by thoroughly researching the creators, verifying the project's legitimacy, and being wary of projects with unrealistic promises or a lack of transparency.

10. **Question:** Explain how the shift from Proof of Work to Proof of Stake in Ethereum has impacted the environmental concerns associated with NFTs. Is the energy consumption issue entirely resolved?

    Answer: The shift from Proof of Work (PoW) to Proof of Stake (PoS) in Ethereum, known as the "Ethereum merge," has significantly reduced the energy consumption associated with NFT transactions on that blockchain. PoS requires far less computational power than PoW, leading to a substantial decrease in the carbon footprint. While this transition has drastically improved the situation, the energy consumption of other blockchains still varies, so the issue is not entirely resolved across the entire NFT ecosystem.

CHAPTER 11: SMART CONTRACTS – CODE THAT RUNS THE WORLD

⬚ What is a Smart Contract?

A smart contract is a self-executing digital agreement stored on a blockchain network. Its essence lies in its ability to automatically enforce the terms of an agreement. Once deployed, it operates precisely as programmed, without the possibility of downtime, fraudulent manipulation, or interference from external parties.

In simpler terms, a smart contract can be conceptualized as a digital vending machine for promises. Upon the receipt of a specified input (such as a payment), it autonomously dispenses the corresponding output (a product or service), thereby eliminating the necessity for a traditional intermediary.

🎁 Example 1: The Digital Vending Machine

Consider the scenario where an individual seeks to acquire a digital artwork NFT.

The smart contract, in this context, performs the following functions:

- **Verification of Conditions:**
  - It meticulously verifies whether the purchaser has transferred the requisite amount of Ether (ETH).
  - It ascertains the availability of the specified NFT.
- **Execution of Transaction (if conditions are met):**
  - Upon confirmation that both conditions are satisfied, the smart contract automatically transfers ownership of the NFT to the purchaser's digital wallet.
  - Simultaneously, it transfers the corresponding ETH payment to the seller's digital wallet.
- **Abortion of Transaction (if conditions are not met):**
  - Conversely, if either condition remains unmet (e.g., insufficient payment or unavailability of the NFT), the smart contract halts the execution of the transaction, ensuring that no unauthorized transfer occurs.

This automated process obviates the need for intermediaries such as lawyers, brokers, or customer service departments. The entire transaction is executed in an automated, transparent, and trustless manner, fostering a secure and efficient exchange between parties.

🔗 Ethereum & Solidity: The Language of Smart Contracts

⬚ Ethereum – The Smart Contract Platform

Ethereum is the **most popular blockchain for deploying smart contracts**. It's like the operating system, and smart contracts are the apps running on it.

Other blockchains that support smart contracts include **Polygon, Binance Smart Chain, Avalanche, Solana**, and more.

🔠 Solidity – The Programming Language of Web3

Solidity is the **primary language** for writing smart contracts on Ethereum.

Here's a simple smart contract written in Solidity:

```solidity
CopyEdit
// SPDX-License-Identifier: MIT
pragma solidity ^0.8.0;

contract HelloStudent {
    string public message = "Welcome to Web3!";

    function setMessage(string memory _newMsg) public {
        message = _newMsg;
    }
}
```

This contract stores a message and lets you update it. It's simple—but the same logic is used in real-world apps for **payments, auctions, identity systems, and more.**

🏛 Real-Life Uses of Smart Contracts

Smart contracts are not merely technological novelties; they are poised to revolutionize traditional industries in ways previously unimaginable. Let us delve into some illustrative examples:

✚ 1. Insurance

Use Case: Flight Delay Insurance

Consider a scenario where an individual purchases flight delay insurance through a smart contract.

The contract is designed to:

- **Real-time Data Verification:** The smart contract autonomously monitors real-time flight data from a trusted and reliable source, often referred to as an "Oracle."
- **Automatic Trigger for Compensation:** In the event that the insured's flight is delayed by a duration exceeding two hours, the smart contract automatically initiates the payment of compensation to the insured. This process occurs seamlessly, eliminating the need for the insured to file a claim or interact with an insurance agent.

This application of smart contracts ensures:

- ✅ **Fairness:** Predetermined conditions guarantee equitable treatment for all parties involved.
- ✅ **Speed:** Automated execution expedites the compensation process, providing timely relief to the insured.
- ✅ **Fraud Prevention:** The immutable nature of the blockchain and the self-executing code minimize the potential for fraudulent claims or manipulation.

🗳️ 2. Voting

Smart contracts are being harnessed to develop transparent and secure voting systems.

Example: University Elections

A university employs a smart contract-based voting application for its student elections. Each student's digital wallet is registered and authorized for a single vote. Upon casting, each vote is immutably recorded on the blockchain, rendering it publicly verifiable, tamper-proof, and anonymous.

This innovative approach significantly mitigates the risks of:

- **Double Voting:** The system prevents any single individual from casting more than one vote.
- **Vote Tampering:** The integrity of the vote is safeguarded by the immutability of the blockchain, making it virtually impossible to alter the recorded votes.
- **Human Error:** The automated process minimizes the potential for human error in vote counting and tabulation.

🏠 3. Real Estate

The traditional process of buying a house involves a multitude of intermediaries, including brokers, lawyers, and banks, and is often characterized by extensive paperwork.

Smart contracts offer a streamlined alternative:

- **Automated Transaction:** The buyer initiates the process by transferring the funds to a designated smart contract.

- **Title and Document Verification:** The smart contract automatically verifies the property title and relevant digital documents, ensuring the legitimacy of the transaction.
- **Ownership Transfer:** Upon successful verification, the smart contract transfers the Ownership NFT (a unique digital asset representing ownership of the house) to the buyer's digital wallet.
- **Funds Disbursement:** Simultaneously, the funds held in escrow by the smart contract are released to the seller.

This automation of the real estate transaction process significantly reduces the time and cost involved, potentially compressing a process that traditionally spans months into a matter of minutes.

Why Smart Contracts Matter for Students

For today's students, smart contracts represent a transformative technology, akin to the emergence of websites in the 1990s or mobile applications in the 2010s—a nascent wave of unprecedented opportunity.

Careers

The burgeoning field of smart contracts is spawning a plethora of novel career paths, including:

- **Smart Contract Developer:** Professionals proficient in programming languages such as Solidity and Vyper, responsible for crafting and implementing the self-executing agreements that underpin decentralized applications.
- **Blockchain Auditor:** Specialists who meticulously examine smart contract code to identify potential vulnerabilities, security flaws, and inefficiencies, ensuring the integrity and reliability of blockchain-based systems.
- **Web3 App Builder:** Visionaries who design and develop decentralized applications (dApps) that leverage smart contracts to provide users with novel functionalities and experiences, often within the broader context of Web3.

Innovation

Smart contracts empower students to become pioneers of innovation, enabling them to:

- **Create Decentralized Finance (DeFi) Platforms:** Develop novel financial instruments and platforms that operate without traditional intermediaries, offering services such as lending, borrowing, and trading in a decentralized and transparent manner.
- **Build Decentralized Autonomous Organizations (DAOs):** Construct and participate in organizations governed by community-defined rules encoded in smart contracts, fostering decentralized decision-making and collective ownership.

- **Launch NFT Projects with Automatic Royalties:** Create and deploy Non-Fungible Tokens (NFTs) with embedded royalty mechanisms, allowing creators to earn a percentage of future sales, thereby establishing sustainable income streams.

💰 Income

The demand for smart contract expertise translates into lucrative income opportunities for students:

- **Freelance Smart Contract Gigs:** Independent smart contract developers can command substantial fees, ranging from $500 to $10,000 or more per project, depending on complexity and scope.
- **dApp Ownership and Revenue Generation:** Students can launch their own decentralized applications and generate income through transaction fees, subscriptions, or other innovative monetization models.

🔐 Real-World Example: The Student DAO

Consider a group of college students who establish a Decentralized Autonomous Organization (DAO) to manage their club funds with utmost transparency.

- **Governance Token Allocation:** Each member receives a predetermined number of governance tokens, with each token representing a single vote in the decision-making process.
- **Smart Contract-Enforced Fund Disbursement:** Funds earmarked for club events or activities are held within a smart contract. These funds are released only when a specified threshold, such as 80% member approval, is reached through on-chain voting.

This system eliminates the need for manual record-keeping, mitigates the risk of corruption or embezzlement, and prevents the misuse of funds. In essence, blockchain technology empowers these students to create their own system of digital democracy, characterized by transparency, security, and immutability.

✅ Final Thoughts

Smart contracts are not just code—they are the **building blocks of trust** in the digital age. Whether you're a developer, designer, or dreamer, learning to work with smart contracts means **building apps, systems, and even businesses** that run with mathematical precision and zero bias.

The world is moving toward automation and decentralization. **You can either watch it happen, or build it yourself.**

30 multiple-choice questions (MCQs) on smart contracts:

What is a Smart Contract?

1. A smart contract is: a) A traditional legal agreement. b) A self-executing agreement written in code. c) A contract with AI. d) An agreement enforced by a third party.
2. Smart contracts run on: a) Centralized servers. b) Personal computers. c) A blockchain. d) Cloud storage.
3. Which of the following is a key feature of smart contracts? a) They require intermediaries. b) They are self-executing. c) They are easily modified after deployment. d) They are always written in legal language.
4. The primary purpose of a smart contract is to: a) Replace all legal systems. b) Automate agreements. c) Create digital art. d) Manage social media accounts.
5. Smart contracts eliminate the need for: a) Computers. b) Electricity. c) Intermediaries. d) Blockchains.
6. What triggers the execution of a smart contract? a) A judge's order. b) A specific date. c) Predetermined conditions. d) A user's request.
7. Once deployed, smart contracts are generally: a) Easily editable. b) Immutable. c) Stored on a central server. d) Executable only once

Ethereum and Solidity Basics

8. Ethereum is a: a) Cryptocurrency only. b) Platform for building smart contracts. c) Web browser. d) Social media platform.
9. The programming language most commonly used to write smart contracts on Ethereum is: a) Java. b) Python. c) Solidity. d) C++.
10. In Ethereum, "Gas" refers to: a) A type of cryptocurrency. b) The computational cost of executing a transaction. c) A unit of energy. d) A storage unit.
11. The Ethereum Virtual Machine (EVM) is: a) A hardware component. b) A software that executes smart contracts. c) A database. d) A programming language.
12. Which of the following is NOT a data type in Solidity? a) uint b) string c) address d) float
13. A "fallback function" in Solidity is used for: a) Error handling. b) Receiving Ether when no other function matches. c) Performing complex calculations. d) Deploying the contract.
14. What is an "address" in Solidity? a) A physical location. b) An identifier for an account or contract. c) A web address. d) An email address.
15. What does ABI stand for? a) Application Binary Interface b) Abstract Binary Interaction c) Application Blockchain Integration d) Abstract Blockchain Interface

Real-Life Use: Insurance, Voting, Real Estate

16. In the context of flight delay insurance, a smart contract can: a) Determine the weather. b) Automatically pay compensation. c) File a claim with an agent. d) Negotiate with the airline.

17. How do smart contracts enhance voting systems? a) By centralizing vote counting. b) By ensuring votes are public and tamper-proof. c) By allowing multiple votes per person. d) By eliminating the need for voters.
18. In a real estate transaction, a smart contract can automate: a) Property viewings. b) Loan applications. c) Ownership transfer. d) Home staging.
19. A smart contract in insurance relies on what to get external data? a) Another smart contract b) An Oracle c) A legal team d) The insured person
20. What is a benefit of using smart contracts for voting? a) Slower vote counting b) Increased risk of fraud c) Reduced transparency d) Tamper-proof records
21. In real estate, what does the buyer send to a smart contract? a) A handshake agreement b) Funds c) A property title d) Moving boxes
22. What does an Ownership NFT represent in a real estate smart contract? a) The buyer's credit score b) The seller's address c) Ownership of the property d) The mortgage terms
23. How do smart contracts help to reduce fraud in insurance? a) By increasing the number of intermediaries b) By automating and enforcing the terms c) By relying on subjective human judgment d) By keeping the process completely opaque
24. Why might a university use smart contracts for elections? a) To increase the cost of running elections b) To allow non-students to vote c) To ensure transparency and reduce tampering d) To make the process less efficient
25. What is a disadvantage of the traditional real estate process that smart contracts address? a) Too few brokers are involved b) Transactions are too fast c) It involves many intermediaries and paperwork d) It's too transparent
26. In a smart contract-based insurance claim, when is the payout typically made? a) After a long investigation b) Only if a lawyer is involved c) Automatically, when conditions are met d) At the discretion of the insurance company
27. What role does a blockchain play in smart contract voting systems? a) It stores votes in a central database b) It makes votes easily changeable c) It provides a tamper-proof record of votes d) It allows for anonymous voting
28. For a buyer, what is the advantage of using a smart contract in real estate? a) More paperwork b) Faster transaction c) Need for more intermediaries d) Increased costs
29. What is a key benefit of using smart contracts in the insurance industry? a) Slower processing b) Increased paperwork c) Faster and fairer payouts d) More intermediaries
30. In what way do smart contracts make voting systems more secure? a) By keeping votes secret from everyone b) By allowing votes to be altered easily c) By making votes public and unchangeable d) By centralizing the voting process

10 mid-size questions with answers on smart contracts:

What is a Smart Contract?

1. **Question:** Define a smart contract and explain how it differs from a traditional legal contract.

   Answer: A smart contract is a self-executing agreement written in code and stored on a blockchain. Unlike a traditional legal contract, which is governed by legal systems and requires intermediaries for enforcement, a smart contract automatically enforces its terms when the predetermined conditions are met. It operates on the principle of "code is law," reducing the need for trust and third-party involvement.

Ethereum and Solidity Basics

2. **Question:** Describe the role of Ethereum in the smart contract ecosystem and explain why Solidity is the primary language used for writing smart contracts on this platform.

   Answer: Ethereum is a decentralized platform that enables the creation and deployment of smart contracts. It provides the infrastructure and tools necessary for developers to build and run decentralized applications (dApps). Solidity is the primary language for Ethereum because it was specifically designed to target the Ethereum Virtual Machine (EVM). Solidity is well-suited to express the logic of contracts, handle cryptocurrency, and interact with the Ethereum blockchain.

3. **Question:** Explain the concept of "Gas" in Ethereum. Why is it necessary, and how does it work?

   Answer: In Ethereum, "Gas" is the unit of computational effort required to execute an operation or a smart contract. It is necessary to prevent malicious actors from spamming the network with computationally intensive operations, which could lead to network congestion or denial-of-service attacks. Users pay for Gas to compensate the network for the computational resources used. Each transaction specifies a Gas limit (the maximum Gas the sender is willing to pay) and a Gas price (the price per unit of Gas).

Real-Life Use: Insurance

4. **Question:** How can smart contracts be used to improve the efficiency and transparency of insurance claims processing? Provide an example.

   Answer: Smart contracts can automate claims processing by defining the conditions for a payout in code. For example, a flight delay insurance smart contract can automatically check flight data from a trusted oracle. If a flight is delayed by a specified time, the contract automatically triggers a payout to the insured, eliminating the need for manual claim filing and processing. This increases efficiency, reduces administrative costs, and enhances transparency, as all transactions are recorded on the blockchain.

5. **Question:** Discuss the potential benefits and challenges of using smart contracts in the insurance industry.

   Answer: Benefits include reduced fraud, faster payouts, lower administrative costs, and increased transparency. Challenges include the need for reliable data oracles, the complexity of handling complex or subjective claims, and regulatory uncertainty.

Real-Life Use: Voting

6. **Question:** Explain how smart contracts can be used to create more secure and transparent voting systems.

   Answer: Smart contracts can ensure that each vote is recorded immutably on the blockchain, making it virtually impossible to alter or delete. They can also enforce rules such as one vote per voter and can provide a transparent audit trail of all votes cast. This reduces the risk of voter fraud and increases trust in the electoral process.

7. **Question:** What are some of the obstacles to the widespread adoption of smart contract-based voting systems? **Answer:** Obstacles include voter education and adoption, the need for secure and reliable digital identity solutions, scalability challenges, and regulatory hurdles. There are also concerns about the accessibility of such systems to all demographics.

Real-Life Use: Real Estate

8. **Question:** Describe how smart contracts can streamline the real estate transaction process and benefit both buyers and sellers.

   Answer: Smart contracts can automate many steps in a real estate transaction, such as verifying property titles, managing escrow funds, and transferring ownership. This can reduce the time and cost involved, minimize paperwork, and increase transparency. For buyers, it can mean faster and more secure transactions. For sellers, it can mean quicker access to funds and a more efficient sales process.

9. **Question:** Discuss the role of NFTs in representing property ownership in a smart contract-based real estate transaction.

   Answer: Non-Fungible Tokens (NFTs) can be used to represent ownership of a specific property. The smart contract can transfer this NFT from the seller to the buyer once all conditions of the sale are met. This provides a clear, digital, and easily transferable record of ownership on the blockchain, replacing traditional paper deeds and titles.

10. **Question:** What are the potential risks and rewards associated with using smart contracts in real estate transactions?

    Answer: Potential rewards include increased efficiency, reduced costs, greater transparency, and faster transaction times. Potential risks include the complexity of coding and deploying such contracts, the potential for errors or vulnerabilities in the code, and the need for clear legal and regulatory frameworks.

CHAPTER 12: MAKE YOUR FIRST SMART CONTRACT (NO-CODE / LOW-CODE)

⬜⬜ Essential Tools for Building Smart Contracts

Before embarking on the journey of smart contract development, it is prudent to familiarize oneself with the platforms and tools that can facilitate the process, often without necessitating intricate or cumbersome setups.

🔧 1. Remix IDE (Low-Code/Code)

- **Description:** Remix Integrated Development Environment (IDE) is a browser-based development environment specifically designed for Ethereum smart contracts. It provides a comprehensive suite of tools within a single interface, accessible directly from a web browser.
- **Key Features:**
  - **Browser-Based Environment:** Remix operates directly within a web browser, eliminating the need for local software installation and configuration.
  - **Built-in Compiler:** Remix includes a compiler that translates Solidity code into bytecode, the format executable by the Ethereum Virtual Machine (EVM).
  - **Deployment Capabilities:** Remix allows developers to deploy smart contracts to various Ethereum environments, including test networks and the main network.
  - **Debugging Tools:** Remix provides debugging tools to help developers identify and resolve issues in their Solidity code.
  - **User-Friendly Interface:** Remix offers an intuitive interface, making it an excellent choice for beginners to learn and experiment with Solidity.
- **Use Case:** Remix is particularly well-suited for writing, testing, and deploying simple to moderately complex smart contracts. It serves as an invaluable tool for learning Solidity and prototyping dApps.
- **Website:** https://remix.ethereum.org

⬜ 2. Moralis (No-Code Backend)

- **Description:** Moralis is a comprehensive Web3 backend platform that simplifies the development of decentralized applications by providing a suite of pre-built tools and services.
- **Key Features:**
  - **User Authentication:** Moralis offers tools for user authentication, allowing dApps to securely manage user accounts.
  - **Decentralized Storage:** Moralis provides seamless integration with the InterPlanetary File System (IPFS) for decentralized file storage.
  - **Smart Contract Interaction:** Moralis simplifies the process of interacting with deployed smart contracts, allowing developers to easily read data from and write data to the blockchain.
  - **No Server Management:** Moralis abstracts away the complexities of server management, allowing developers to focus on building the front-end and smart contract logic of their applications.

- **Use Case:** Moralis is ideal for developers who want to quickly build dApps without the overhead of setting up and managing their own backend infrastructure. It is particularly useful for projects that require user authentication, decentralized storage, and interaction with smart contracts.
- **Website:** https://moralis.io

⚙️ 3. Alchemy (Node-as-a-Service)

- **Description:** Alchemy is a blockchain developer platform that provides reliable and scalable infrastructure for interacting with blockchain networks. It functions as a Node-as-a-Service provider.
- **Key Features:**
    - **Blockchain Connectivity:** Alchemy allows smart contracts and dApps to communicate with various blockchain networks, including Ethereum and Polygon, through its robust APIs.
    - **Enhanced Reliability:** Alchemy provides highly reliable and scalable access to blockchain data, ensuring that dApps can function smoothly even under heavy load.
    - **Developer Tools:** Alchemy offers a suite of developer tools, including dashboards, performance metrics, and webhooks, to help developers monitor and optimize their dApps.
- **Use Case:** Alchemy is designed for developers who require robust, reliable, and scalable infrastructure to support their dApps. It is particularly well-suited for production-grade applications that demand high performance and availability.
- **Website:** https://www.alchemy.com

🛠️ Let's Build: A Simple Digital Certificate Contract

🔐 Real-World Use Case: College Certificate on Blockchain

Imagine a university seeking to issue digital graduation certificates on the blockchain. This approach would offer certificates that are tamper-proof, easily verifiable, and permanently accessible.

💡 What the contract will do:

- Store the name and academic details of a student.
- Restrict the issuance of certificates to the designated administrator.
- Enable anyone to verify the authenticity of a certificate by querying the blockchain.

✍️ Step-by-Step: Smart Contract Code (Remix IDE)

To begin, navigate to the Remix IDE (an online Solidity development environment) and paste the following code:

```solidity
// SPDX-License-Identifier: MIT
pragma solidity ^0.8.0;

contract DigitalCertificate {
    address public admin;

    struct Certificate {
        string studentName;
        string course;
        uint256 issueDate;
    }

    mapping(address => Certificate) public certificates;

    constructor() {
        admin = msg.sender;
    }

    function issueCertificate(address student, string memory name, string
memory course) public {
        require(msg.sender == admin, "Only admin can issue");
        certificates[student] = Certificate(name, course, block.timestamp);
    }

    function viewCertificate(address student) public view returns (string
memory, string memory, uint256) {
        Certificate memory cert = certificates[student];
        return (cert.studentName, cert.course, cert.issueDate);
    }
}
```

Explanation of the Code:

- `SPDX-License-Identifier: MIT`: This line specifies the license under which the code is released.
- `pragma solidity ^0.8.0;`: This indicates that the code is compatible with Solidity version 0.8.0 and above.
- `contract DigitalCertificate { ... }`: This defines the smart contract named "DigitalCertificate".
- `address public admin;`: This declares a state variable `admin` of type `address` (representing an Ethereum address) and makes it publicly readable. The `admin` is the address of the account that deployed the contract.
- `struct Certificate { ... }`: This defines a structure named `Certificate` to hold the details of a certificate, including the student's name, course, and issue date.
- `mapping(address => Certificate) public certificates;`: This declares a mapping named `certificates`. A mapping is like a dictionary or hash table. In this case, it maps a student's Ethereum address to their `Certificate` data.
- `constructor() { ... }`: This is a special function that is executed only once when the contract is deployed. It sets the `admin` to the address of the account that deployed the contract (`msg.sender`).

- **`function issueCertificate(...) public { ... }`**: This function allows the admin to issue a certificate to a student.
    - It takes the student's address, name, and course as input.
    - It uses `require(msg.sender == admin, "Only admin can issue");` to ensure that only the admin can call this function.
    - It creates a new `Certificate` object and stores it in the `certificates` mapping, using the student's address as the key. The `block.timestamp` variable stores the time the certificate is issued.
- **`function viewCertificate(address student) public view returns (...) { ... }`**: This function allows anyone to view a student's certificate details.
    - It takes the student's address as input.
    - It retrieves the `Certificate` from the `certificates` mapping using the student's address.
    - It returns the student's name, course, and issue date. The `view` keyword indicates that this function does not modify the contract's state.

□ Testing the Smart Contract

1. **Compile the contract:** In Remix, use the "Solidity Compiler" tab to compile the `DigitalCertificate` contract.
2. **Deploy the contract:** Use the "Deploy & Run Transactions" tab to deploy the compiled contract. You'll need to select an environment (e.g., Remix VM for testing) and an account.
3. **Issue a certificate:** In the "Deploy & Run Transactions" tab, find the deployed `DigitalCertificate` contract and interact with it.
    - Call the `issueCertificate()` function.
    - Enter the student's wallet address, name (e.g., "Alice Johnson"), and course (e.g., "BSc Computer Science").
    - Click "Transact" to execute the function.
4. **View the certificate:** Call the `viewCertificate()` function, entering the student's address. The function will return the student's name, course, and issue date, verifying that the certificate has been successfully issued and stored on the blockchain.

✅ You have now successfully issued a digital certificate on the blockchain!

□□ Build Option: Voting App (No-Code)

For those inclined towards creating interactive applications with minimal coding, a voting app presents an excellent project. Platforms like Moralis Templates and ThirdWeb offer a streamlined approach to building such applications. These platforms enable the creation of a voting contract with the following key features:

- **Student Participation:** Students can cast their votes on pertinent campus issues.

- **On-Chain Vote Tracking:** All votes are recorded on the blockchain, ensuring transparency and immutability.
- **One-Wallet-One-Vote Mechanism:** The system enforces a rule where each digital wallet is entitled to a single vote, preventing voter fraud.

These tools abstract away much of the complexity associated with smart contract development, allowing developers to deploy and manage contracts with a few clicks.

Example using Moralis (Conceptual):

While Moralis is more of a backend platform, you'd generally use it in conjunction with a frontend to build a voting app. Here's a conceptual outline:

1. **Set up Moralis:** Create a Moralis account and set up a new Moralis application, connecting it to the desired blockchain network (e.g., Ethereum, Polygon).
2. **Smart Contract (Pre-built or Uploaded):**
   o Moralis might provide pre-built smart contract templates for voting, which you could customize.
   o Alternatively, you could write your own smart contract (using Remix, for example) and then use Moralis to deploy and interact with it. This contract would define the voting logic (one-wallet-one-vote, etc.).
3. **Frontend Development:**
   o Use a framework like React to build the user interface for the voting app.
   o Integrate the frontend with Moralis using the Moralis SDK. This allows the frontend to:
     ▪ Authenticate users (e.g., using their MetaMask wallets).
     ▪ Interact with the deployed smart contract to submit votes.
     ▪ Retrieve voting results from the blockchain.
4. **User Authentication:** Moralis provides functions to authenticate users using their Web3 wallets (like MetaMask). This ensures that only eligible voters can participate.
5. **Vote Submission:** When a student casts a vote, the frontend sends a transaction to the smart contract, recording the vote on the blockchain.
6. **Vote Tracking and Results:** The frontend can query the smart contract to retrieve the voting results, which are stored on the blockchain. This ensures that the results are transparent and cannot be tampered with.

Example using ThirdWeb:

ThirdWeb provides an even more abstracted approach, often with pre-built components:

1. **ThirdWeb Project:** Create a project on ThirdWeb.
2. **Deploy Voting Contract:** Use ThirdWeb's interface to deploy a pre-built voting contract. ThirdWeb handles the deployment to the blockchain.
3. **Frontend Integration:** Use ThirdWeb's SDK to connect your frontend (React, etc.) to the deployed contract.
4. **User Interface:** Build a UI where students can:

- Connect their wallets.
- View the voting options.
- Submit their vote with a button click.

5. **Vote Recording:** ThirdWeb and the smart contract ensure each vote is recorded on-chain, associated with the voter's wallet.

6. **Results Display:** The UI can then display the on-chain voting results.

In essence, these no-code/low-code platforms simplify the process of creating and deploying smart contracts, enabling individuals with limited coding expertise to build functional and interactive voting applications.

☐ Deploying to a Testnet (Goerli or Polygon Mumbai)

With your smart contract successfully compiled and tested, the next step is to deploy it to a blockchain testnet. A testnet is a blockchain environment that mimics the main network but uses non-real-value cryptocurrency, allowing developers to experiment and deploy their contracts without risking actual funds.

☐ What You Need:

To deploy your smart contract to a testnet, you will require the following:

- **MetaMask Wallet:** A browser extension that allows you to manage your Ethereum accounts and interact with blockchain networks. Ensure that MetaMask is installed and connected to your browser.
- **Test ETH from a Faucet:** Since testnets use non-real-value cryptocurrency, you will need some test ETH to pay for the transaction fees associated with deploying your contract. You can obtain test ETH from a "faucet," which is a service that provides small amounts of cryptocurrency for testing purposes.
- **Connection to Goerli or Polygon Mumbai:** You will need to configure Remix to connect to the specific testnet you wish to use, such as Goerli (for Ethereum) or Polygon Mumbai (for the Polygon network).

Deployment Steps:

The following steps outline the process of deploying your smart contract using Remix IDE:

1. **Select "Injected Web3" as the Environment in Remix:** In the Remix IDE, navigate to the "Deploy & Run Transactions" tab. In the "ENVIRONMENT" dropdown menu, select "Injected Web3." This option instructs Remix to use your MetaMask wallet to interact with the blockchain.

2. **Connect MetaMask and Select the Correct Network:** Ensure that your MetaMask wallet is unlocked and connected to the correct testnet (e.g., Goerli or Polygon Mumbai). You can select the network from the network selection dropdown menu in MetaMask.

3. **Initiate Deployment:** In Remix, with the correct contract selected, click the "Deploy" button. This action will send a transaction to the selected testnet to deploy your smart contract.
4. **Confirm the Transaction in MetaMask:** Upon clicking "Deploy," MetaMask will prompt you to confirm the transaction. The confirmation window will display the transaction details, including the estimated Gas fee. Review the details and click "Confirm" to proceed with the deployment.
5. **Contract Deployed Successfully:** Once the transaction is confirmed and processed by the network, your smart contract will be live on the blockchain. Remix will display the contract address, which is a unique identifier for your deployed contract.

🎉 **Congratulations!** Your smart contract is now deployed and accessible on the blockchain. You can share the contract address with others, allowing them to interact with your contract's functions.

📚 Summary

You've now: ✔ Built a smart contract
✔ Deployed it on a test blockchain
✔ Taken your first real step into Web3 development

This may seem small—but remember, **every Web3 company, DAO, NFT project, and DeFi app starts here**.

30 multiple-choice questions (MCQs) on the tools, a simple project, and testing/deploying your contract:

Tools: Remix IDE, Moralis, Alchemy

1. Remix IDE is primarily used for: a) Deploying web servers. b) Developing Ethereum smart contracts. c) Managing databases. d) Creating mobile apps.
2. Which tool is a browser-based IDE? a) Alchemy b) Moralis c) Remix IDE d) Truffle
3. Moralis is best described as a: a) Code editor. b) Web3 backend platform. c) Blockchain network. d) Virtual machine.
4. Which tool provides a no-code backend for dApp development? a) Remix IDE b) Alchemy c) Moralis d) Solidity
5. Alchemy is a: a) Smart contract language. b) Node-as-a-Service platform. c) Decentralized exchange. d) Operating system.
6. Which tool helps smart contracts communicate with blockchain networks? a) Remix IDE b) Moralis c) Alchemy d) IPFS
7. Which tool offers a built-in Solidity compiler? a) Moralis b) Alchemy c) Remix IDE d) Web3.js

8. Which tool provides user authentication in Web3? a) Remix IDE b) Alchemy c) Moralis d) Hardhat
9. Which tool provides dashboards and metrics for dApps? a) Remix IDE b) Moralis c) Alchemy d) Ethers.js
10. Which tool is suitable for beginners to write and test Solidity code? a) Alchemy b) Moralis c) Remix IDE d) Web3.py

A Simple Project: Digital Certificate, Voting App

11. In a digital certificate contract, who typically has the authority to issue certificates? a) Any user b) The student c) The contract creator/admin d) An external oracle
12. What is the primary purpose of storing a digital certificate on a blockchain? a) To make it editable b) To ensure it is tamper-proof and verifiable c) To reduce storage costs d) To make it inaccessible
13. In a voting app built with smart contracts, each vote is associated with: a) The voter's name b) The voter's physical address c) The voter's wallet address d) The voter's social security number
14. What does a voting app smart contract typically enforce? a) One vote per person (or wallet) b) Unlimited votes per person c) Votes being editable after casting d) Centralized vote counting
15. Which of the following is a key advantage of a blockchain-based voting system? a) Increased central control b) Reduced transparency c) Tamper-proof vote records d) Faster vote manipulation
16. In a digital certificate smart contract, what data is typically stored? a) Student's grades only b) Student's name and course c) Student's attendance record d) Student's financial information
17. What is the role of a smart contract in a voting application? a) To collect personal data b) To manage and record votes c) To design the user interface d) To advertise the election
18. Why is a blockchain suitable for storing digital certificates? a) It's easy to modify the data b) It ensures data is permanent and verifiable c) It's a cheap storage solution d) It allows for centralized control
19. In a voting dApp, what is the purpose of the "one wallet = one vote" rule? a) To allow users to vote multiple times b) To prevent voter fraud c) To complicate the voting process d) To track users' personal information
20. What is the primary benefit of using a smart contract for issuing certificates? a) Increased processing time b) Reduced security c) Enhanced verification and trust d) Higher costs

Testing and Deploying Your Contract

21. Before deploying a smart contract, it is crucial to: a) Delete the code b) Test it thoroughly c) Send it to a lawyer d) Mine cryptocurrency
22. A blockchain testnet is: a) The main blockchain network b) A network for testing smart contracts c) A type of cryptocurrency d) A government database
23. Which tool is commonly used to interact with blockchain networks during deployment? a) Microsoft Word b) MetaMask c) Adobe Photoshop d) Excel

24. What is the purpose of getting test ETH from a faucet? a) To pay for real-world goods b) To pay for transaction fees on a testnet c) To invest in cryptocurrency d) To mine new ETH

25. In Remix, which environment is used to connect to a blockchain via MetaMask? a) JavaScript VM b) Injected Web3 c) Web3 Provider d) Solidity Compiler

26. What does "Deploy" mean in the context of smart contracts? a) To delete the contract b) To write the contract code c) To execute the contract d) To put the contract on the blockchain

27. After deploying a contract, you receive a: a) QR code b) Contract address c) Private key d) Public announcement

28. What is the first step in deploying a smart contract using Remix and MetaMask? a) Write the Solidity code b) Compile the contract c) Connect MetaMask to a testnet d) Select "Injected Web3" in Remix

29. Where do you confirm a transaction when deploying a contract with MetaMask? a) In Remix IDE b) In the browser console c) In MetaMask d) On a centralized exchange

30. What is the significance of the contract address after deployment? a) It is used to edit the contract code. b) It is used to interact with the contract. c) It represents the contract's private key. d) It is used to delete the contract.

10 mid-size questions with answers on Smart Contract Tools:

Tools: Remix IDE, Moralis, Alchemy

1. **Question:** Compare and contrast Remix IDE and Alchemy in terms of their primary functions and target users.

   Answer: Remix IDE is a browser-based IDE primarily for developing, testing, and deploying Ethereum smart contracts. It's beginner-friendly and great for quick prototyping. Alchemy, on the other hand, is a Node-as-a-Service platform that provides developers with reliable and scalable infrastructure to interact with blockchain networks like Ethereum. Alchemy is geared towards developers building production-ready dApps that require robust blockchain connectivity.

2. **Question:** Explain the role of Moralis in simplifying Web3 development. Provide examples of the services it offers.

   Answer: Moralis simplifies Web3 development by providing a backend platform that eliminates the need for developers to manage their own servers and infrastructure. It offers services like user authentication (integrating with wallets like MetaMask), decentralized storage (IPFS integration), and simplified smart contract interaction, allowing developers to focus on frontend development and smart contract logic.

A Simple Project: Digital Certificate, Voting App

3. **Question:** Describe the key features and benefits of implementing a digital certificate system using a smart contract.

Answer: Implementing a digital certificate system using a smart contract offers benefits like immutability (certificates cannot be altered), verifiability (anyone can verify a certificate's authenticity on the blockchain), and accessibility (certificates are permanently available on the blockchain). Key features include storing student details on-chain and restricting certificate issuance to authorized parties.

4. **Question:** Explain how a smart contract-based voting app can ensure transparency and prevent fraud.

   Answer: A smart contract-based voting app ensures transparency by recording each vote on the blockchain, creating a public and auditable record. It can prevent fraud by enforcing rules like "one wallet, one vote," making it difficult for individuals to cast multiple ballots. The immutability of the blockchain ensures that votes cannot be tampered with after they are cast.

Testing and Deploying Your Contract

5. **Question:** Why is it important to test smart contracts thoroughly before deploying them to a mainnet? What are some potential consequences of deploying an untested contract?

   Answer: Thorough testing is crucial because smart contracts are immutable once deployed, and any bugs or vulnerabilities in the code can lead to significant financial losses or security breaches. Potential consequences of deploying an untested contract include loss of funds due to exploits, contract malfunctions, and the need to redeploy (if possible) at significant cost.

6. **Question:** Describe the process of deploying a smart contract to a testnet using Remix and MetaMask.

   Answer: The process involves: 1) Selecting "Injected Web3" as the environment in Remix, 2) Connecting MetaMask to the desired testnet (e.g., Goerli), 3) Deploying the contract from Remix, and 4) Confirming the deployment transaction in MetaMask. This sends the contract's bytecode to the testnet, making it accessible on the blockchain.

7. **Question:** What is a blockchain testnet, and why are they used in smart contract development?

   Answer: A blockchain testnet is a separate blockchain environment that mirrors the functionality of the mainnet but uses non-real-value cryptocurrency. They are used in smart contract development to allow developers to deploy and test their contracts without risking real funds. This provides a safe environment to identify and fix bugs before deploying to the mainnet.

8. **Question:** Explain the role of MetaMask in deploying and interacting with smart contracts.

Answer: MetaMask acts as a bridge between the user's browser and the blockchain. It allows users to manage their Ethereum accounts, connect to different blockchain networks (including testnets and the mainnet), and sign transactions, including those for deploying contracts and interacting with contract functions.

9. **Question:** What information is needed to interact with a deployed smart contract, and how can you obtain it?

   Answer: To interact with a deployed smart contract, you need its address (a unique identifier on the blockchain) and its Application Binary Interface (ABI), which defines the contract's functions and how to interact with them. The contract address is provided after successful deployment, and the ABI is generated by the Solidity compiler during the compilation process.

10. **Question:** Describe the difference between deploying a smart contract to a testnet versus a mainnet.

    Answer: Deploying to a testnet uses non-real-value cryptocurrency and is for testing purposes, allowing developers to find and fix bugs without financial risk. Deploying to a mainnet uses real cryptocurrency and makes the contract live and operational for real-world use, involving actual financial transactions.

CHAPTER 13: DAPPS – DECENTRALIZED APPLICATIONS FOR A DECENTRALIZED WORLD

In today's Web2 world, most applications we use—from Instagram to YouTube to Uber—are controlled by centralized companies. These companies store all user data, run the servers, control the rules, and can change policies at any moment.

But imagine a world where **no single authority** controls an application. A world where users truly **own their data**, **participate in governance**, and even **earn from their engagement**.

Welcome to the world of **DApps**—Decentralized Applications.

☐ What is a DApp?

A Decentralized Application, or DApp, is a software application that, unlike traditional applications, operates on a blockchain network rather than relying on a centralized server. This fundamental difference gives DApps a unique set of characteristics and advantages.

Here are four defining characteristics of a DApp:

- **Open-Source:** The source code of a DApp is typically open and available for anyone to inspect, verify, and use. This promotes transparency and allows the community to contribute to the application's development.
- **Decentralized Backend:** Unlike traditional applications that store data on centralized servers, DApps store their data and logic on a blockchain network, such as Ethereum. This decentralization ensures that no single entity controls the application or its data.
- **Smart Contracts:** The rules and logic of a DApp are governed by smart contracts, which are self-executing agreements written in code. These contracts automatically enforce the terms of the application, eliminating the need for intermediaries and ensuring that the application functions as intended.
- **Tokens:** Many DApps utilize their own cryptocurrency tokens for transactions, incentivizing participation, and governing the application. These tokens can represent various things, such as ownership, access rights, or voting power within the DApp.

📌 Example: A Decentralized Music Streaming App

Consider a decentralized music streaming application. In this scenario, artists can upload their music directly to the blockchain, and listeners can pay artists directly using cryptocurrency every time they play a song. This system operates without intermediaries like Spotify or YouTube, allowing artists to retain a greater share of their earnings and providing listeners with more transparent and direct access to music.

☐ DApp vs. Traditional App

The following table highlights the key differences between traditional (Web2) applications and decentralized (Web3) applications:

Feature	Traditional App (Web2)	DApp (Web3)
Hosting	Centralized server	Blockchain network
Control	Single company	Community / Smart contracts
User Data	Owned by the company	Owned by the user
Payments	Bank / Fiat	Crypto-based
Downtime risk	Yes, server-dependent	Minimal (due to distributed nodes)

✏ Real-World Examples of DApps

Let us explore some prominent DApps that are currently accessible and operational:

☐ 1. Uniswap – The Decentralized Exchange (DEX)

Uniswap is a decentralized exchange (DEX) operating on the Ethereum blockchain. It enables users to swap cryptocurrencies directly with each other, eliminating the need for a central authority or intermediary.

- **Key Features:**
  - **Permissionless:** Users can access and use Uniswap without creating an account or undergoing Know Your Customer (KYC) procedures.
  - **Decentralized:** Transactions are executed directly between users through smart contracts, ensuring that no single entity controls the exchange.
  - **Automated Liquidity Provision:** Liquidity on Uniswap is provided by users who deposit their cryptocurrency assets into liquidity pools. In return, these liquidity providers earn fees from the trades that occur within their pools.
- **Use Case:** A user can connect their MetaMask wallet to Uniswap directly through their web browser and swap Ether (ETH) for USD Coin (USDC) or any other supported cryptocurrency.
- **Website:** https://uniswap.org

🏛 2. Compound – DeFi Lending & Borrowing

Compound is a decentralized finance (DeFi) protocol that allows users to lend or borrow cryptocurrency assets in a permissionless and automated manner.

- **Key Features:**
  - **Lenders Earn Interest:** Users can supply their crypto assets to Compound and earn interest, with the interest rates determined algorithmically based on supply and demand.

- o **Borrowers Pay Interest:** Users can borrow crypto assets from Compound by providing collateral, typically in the form of other cryptocurrencies. The interest rates for borrowing also vary based on market conditions.
- o **Smart Contract Automation:** All lending and borrowing activities are governed by smart contracts, which automate the process of interest calculation, collateral management, and loan repayment.
- **Use Case:** A user can deposit 100 USDC into Compound and earn a variable interest rate (e.g., 3%) or borrow Dai (DAI) by providing ETH as collateral.
- **Website:** https://compound.finance

🎶 3. Audius – Decentralized Music Streaming

Audius is a decentralized music streaming platform that provides an alternative to traditional streaming services like Spotify. It is built on blockchain technology.

- **Key Features:**
  - o **Direct Artist Uploads:** Artists can upload their music directly to the Audius platform, bypassing traditional intermediaries such as record labels.
  - o **Free Streaming for Fans:** Fans can stream music on Audius for free, supporting artists directly.
  - o **Direct Artist Compensation:** Revenue generated on the platform is distributed directly to artists through the platform's native token, AUDIO.
- **Use Case:** Independent musicians can monetize their music and connect with their audience without relying on traditional record labels or streaming services.
- **Website:** https://audius.co

To understand the architecture of a DApp, let us break down its components.

🎨 Frontend (User Interface)

- **Description:** The frontend of a DApp is what the user directly interacts with. It is responsible for the application's visual presentation and user experience.
- **Technology:** DApp frontends are typically built using standard web technologies such as HTML for structuring content, CSS for styling, and JavaScript for adding interactivity. Frameworks like React, Vue, or Angular are often employed to create dynamic and user-friendly interfaces.
- **User Experience:** To the end-user, a DApp frontend often appears and behaves similarly to a traditional web application. It may consist of familiar elements such as login pages, buttons, forms, and data visualizations like charts.
- **Example:** In a decentralized social media DApp, the frontend would include components for creating profiles, posting messages, viewing content, and interacting with other users.

🔲 Backend (Smart Contracts)

- **Description:** In contrast to traditional applications that rely on centralized servers to handle application logic and data storage, DApps utilize smart contracts.
- **Smart Contract Languages:** Smart contracts are written in programming languages specifically designed for blockchain development, such as Solidity (for Ethereum) or Rust (for Solana).
- **Blockchain Deployment:** These smart contracts are then deployed onto a blockchain network, such as Ethereum or Polygon. Once deployed, they become an immutable and self-executing set of rules that govern the application's behavior.
- **Functionality:** Smart contracts define the core logic of the DApp, including how data is stored, how transactions are processed, and how users interact with the application.

⊷ Communication Layer

To enable seamless interaction between the frontend and the smart contracts on the blockchain, DApps employ specific libraries:

- **Web3.js or Ethers.js:** These JavaScript libraries provide a set of tools and functions that allow the frontend to connect to the blockchain network and interact with deployed smart contracts. They facilitate tasks such as sending transactions, reading data from the blockchain, and listening for events emitted by smart contracts.
- **Wallets (e.g., MetaMask):** Digital wallets like MetaMask act as a bridge between the user and the blockchain. They allow users to manage their blockchain accounts, sign transactions, and authorize interactions with DApps. When a user interacts with a DApp, their wallet is used to verify their identity and authorize any transactions.

☐ Illustrative Example: Voting DApp

Consider a simplified voting DApp.

- **Frontend:** The frontend presents a form with voting options, such as "Vote for Alice" or "Vote for Bob."
- **Smart Contract:**

```
mapping(string => uint256) public votes;

function vote(string memory candidate) public {
    votes[candidate]++;
}
```

Explanation:

- `mapping(string => uint256) public votes;`: This line declares a state variable named `votes` which is a mapping (similar to a dictionary). It maps a candidate's name (a string) to the number of votes they have (an unsigned integer). The `public` keyword automatically creates a getter function, allowing anyone to query the current vote count for a candidate.

- `function vote(string memory candidate) public { ... }`: This declares a function named `vote` that takes the name of the candidate being voted for as a string. The `public` keyword means anyone can call this function. The function increments the vote count for the selected candidate.

How it works:

1. **User Interaction:** When a user clicks "Vote for Alice" on the frontend, the DApp uses Web3.js or Ethers.js to call the `vote` function in the smart contract, passing "Alice" as the candidate name.
2. **Transaction Submission:** The user's wallet (e.g., MetaMask) prompts them to authorize this transaction.
3. **Vote Recording:** Once the user approves the transaction, it is sent to the blockchain network. The smart contract's `vote` function is executed, and the vote for Alice is permanently recorded on the blockchain.
4. **Immutability and Transparency:** No administrator or any other entity can subsequently alter, delete, or falsify the recorded vote. The blockchain's inherent immutability and transparency ensure the integrity of the voting process.

☐ The Magic of DApps: Trust Through Transparency

This example illustrates a fundamental principle of DApps: they foster trust through transparency. By leveraging blockchain technology and smart contracts, DApps eliminate the need for intermediaries and central authorities, enabling users to interact directly with each other in a secure and verifiable manner.

⬚ Why Should Students Learn to Build DApps?

The realm of decentralized applications (DApps) presents a unique and compelling opportunity for students today. Here's why:

- **High-Paying Jobs:** The demand for skilled DApp developers is surging globally. As businesses and industries increasingly explore blockchain technology, professionals proficient in building decentralized applications are highly sought after, commanding competitive salaries.
- **Startup Potential:** DApps are at the forefront of the next wave of technological innovation, often referred to as Web3. Students who acquire DApp development skills have the potential to create groundbreaking products and services, potentially leading to successful startups and entrepreneurial ventures.
- **No Gatekeepers:** Unlike traditional app development, which often involves navigating app store approvals and licensing restrictions, DApps offer a more open and permissionless environment. Developers can deploy their applications directly onto the blockchain, giving them greater control over their creations and reducing barriers to entry.

- **Creative Freedom:** DApp development empowers students to explore a wide range of creative possibilities. From decentralized games and marketplaces to innovative social networking platforms, the potential applications of DApps are virtually limitless, allowing students to bring their unique visions to life.

☐ Pro Tip: Start With Templates

For those new to DApp development, there's no need to feel overwhelmed. Several platforms offer tools and templates to simplify the process:

- **ThirdWeb:** This platform provides drag-and-drop tools that streamline the creation and deployment of smart contracts, making it easier for beginners to get started with DApp development.
- **Moralis:** Moralis offers backend infrastructure support, simplifying tasks such as user authentication and transaction management, which are crucial for building functional DApps.
- **Alchemy:** Alchemy provides developers with the tools they need to interact with Ethereum, offering a robust and reliable platform for building and deploying DApps on the Ethereum network.

★ Chapter Recap

✅ DApps are decentralized versions of traditional apps
✅ Smart contracts + frontend = complete Web3 application
✅ You explored real-life DApps like Uniswap, Audius, Compound
✅ You learned how students can build and earn from DApps

30 multiple-choice questions (MCQs) on DApps:

What is a DApp?

1. A DApp is an application that runs on a: a) Centralized server b) Decentralized network c) Local computer d) Cloud service
2. Which of the following is a defining characteristic of a DApp? a) Closed-source code b) Centralized backend c) Smart contracts d) Single point of failure
3. In a DApp, the rules and logic are governed by: a) A company b) A central authority c) Smart contracts d) User agreements
4. Many DApps utilize their own _____ for transactions and governance. a) Traditional currency b) Cryptocurrency c) Stock options d) Loyalty points
5. Which is a core component of a DApp's architecture? a) Centralized database b) Blockchain network c) Single server d) Mainframe computer
6. DApps are different from traditional apps because they have: a) Centralized control b) User data owned by a company c) Minimal downtime risk d) Payments via banks

7. The backend of a DApp typically resides on a: a) Central server b) Cloud storage c) Blockchain d) Local machine
8. Which of the following is NOT a characteristic of DApps? a) Open-source b) Decentralized backend c) Reliance on a central authority d) Use of tokens
9. DApps enhance trust through: a) Centralized control b) Opaque systems c) Transparency d) Intermediaries
10. What is the primary advantage of a decentralized backend? a) Single point of control b) Increased vulnerability c) No single point of failure d) Data manipulation

Examples: Uniswap, Compound, Audius

11. Uniswap is a DApp that functions as a: a) Social media platform b) Decentralized exchange c) Music streaming service d) Lending platform
12. On Uniswap, users can swap cryptocurrencies: a) Through a central authority b) Without KYC c) With traditional currency d) Using a bank account
13. The liquidity on Uniswap is provided by: a) A central bank b) The exchange itself c) Users d) Market makers
14. Compound is a DApp for: a) Trading stocks b) Lending and borrowing crypto assets c) Streaming videos d) Social networking
15. On Compound, lenders can: a) Borrow crypto b) Earn interest c) Pay interest d) Trade derivatives
16. In Compound, borrowers provide _____ to take loans. a) Their credit score b) Collateral c) Personal information d) A signed agreement
17. Audius is a DApp in the domain of: a) Finance b) Social media c) Music streaming d) E-commerce
18. On Audius, artists can: a) Only upload to record labels b) Upload songs directly c) Only stream music d) Manage user data
19. The revenue on Audius goes directly to: a) The platform b) Record labels c) Creators d) Advertisers
20. Which token is used in the Audius platform? a) ETH b) USDC c) AUDIO d) DAI

Frontend + Blockchain Integration Basics

21. The user interface of a DApp is called the: a) Backend b) Frontend c) Smart contract d) Database
22. DApp frontends are built using technologies like: a) Solidity b) Python c) HTML, CSS, and JavaScript d) Java
23. Instead of a centralized server, DApps use _____ for backend logic. a) Frontend frameworks b) Smart contracts c) Cloud storage d) APIs
24. Smart contracts are written in languages like: a) JavaScript b) Python c) Solidity d) HTML
25. Which blockchain is commonly used to deploy smart contracts? a) Bitcoin b) Ripple c) Ethereum d) Dogecoin
26. To connect the frontend to smart contracts, DApps use libraries like: a) React Native b) Angular c) Web3.js or Ethers.js d) Node.js

27. Which acts as a bridge between users and the blockchain? a) A web browser b) A search engine c) A digital wallet (like MetaMask) d) An operating system
28. In a voting DApp example, the smart contract records the votes: a) In a central database b) On the blockchain c) In a server log d) In the user's browser
29. In a DApp, who has the authority to edit the recorded data? a) An admin b) A company c) No one d) The users
30. What does a DApp use to ensure trust and transparency? a) Centralized control b) Opaque systems c) Blockchain d) Intermediaries

10 mid-size questions with answers on DApps:

What is a DApp?

1. **Question:** Define a Decentralized Application (DApp) and explain how it differs from a traditional web application.

   Answer: A Decentralized Application (DApp) is an application that runs on a decentralized network, such as a blockchain, rather than a centralized server. Unlike traditional web applications, where a single entity controls the server and data, DApps operate autonomously based on smart contracts. This results in increased transparency, security, and user control.

2. **Question:** What are the key characteristics that define a DApp?

   Answer: The key characteristics of a DApp include:

   o   Open-source code: Anyone can view and verify the code.
   o   Decentralized backend: Data and logic reside on a blockchain.
   o   Smart contracts: Rules are enforced by code, not intermediaries.
   o   Tokens: Often uses its own cryptocurrency for transactions and governance.

Examples: Uniswap, Compound, Audius

3. **Question:** Explain how Uniswap works as a Decentralized Exchange (DEX).

   Answer: Uniswap is a DEX that allows users to swap cryptocurrencies directly with each other without a central authority. It uses automated market makers (AMMs) and liquidity pools, where users provide liquidity and earn fees. Smart contracts facilitate these swaps, making them trustless and efficient.

4. **Question:** How does Compound enable lending and borrowing of crypto assets?

   Answer: Compound is a DeFi protocol where users can lend or borrow cryptocurrencies. Lenders provide assets to pools and earn interest, while borrowers take loans by providing collateral. Smart contracts manage interest rates, collateral, and loan terms algorithmically, creating a decentralized and transparent lending/borrowing system.

5. **Question:** What problem does Audius solve in the music streaming industry?

   Answer: Audius aims to disrupt the traditional music streaming industry by providing a decentralized platform where artists can upload their music directly to the blockchain and connect with fans without intermediaries. This allows for fairer revenue distribution and greater artist control, addressing issues of centralized control and low payouts in platforms like Spotify.

Frontend + Blockchain Integration Basics

6. **Question:** Describe the role of the frontend in a DApp.

   Answer: The frontend of a DApp is the user interface that users interact with. It is built using standard web technologies (HTML, CSS, JavaScript) and provides a user-friendly way to access the DApp's functionality. It communicates with the backend (smart contracts) to display data and execute transactions.

7. **Question:** What are smart contracts and how do they function as the backend of a DApp?

   Answer: Smart contracts are self-executing agreements written in code and deployed on a blockchain. They define the rules and logic of a DApp, controlling data storage, transaction execution, and user interactions. When conditions are met, smart contracts automatically enforce the terms, ensuring transparency and eliminating the need for intermediaries.

8. **Question:** Explain how a DApp's frontend communicates with smart contracts on the blockchain.

   Answer: DApps use libraries like Web3.js or Ethers.js to facilitate communication between the frontend and smart contracts. These libraries allow the frontend to send transactions to the blockchain, call functions in smart contracts, and retrieve data from the blockchain.

9. **Question:** What is the role of a wallet like MetaMask in the DApp ecosystem?

   Answer: MetaMask acts as a bridge between the user and the blockchain. It allows users to manage their blockchain identity, sign transactions, and interact with DApps. It securely stores the user's private keys and enables them to connect to DApps and authorize operations on the blockchain.

10. **Question:** In a typical DApp, who has control over the data and logic?

    Answer: In a typical DApp, control over data and logic is decentralized. The data is stored on the blockchain, and the logic is governed by smart contracts. This means that no single entity has complete control, and the rules of the application are transparent and immutable.

CHAPTER 14: DAOS – DIGITAL COMMUNITIES THAT RULE THEMSELVES

"What if organizations could run without bosses, banks, or borders—powered by code, and governed by the people?"

Welcome to the world of **DAOs—Decentralized Autonomous Organizations**, a groundbreaking innovation in how people collaborate, govern, and build shared digital futures.

For students and creators entering Web3, DAOs represent **a new era of online community—** where your voice matters, your skills are valued, and your actions help shape real outcomes.

⬛ What is a DAO?

A Decentralized Autonomous Organization (DAO) is a blockchain-based collective of individuals who coordinate, vote, and make decisions in a communal manner. This is achieved through the use of smart contracts, thereby eliminating the need for a central leadership or traditional hierarchical structure.

In essence, a DAO can be conceptualized as:

- A digital cooperative operating without a Chief Executive Officer.
- A global community governed by lines of code.
- A transparent and trustless organization where decisions are enacted through community votes.

DAOs have the potential to govern a wide array of entities and initiatives, including:

- Projects
- Communities
- Funds
- Companies
- Social causes

🎓 Real-Life Analogy:

Consider your college club. In a DAO framework, every member would possess voting rights, the club's finances would be managed transparently on the blockchain, and all decisions, such as event planning or budget allocation, would be executed through smart contracts. This is the essence of a DAO.

⬛ How Does a DAO Work?

To understand the operational framework of a DAO, let's examine its structural components:

Component	Role in DAO
Smart Contracts	The codified rules and logic of the organization, including voting systems and treasury management.
Tokens	Digital assets that represent membership or voting power within the DAO.
Governance	The process by which the community proposes and votes on changes or initiatives.
Treasury	Shared funds held on the blockchain, managed transparently through smart contracts.

🔐 Example:

Consider an ArtDAO established to fund student digital artists.

- Members can submit proposals, such as "Allocate $500 to Sarah for her NFT series."
- Token holders then vote to approve or reject the proposal.
- If the proposal is approved, the smart contract automatically disburses the funds.

In this system, no single individual is required to approve the transaction. The process is entirely autonomous and collective.

📚 Benefits of Joining a DAO (Especially as a Student)

For students, participating in a Decentralized Autonomous Organization (DAO) offers a unique set of advantages:

✅ 1. Learn by Doing

- **Practical Experience:** DAOs provide hands-on opportunities to contribute to real-world Web3 projects.
- **Skill Development:** Members gain practical experience with smart contract tools, decentralized governance mechanisms, and community management practices.

✅ 2. Earn Crypto & Build Reputation

- **Cryptocurrency Compensation:** DAOs often compensate contributors with cryptocurrency, such as ETH, USDC, or the DAO's native tokens.
- **On-Chain Portfolio:** Contributions and voting activity are recorded transparently on the blockchain, creating a verifiable and publicly accessible record of your work and participation. This serves as a transparent and immutable resume.

✅ 3. Build a Global Network

- **Global Collaboration:** DAOs facilitate collaboration with a diverse group of individuals, including developers, designers, marketers, and creators from around the world.
- **Community Engagement:** Many DAO contributors are students, freelancers, and independent builders, providing valuable networking and learning opportunities.

🚀 How to Join or Start a DAO as a Student

✋ Step 1: Explore Existing DAOs

Begin by exploring platforms that list and provide information about various DAOs:

- https://daocentral.com
- https://snapshot.org
- https://deepdao.io

Select a DAO that aligns with your interests, such as those focused on art, coding, education, social impact, or cryptocurrency.

☐ Step 2: Join the Community

Once you've identified a DAO, take the following steps to engage with the community:

- Follow the DAO's communication channels on platforms like Discord or Telegram.
- Review the DAO's governance documents, which are often hosted on platforms like Notion or GitHub.
- Look for channels or sections dedicated to "Contribute" or "Bounties," where you can find opportunities to get involved.

Remember that you don't need to be an expert to join a DAO. Many DAOs welcome new members who are eager to learn and contribute.

☐☐ Step 3: Start Your Own DAO (Beginner-Friendly Path)

For students interested in creating their own DAOs, several user-friendly tools are available:

- **Aragon:** A platform that simplifies the process of launching DAOs with customizable governance structures.
- **DAOhaus:** A no-code DAO builder that allows users to create DAOs without extensive technical knowledge.
- **Juicebox:** A platform for creating crowdfunded DAOs, which is particularly well-suited for student clubs and creator initiatives.

With these tools, you can establish DAOs for various purposes, such as:

- Funding student hackathons
- Promoting digital art
- Organizing educational projects
- Managing a decentralized study group

☐☐♂☐ Case Studies – DAOs Changing the Game

DAOs are demonstrating their transformative potential across various sectors. Let's explore some notable examples:

💰 1. MakerDAO – The Pioneer

- **Description:** MakerDAO is one of the earliest and most influential DAOs, primarily known for managing Dai, a decentralized stablecoin pegged to the US dollar.
- **Function:** The MakerDAO community governs the monetary policy of the Dai stablecoin through a system of on-chain votes. This includes decisions related to stability fees, collateral types, and system upgrades.
- **Impact:** Dai is widely used in decentralized finance (DeFi) applications worldwide, providing a stable and reliable medium of exchange.
- **Governance:** Members who hold Maker's governance token (MKR) vote on proposals to update the Maker Protocol and adjust various risk parameters.
- **Website:** https://makerdao.com

🖥 2. Gitcoin DAO – Funding Open Source

- **Description:** Gitcoin DAO is focused on funding the development of public goods, particularly open-source software projects.
- **Function:** Gitcoin DAO provides grants and funding to developers, students, and non-profit organizations working on open-source initiatives. It also facilitates quadratic funding, a mechanism designed to allocate funds more equitably based on community support.
- **Impact:** Gitcoin has become a crucial source of funding for many open-source projects that benefit the entire Web3 ecosystem.
- **Example:** A student in India can receive a grant of $300 through Gitcoin to contribute to a specific GitHub project, enabling them to participate in and contribute to the open-source community.
- **Website:** https://gitcoin.co

☐ 3. Friends With Benefits (FWB) – The Social DAO

- **Description:** Friends With Benefits (FWB) is a token-gated social DAO that brings together creators, artists, and cultural influencers.

- **Function:** FWB focuses on fostering community, collaboration, and cultural production across art, music, and various creative fields. The DAO organizes both online and in-person events, supports member projects, and facilitates learning opportunities.
- **Impact:** FWB has become a prominent example of how DAOs can be used to cultivate vibrant online and offline communities centered around shared interests and creative endeavors.
- **Example:** Musicians and digital artists within the FWB DAO can collaborate on projects, launch NFTs, and organize DAO-funded concerts, leveraging the community's resources and network.
- **Website:** https://www.fwb.help

⚠️ Risks and Responsibilities

While DAOs offer numerous advantages, it's crucial to acknowledge the inherent risks and responsibilities associated with them:

- **Low Participation:** In some DAOs, low voter turnout can lead to the passage of proposals that do not reflect the best interests of the community.
- **Smart Contract Vulnerabilities:** If the smart contracts governing a DAO are poorly written or contain bugs, they can be exploited, potentially leading to loss of funds or governance attacks.
- **Legal Uncertainty:** The legal status of DAOs remains ambiguous in many jurisdictions, which can create regulatory challenges and uncertainties.

🔒 A Word of Caution:

Remember that in DAOs, users are not only participants but also owners. Therefore, it's essential to exercise prudence and make informed decisions when joining and engaging with these organizations.

☐ Chapter Recap

✓ DAOs are digital communities governed by members via smart contracts
✓ They offer global collaboration, income, learning, and leadership
✓ You can **join or start** one using beginner-friendly tools
✓ Real-world DAOs like Gitcoin, MakerDAO, and FWB are reshaping industries

30 multiple-choice questions (MCQs) on DAOs:

What is a DAO?

1. What does DAO stand for? a) Digital Autonomous Organization b) Decentralized Autonomous Organization c) Distributed Autonomous Operation d) Dynamic Autonomous Organization
2. A DAO is primarily based on: a) Centralized servers b) Blockchain technology c) Cloud computing d) Traditional databases
3. In a DAO, decisions are made: a) By a central leader b) Collectively using smart contracts c) Through a traditional hierarchy d) By a board of directors
4. Which of the following is a key component of a DAO? a) CEO b) Smart contracts c) Headquarters d) Physical office
5. What does a DAO eliminate the need for? a) Community b) Blockchain c) Central leadership d) Technology
6. A DAO can be described as a: a) Traditional corporation b) Digital co-op c) Government agency d) Non-profit organization
7. What governs the rules and logic of a DAO? a) Human managers b) Government regulations c) Smart contracts d) User agreements
8. How are changes typically implemented in a DAO? a) Through executive orders b) Via community votes c) By a single authority d) Through legal processes
9. What is used to represent membership or voting power in a DAO? a) Shares b) Tokens c) IDs d) Passwords
10. Where are a DAO's shared funds typically stored? a) In a bank account b) On a centralized server c) On a blockchain d) In a company vault

How to Join/Start a DAO as a Student

11. Which platform can be used to explore existing DAOs? a) Google Search b) Facebook c) daocentral.com d) Wikipedia
12. What is a common platform for DAO communication? a) Email b) Discord or Telegram c) Postal service d) Fax
13. Where can you typically find a DAO's governance documents? a) Twitter b) Instagram c) Notion or GitHub d) LinkedIn
14. What should a student look for to get involved in a DAO? a) "About Us" page b) "Contact Us" form c) "Contribute" or "Bounty" channels d) "Terms of Service" agreement
15. Do you need to be an expert to join a DAO? a) Yes b) No, DAOs often welcome newcomers c) Only for leadership roles d) Only for technical roles
16. Which tool is mentioned for launching DAOs with easy governance structures? a) WordPress b) Aragon c) Salesforce d) Zoom
17. Which tool is described as a no-code DAO builder? a) Slack b) DAOhaus c) Trello d) Airtable
18. Which tool is suitable for creating crowdfunded DAOs? a) Photoshop b) Juicebox c) Canva d) Premiere Pro

19. What is a potential use case for a student-led DAO? a) Running a centralized university b) Funding student hackathons c) Managing a traditional bank d) Operating a government agency

20. What type of projects can a student DAO promote? a) Only physical art b) Digital art c) Only commercial products d) Only political campaigns

Case Studies: MakerDAO, Gitcoin, Friends With Benefits

21. What does MakerDAO primarily manage? a) Bitcoin b) Dai stablecoin c) Ethereum d) Dogecoin

22. How does MakerDAO govern its monetary policy? a) Through a CEO b) Via government regulations c) Through community votes d) By a central bank

23. What is a key use case of Dai? a) Stock trading b) DeFi applications c) Real estate transactions d) International diplomacy

24. What does Gitcoin DAO primarily fund? a) Large corporations b) Open-source projects c) Government initiatives d) Private businesses

25. What does Gitcoin offer to developers and students? a) High-interest loans b) Bounties and grants c) Free software d) Legal services

26. What funding mechanism does Gitcoin use to ensure fairness? a) First-come, first-served b) Equal distribution c) Quadratic funding d) Lottery system

27. Friends With Benefits (FWB) is described as a: a) Financial institution b) Social DAO c) Political party d) Educational organization

28. What is the primary focus of FWB? a) International trade b) Art, music, culture, and collaboration c) Scientific research d) Space exploration

29. What do FWB members hold to vote and access benefits? a) Company shares b) $FWB tokens c) Membership cards d) Social security numbers

30. What type of events does FWB host? a) Only online webinars b) IRL events c) Only academic conferences d) Only business meetings

10 mid-size questions with answers on DAOs:

What is a DAO?

1. **Question:** Explain the core concept of a DAO and how it differs from a traditional organization.

   Answer: A Decentralized Autonomous Organization (DAO) is a group of people who coordinate and make decisions collectively using smart contracts on a blockchain, rather than relying on a central authority or traditional hierarchy. Unlike traditional organizations with a CEO and management structure, DAOs operate based on rules encoded in smart contracts, ensuring transparency and community-driven governance.

2. **Question:** Describe the key components of a DAO and their respective roles.

Answer: The key components of a DAO include:

- **Smart Contracts:** These define the rules and logic, such as voting systems and treasury management.
- **Tokens:** These represent membership or voting power within the DAO.
- **Governance:** This is the process by which the community proposes and votes on changes.
- **Treasury:** This refers to the shared funds stored on the blockchain, managed transparently through smart contracts.

How to Join/Start a DAO as a Student

3. **Question:** What are the typical steps a student should take to join an existing DAO?

   Answer: A student can typically join a DAO by:

   1. Exploring DAO platforms like daocentral.com to find a suitable DAO.
   2. Joining the DAO's community channels on platforms like Discord or Telegram.
   3. Reviewing the DAO's governance documents (often on Notion or GitHub).
   4. Looking for ways to contribute, such as through "Contribute" or "Bounty" channels.

4. **Question:** What tools are available for students who want to start their own DAOs, and what are some potential use cases for a student-led DAO?

   Answer: Tools like Aragon, DAOhaus, and Juicebox can help students start DAOs. Potential use cases include:

   - Funding student hackathons.
   - Promoting digital art.
   - Running educational projects.
   - Managing a decentralized study group.

Case Studies: MakerDAO, Gitcoin, Friends With Benefits

5. **Question:** What is MakerDAO, and what is its primary function?

   Answer: MakerDAO is a pioneering DAO that manages Dai, a decentralized stablecoin. Its primary function is to maintain the stability of Dai and govern its monetary policy through community votes.

6. **Question:** How does Gitcoin DAO support the development of open-source software?

   Answer: Gitcoin DAO funds developers working on public goods (open-source projects) by offering bounties and grants. It uses mechanisms like quadratic funding to distribute funds in a way that reflects community support.

7. **Question:** What is Friends With Benefits (FWB), and what is its focus as a DAO?

   Answer: Friends With Benefits (FWB) is a social DAO that serves as an exclusive, token-gated community for creators. Its focus is on art, music, culture, and collaboration, and it organizes both online and in-person events.

8. **Question:** What are some of the risks associated with participating in DAOs?

   Answer: Risks associated with DAOs include:

   o   Low participation, which can lead to unrepresentative decisions.
   o   Smart contract bugs that can be exploited.
   o   Legal uncertainty surrounding the status of DAOs in some jurisdictions.

9. **Question:** Explain the concept of ""quadratic funding"" as used by Gitcoin.

   Answer: Quadratic funding is a mechanism used by Gitcoin to allocate donations to projects. It's designed to give more weight to a larger number of smaller contributions than to a few large ones, aiming to better reflect the broad support of a community for a project.

10. **Question:** How does MakerDAO ensure the stability of the Dai stablecoin?

    Answer: MakerDAO uses a system of smart contracts and collateralized debt positions (CDPs) to ensure the stability of Dai. Users can lock up collateral (like ETH) in these CDPs to generate Dai. The system is designed to maintain Dai's peg to the US dollar through algorithmic adjustments and community governance.

CHAPTER 15: WEB3 CAREERS – YOUR ROADMAP TO SUCCESS

"Web3 is not just a technology shift—it's a career revolution. The earlier you enter, the greater your impact."

As students, you stand at a historic turning point. The digital economy is evolving—and with it, the job market is being rewritten. Web3 is not just about blockchain or crypto; it is about **rebuilding the internet from the ground up**, and with that comes a **new universe of careers** that didn't exist just a few years ago.

This chapter will help you **identify your path in Web3**, build a resume that stands out in a decentralized world, and find real-world opportunities to **learn, earn, and grow**.

🚀 Top Web3 Roles – Where You Fit In

The Web3 space offers a diverse array of opportunities for individuals with various skill sets and interests. Whether you possess a knack for coding, communication, or creative thinking, there's a place for you in this burgeoning ecosystem.

👨‍💻 1. Blockchain Developer

- **Role:** Blockchain developers are responsible for building the foundational infrastructure of Web3. Their duties include writing smart contracts, developing decentralized applications (DApps), and managing the logic behind token systems.
- **Languages/Tools:** Proficiency in languages and tools such as Solidity, Rust, and JavaScript is essential. Developers also work with platforms like Ethereum, Solana, Near, and Polkadot, and utilize libraries like Web3.js.
- **Example:** A blockchain developer might create a voting DApp for student elections using Solidity and deploy it on a testnet to ensure its functionality and security.

🎨 2. Web3 UI/UX Designer

- **Role:** Web3 UI/UX designers focus on creating user-friendly interfaces for various Web3 applications, including DApps, wallets, and NFT marketplaces. Their goal is to make these decentralized technologies accessible and intuitive for a broad audience.
- **Skills:** Key skills include proficiency in design tools like Figma and Webflow, as well as a strong understanding of HTML/CSS, responsive design principles, and cryptocurrency wallet integration.
- **Example:** A Web3 UI/UX designer could design a clean and mobile-friendly interface for a decentralized finance (DeFi) staking application, ensuring a seamless user experience.

📊 3. Data Analyst / Token Economist

- **Role:** Data analysts and token economists play a crucial role in understanding and optimizing Web3 ecosystems. They analyze blockchain data, design tokenomics models, and forecast market trends to inform strategic decision-making.
- **Tools:** These professionals utilize tools like Dune Analytics, The Graph, Excel, and data visualization dashboards to extract insights and present their findings.
- **Example:** A data analyst might track the user growth of a Decentralized Autonomous Organization (DAO) and prepare a funding proposal based on the analysis of relevant metrics, demonstrating the DAO's progress and potential.

4. Community Manager

- **Role:** Community managers are the voice and face of Web3 projects, responsible for engaging with and growing online communities across platforms like Discord, Twitter, and Telegram. They foster a sense of belonging, facilitate communication, and build a strong community around the project.
- **Skills:** Effective communication, branding expertise, event hosting capabilities, and moderation skills are essential for this role.
- **Example:** A community manager might organize a meme contest to generate excitement around an upcoming NFT launch or host Twitter AMAs (Ask Me Anything) sessions with project developers to engage the community and address their questions.

5. Content Creator / Educator

- **Role:** Content creators and educators play a vital role in simplifying complex Web3 concepts and making them accessible to a wider audience. They create content in various formats, including blog posts, YouTube videos, podcasts, and tutorials.
- **Platforms:** These individuals utilize platforms like Medium, Mirror.xyz, YouTube, and Substack to share their knowledge and insights.
- **Example:** A student could start a newsletter that breaks down the latest cryptocurrency news and trends in a clear and concise manner, catering to beginners and those new to the space.

6. Product Manager

- **Role:** Product managers in Web3 act as a bridge between developers, designers, and users. They define the product vision, create roadmaps, and ensure that the product meets the needs of its target audience.
- **Skills:** A strong understanding of Agile methodologies, roadmap planning, and user research is crucial for this role.
- **Example:** A product manager could lead a student team in the development of a decentralized library application, coordinating the efforts of developers and designers while ensuring the application aligns with user needs and expectations.

□□ How to Build Your Web3 Resume

In the Web3 space, practical experience and demonstrated skills are often valued more highly than traditional academic credentials. This means that your resume should emphasize your contributions and on-chain activity.

✅ 1. GitHub > GPA

- **Open-Source Contributions:** Actively contribute to open-source projects related to Web3. This demonstrates your ability to collaborate, write code, and engage with the community.
- **Project Portfolio:** Upload your smart contracts, DApp projects, and project documentation to GitHub. This provides tangible evidence of your technical skills and development process.

✅ 2. Showcase Your Wallet

- **ENS Name:** Include your Ethereum Name Service (ENS) name (e.g., studentxyz.eth). This provides a human-readable identifier for your blockchain address and demonstrates your familiarity with Web3 naming conventions.
- **On-Chain Assets:** Showcase your NFTs, tokens, and DAO memberships by listing them or providing links to where they can be viewed. This illustrates your active participation in the Web3 ecosystem.

✅ 3. On-Chain Proof

- **Verifiable Contributions:** Highlight your contributions to DAOs, including specific proposals you've made, votes you've cast, and any bounties you've earned and completed.
- **Web3 Resume Platforms:** Utilize platforms like Questbook, Showwcase, and TalentLayer, which are specifically designed to help you create and showcase your Web3 experience and credentials. These platforms allow you to present your on-chain activity in a structured and verifiable manner.

Getting Started in Web3: A Step-by-Step Guide

The most effective way to enter the Web3 space is by actively building and collaborating. Here's a detailed breakdown of how you can gain practical experience:

💡 Web3 Hackathons

Web3 hackathons are intensive events where individuals and teams collaborate to build functional projects within a short period, typically 48-72 hours. They offer a dynamic and immersive introduction to Web3 development.

- **Platforms:** Participate in Web3 hackathons organized by platforms like:
  - **ETHGlobal:** A global community organizing Ethereum hackathons.
  - **Devfolio:** A platform for organizing and participating in developer events, including many Web3 hackathons.
  - **Gitcoin:** A platform that supports open-source development and frequently hosts hackathons focused on Web3.
  - **Chainlink:** A provider of oracle services that often sponsors and supports Web3 hackathons.
- **Experience:** These events provide an immersive experience where you can:
  - Form teams with other participants, including students and experienced developers.
  - Brainstorm and develop a project from scratch, which could be a DApp, a smart contract, or a Web3 tool.
  - Work under pressure to meet deadlines, simulating a real-world development environment.
  - Learn new technologies and tools quickly through hands-on experience.
- **Benefits:** Hackathons offer numerous benefits:
  - **Skill Development:** Gain practical experience in blockchain development, smart contracts, and DApp development.
  - **Networking:** Connect with other developers, industry experts, and potential employers.
  - **Portfolio Building:** Create tangible projects that you can showcase in your portfolio.
  - **Prizes and Recognition:** Win prizes, secure grants, and gain recognition for your work.
  - **Job Opportunities:** Attract job offers from Web3 companies that often scout for talent at these events.
- **Example:** A group of students developed a decentralized freelance portal during an ETHIndia hackathon. Their project addressed a real-world problem, garnered attention from investors, and they received funding to further develop and scale their platform into a полноценный business.

☐ Open Source Projects

Contributing to open-source Web3 projects is an excellent way to gain practical experience, collaborate with the community, and build a reputation.

- **Platforms:** Contribute to open-source Web3 projects through platforms like:
  - **Gitcoin:** A platform that connects developers with open-source projects and funding opportunities.
  - **Buidlbox:** A platform focused on Web3 education and providing resources for developers to contribute to open-source.
  - **DAOs:** Many DAOs maintain open-source projects and welcome contributions from the community.
- **Contribution Opportunities:** Look for various ways to contribute:

- o **Bounties:** Work on specific tasks or issues for which you can earn cryptocurrency rewards.
- o **"Starter-friendly" tags:** Find projects with tasks specifically designed for newcomers, such as documentation improvements, bug fixes, or small feature implementations.
- o **Code contributions:** Contribute to the core code of a project, such as implementing new features or optimizing existing code.
- o **Documentation:** Improve the project's documentation, making it more accessible and user-friendly.
- o **Community support:** Help other users, answer questions, and participate in discussions.
- **Example:** A student could contribute by fixing documentation bugs for an NFT marketplace like Rarible. This involves identifying and correcting errors or inconsistencies in the documentation, and the student could receive payment in USDC for their contribution, gaining both experience and earning cryptocurrency.

☌ Web3 Internships

Web3 internships provide structured learning experiences within established Web3 companies and DAOs, allowing you to gain practical skills and industry insights.

- **Platforms:** Explore internship opportunities on Web3-focused job boards such as:
  - o **CryptoJobs:** A job board specializing in blockchain and cryptocurrency-related roles.
  - o **Web3Internships:** A platform specifically focused on connecting students with internships in the Web3 space.
  - o **DAOTalent:** A platform that connects talent with opportunities in DAOs.
- **Opportunities:** Many companies and DAOs offer various internship arrangements:
  - o **Remote internships:** Work from anywhere with an internet connection.
  - o **Part-time internships:** Balance your internship with your studies.
  - o **Full-time internships:** Immerse yourself in the Web3 world for a more intensive experience.
  - o **Paid internships:** Earn compensation for your work.
  - o **Unpaid internships:** Gain valuable experience and build your portfolio.
- **Example:** A student could secure a part-time position as a community moderator for a new metaverse project. This would involve engaging with the community on platforms like Discord, managing discussions, organizing events, and gaining experience in community engagement and management within the Web3 space.

☐☐ Your Personalized Web3 Roadmap (for Students)

Here's a structured roadmap to help you navigate your Web3 journey:

Stage	Action Plan
Beginner	Learn Solidity basics, create a MetaMask wallet, explore DApps, join relevant Discord communities.
Intermediate	Contribute to GitHub projects, mint an NFT, deploy a basic smart contract on a testnet.
Advanced	Join a DAO, launch your own Web3 project, take a leadership role in a hackathon team.

✦ Bonus Tips to Accelerate Your Web3 Career

- **Build in Public:** Share your learning journey, projects, and insights on platforms like Twitter, LinkedIn, or Mirror.xyz. This helps you build a personal brand, attract attention from potential collaborators and employers, and connect with the broader Web3 community.
- **Create a Web3 Blog:** Document your learning process, share your knowledge, and showcase your projects on platforms like Medium, your own website, or Mirror.xyz. This will serve as a valuable digital resume, demonstrate your expertise, and establish you as a thought leader in the space.
- **Network Smartly:** Attend online events, participate in Twitter chats, and attend Web3 meetups (virtual or in-person) to connect with other developers, entrepreneurs, investors, and potential collaborators. Building relationships is crucial in the Web3 space.
- **Certify Your Learning:** Consider pursuing Web3-specific certifications from platforms like Coursera, LearnWeb3DAO, and Alchemy University to validate your skills and knowledge, enhance your credibility, and demonstrate your commitment to the field.

🎁 Chapter Recap

✅ Web3 careers span coding, design, community, data, and content creation
✅ Your wallet, GitHub, and on-chain actions **speak louder than your resume**
✅ Start by joining hackathons, DAOs, and open-source projects
✅ Build in public, network globally, and always stay curious

30 multiple-choice questions with answers on the topics you requested:

Top Roles in Web3

1. Which role is responsible for writing smart contracts? a) Web3 UI/UX Designer b) Blockchain Developer c) Data Analyst d) Community Manager
2. Which of these languages is commonly used by Blockchain Developers? a) HTML b) CSS c) Solidity d) Figma
3. Which role focuses on designing user-friendly interfaces for DApps? a) Blockchain Developer b) Data Analyst c) Web3 UI/UX Designer d) Content Creator
4. Which skill is essential for a Web3 UI/UX Designer? a) Smart contract development b) Responsive design c) Blockchain data analysis d) Community moderation
5. Which role involves analyzing blockchain data and designing tokenomics? a) Community Manager b) Web3 UI/UX Designer c) Data Analyst / Token Economist d) Blockchain Developer
6. Which tool is used by Data Analysts in Web3? a) Figma b) Solidity c) Dune Analytics d) JavaScript
7. Which role is responsible for engaging and growing online communities? a) Blockchain Developer b) Content Creator / Educator c) Community Manager d) Web3 UI/UX Designer
8. Which platform is commonly used by Community Managers? a) GitHub b) Discord c) Mirror.xyz d) Solana
9. Which role simplifies Web3 concepts through various forms of media? a) Web3 UI/UX Designer b) Data Analyst / Token Economist c) Content Creator / Educator d) Blockchain Developer
10. Which platform is used by Content Creators? a) Dune Analytics b) Medium c) Ethers.js d) React
11. Which role bridges the gap between developers, designers, and users? a) Community Manager b) Product Manager c) Data Analyst d) Blockchain Developer
12. Which methodology is commonly used by Product Managers? a) Waterfall b) Agile c) Spiral d) Six Sigma

How to Build Your Web3 Resume

13. What is more valued in Web3 than paper degrees? a) Years of experience b) Proof of work c) Certifications d) Formal education
14. What should you contribute to on GitHub? a) Only your GPA b) Open-source projects c) Personal information d) Financial records
15. What should you upload to your GitHub? a) فقط your resume b) Smart contracts and DApp projects c) School transcripts d) Confidential documents
16. What is an ENS name? a) A type of cryptocurrency b) A human-readable blockchain address c) A programming language d) A design tool
17. What should you showcase in your Web3 resume? a) Only your grades b) NFTs, tokens, and DAO memberships c) Personal opinions d) Private keys
18. What kind of proof should you mention on your Web3 resume? a) Attendance records b) DAO contributions and on-chain votes c) Social media activity d) Personal beliefs

19. Which platform offers Web3-specific resumes? a) LinkedIn b) Indeed c) Questbook d) Glassdoor
20. Which is another platform that offers Web3-specific resumes? a) Monster.com b) Showwcase c) Upwork d) Fiverr
21. Which is a third platform that offers Web3-specific resumes? a) Craigslist b) TalentLayer c) Reddit d) YouTube

Internships, Hackathons, and Open-Source Projects

22. What is the best way to start in Web3? a) Attending conferences b) Reading books c) Building and collaborating d) Getting a degree
23. Which platform organizes Web3 hackathons? a) Google b) ETHGlobal c) Microsoft d) Amazon
24. How long do Web3 hackathons typically last? a) 1-2 days b) 48-72 hours c) 1 week d) 1 month
25. What can you win at Web3 hackathons? a) Only experience b) Prizes, grants, and job offers c) Free food d) Certificates of attendance
26. What did a group of students build at a hackathon in the example? a) A social media app b) A decentralized freelance portal c) A new cryptocurrency d) A video game
27. Which platform can you use to contribute to open-source Web3 projects? a) Facebook b) Gitcoin c) Twitter d) Instagram
28. What are "bounties" in open-source projects? a) Free software b) Paid tasks c) Volunteer work d) Community events
29. What kind of tags are designed for newcomers in open-source projects? a) "Expert-level" b) "Starter-friendly" c) "Advanced" d) "Complex"
30. Where can you find Web3 internships? a) Traditional job boards b) Web3-focused job boards c) Government websites d) Newspapers

10 mid-size questions with answers on the topics you requested:

Top Roles in Web3

1. **Question:** Describe the responsibilities of a Blockchain Developer and list some of the key tools and languages they use.

   Answer: Blockchain Developers are responsible for building the core infrastructure of Web3. This includes writing smart contracts, developing decentralized applications (DApps), and managing token logic. They use languages like Solidity and Rust, and work with platforms like Ethereum and Solana, along with tools like Web3.js.

2. **Question:** Explain the role of a Web3 UI/UX Designer and what skills are essential for this position.

   Answer: Web3 UI/UX Designers focus on creating user-friendly interfaces for DApps, wallets, and NFT marketplaces. Essential skills include proficiency in design tools like

Figma and Webflow, a strong understanding of HTML/CSS, responsive design principles, and knowledge of crypto wallet integration.

How to Build Your Web3 Resume

3. **Question:** How does building a Web3 resume differ from creating a traditional resume?

   Answer: A Web3 resume emphasizes practical experience and on-chain activity over traditional academic credentials. It highlights contributions to open-source projects on platforms like GitHub, showcases your crypto wallet and holdings, and mentions on-chain contributions to DAOs.

4. **Question:** What are the key elements to include in a Web3 resume to demonstrate your skills and experience?

   Answer: Key elements include:

   - Contributions to open-source projects on GitHub.
   - Your ENS name and showcased NFTs/tokens.
   - On-chain proof of DAO contributions and votes.
   - Links to platforms like Questbook or Showwcase where you've built a Web3-specific resume.

Internships, Hackathons, and Open-Source Projects

5. **Question:** What are Web3 hackathons and what benefits do they offer to participants?

   Answer: Web3 hackathons are events where developers and students collaborate to build projects within a short timeframe. They offer benefits like hands-on experience, networking opportunities, portfolio building, the chance to win prizes, and potential job offers.

6. **Question:** How can students contribute to open-source projects in the Web3 space?

   Answer: Students can contribute by finding projects on platforms like Gitcoin, looking for bounties (paid tasks), working on "starter-friendly" tasks, contributing code, improving documentation, and providing community support.

7. **Question:** Where can students find Web3 internship opportunities, and what types of roles are commonly available?

   Answer: Students can find internships on Web3-focused job boards like CryptoJobs and Web3Internships. Common roles include developer positions, community management, marketing, and content creation.

8. **Question:** Describe the role of a Community Manager in a Web3 project.

Answer: Community Managers are responsible for engaging with and growing online communities on platforms like Discord and Twitter. They focus on communication, branding, event hosting, and moderation to build a strong and active community around a Web3 project.

9. **Question:** What does a Data Analyst/Token Economist do in the Web3 space, and what tools do they use?

   Answer: Data Analysts/Token Economists analyze blockchain data, design tokenomics, and forecast market trends. They use tools like Dune Analytics, The Graph, Excel, and Python.

10. **Question:** What is the significance of "building in public" in the Web3 space, and how can students do it?

    Answer: "Building in public" means sharing your learning journey and projects online (e.g., on Twitter or Mirror.xyz). It helps students build a personal brand, connect with the community, and demonstrate their progress and skills.

CHAPTER 16: WEB3 ETHICS, CHALLENGES & RESPONSIBILITY

"With great power comes great responsibility. Web3 gives you control—but it also demands ethical choices."

As students step into the world of Web3, it is crucial to recognize not only its potential but also the **challenges, risks, and responsibilities** that come along. The decentralized world is still young. Like the early days of the internet, there are loopholes, gray areas, and decisions that can shape the future—for better or worse.

This chapter will equip you with the **ethical lens** required to be a responsible builder, creator, and participant in the Web3 space.

---

1. Environmental Concerns – The Cost of Crypto on Nature

The rise of cryptocurrencies has brought about significant environmental concerns, primarily due to the energy-intensive processes involved in their operation.

? The Problem

Cryptocurrencies like Bitcoin utilize a consensus mechanism known as Proof of Work (PoW). This mechanism requires vast computational power to solve complex mathematical problems, which are essential for verifying transactions and maintaining the security of the network. This process consumes enormous amounts of electricity.

⚠ Real Impact

The environmental impact of PoW is substantial. According to the Cambridge Bitcoin Electricity Consumption Index:

- Bitcoin mining consumes more electricity annually than entire countries such as Argentina or Sweden.
- A significant portion of this energy is derived from non-renewable sources, such as fossil fuels, leading to a substantial increase in the carbon footprint associated with Bitcoin.

Q Real-World Example

In 2021, Tesla, a company known for its commitment to sustainability, suspended accepting Bitcoin payments. This decision was driven by environmental concerns, as the company cited the "rapidly increasing use of fossil fuels for Bitcoin mining" as a key factor.

✓ What's Being Done?

The cryptocurrency community is actively working to mitigate these environmental concerns:

- **Ethereum's Upgrade to Proof of Stake (PoS):** Ethereum, the second-largest cryptocurrency, underwent a significant upgrade in 2022, transitioning from PoW to Proof of Stake (PoS). This transition has resulted in a remarkable reduction in energy consumption, estimated to be around 99.95%. PoS mechanisms require significantly less computational power, as they rely on validators "staking" their cryptocurrency to secure the network, rather than solving complex mathematical problems.
- **Green Projects:** The emergence of eco-friendly blockchains like Algorand and Chia demonstrates a growing commitment to sustainability within the crypto space. These blockchains employ consensus mechanisms that are far less energy-intensive than PoW.
- **Carbon Offsetting:** Some NFT platforms are incorporating carbon offsetting options, allowing users to compensate for the environmental impact of their transactions by funding projects that reduce greenhouse gas emissions.

☐ Student Role:

Students can play a vital role in promoting sustainability within the cryptocurrency ecosystem:

- **Support Energy-Efficient Chains:** Actively support and utilize energy-efficient blockchains, such as Polygon, Solana, and the upgraded Ethereum (PoS).
- **Promote Green Initiatives:** Participate in or initiate projects focused on green NFTs and environmental awareness campaigns within the Web3 space.

---

2. ☐☐ Scam Awareness & Safety – Navigating the Risks

While Web3 offers numerous opportunities and empowers users with decentralization, its inherent nature also makes it susceptible to various scams and fraudulent activities.

! Why Web3 is Risky

The decentralized and pseudonymous nature of Web3, while providing greater user autonomy, also creates vulnerabilities. Unlike traditional financial systems, there is often no central authority to intervene or help users recover lost funds in the event of a scam. This necessitates a heightened sense of vigilance and security awareness among Web3 participants. Common risks include:

- **Scams:** Deceptive schemes designed to defraud users of their cryptocurrency or digital assets.
- **Rug Pulls:** A type of scam where developers abandon a project after raising funds, leaving investors with worthless tokens.
- **Phishing Attacks:** Attempts to trick users into revealing sensitive information, such as private keys, through deceptive tactics.

- **Fake Airdrops and Fraudulent Tokens:** Scammers distribute fake tokens or airdrops to lure users into interacting with malicious smart contracts.

Common Scams and How They Work

Scam Type	Example
Phishing	Scammers create fake MetaMask login pages or distribute malicious Discord links to steal users' private keys.
Rug Pull	Developers launch a token, generate hype, then withdraw all funds from the liquidity pool, causing the token price to crash and leaving investors with losses.
Pump-and-Dump	Groups on platforms like Telegram artificially inflate the price of a token through coordinated buying, only to sell off their holdings quickly for a profit, leaving later investors with losses as the price plummets.
Fake Airdrops	Scammers create fake airdrop announcements to trick users into clicking malicious links or interacting with harmful smart contracts, which can drain their wallets.

✅ **Safety Practices for Students**

To mitigate these risks, students entering the Web3 space should adhere to the following safety practices:

- **Never Share Your Private Key or Seed Phrase:** This is the most critical rule. Your private key and seed phrase are the keys to your cryptocurrency and digital assets. Sharing them with anyone grants them complete control over your funds.
- **Verify All Smart Contracts Before Interacting:** Before approving any transaction or interacting with a smart contract, carefully review its code to ensure it is legitimate and doesn't contain malicious functions. Tools and blockchain explorers can help with this.
- **Use Trusted Wallets:** Opt for reputable and secure wallets such as MetaMask, Trust Wallet, or hardware wallets like Ledger. These wallets have security features designed to protect your assets.
- **Double-Check Website URLs:** Scammers often create fake websites that closely resemble legitimate platforms. Always verify the URL and ensure you are on the correct site before entering any sensitive information or connecting your wallet.
- **Join Official Discord/Twitter Pages for Project Updates:** Stay updated on project news and announcements by following the official Discord and Twitter accounts of legitimate projects. This helps you avoid falling for fake airdrop announcements or other scams distributed through unofficial channels.

Real-Life Learning

In 2022, a fake airdrop link designed to look like it was from the popular NFT project Bored Ape Yacht Club resulted in the theft of over $2.8 million worth of NFTs. Victims, believing the airdrop was legitimate, unknowingly approved a malicious smart contract that granted the scammers access to their wallets, highlighting the critical importance of verifying the legitimacy of links and smart contracts.

⚖️ 3. Regulation vs. Decentralization – Striking the Balance

The inherent tension between the principles of decentralization and the need for regulatory oversight presents a complex challenge for the Web3 ecosystem.

⬜ The Ethical Dilemma

Web3's core value proposition lies in its promise of enhanced freedom, user privacy, and decentralized control. However, this very freedom can be exploited and misused in the absence of appropriate checks and balances. This has led governments worldwide to grapple with fundamental questions:

- Should cryptocurrencies be banned entirely, or should they be integrated into the existing financial framework through regulation?
- How should digital assets be classified and taxed?
- To what extent should creators be held accountable for illegal or harmful content distributed on the blockchain?

🔍 Example: India's Regulatory Shift

India's approach to cryptocurrency regulation provides a compelling case study. Initially, there was significant skepticism, with the government considering a ban. However, the regulatory landscape evolved, and in 2022, India imposed a 30% tax on income derived from cryptocurrency transactions, along with a 1% tax deducted at source (TDS) on such transactions.

This regulatory move sparked a debate. While some welcomed the increased clarity and potential legitimacy that regulation could bring, others expressed concern that it would stifle innovation and drive developers and businesses to more favorable regulatory environments.

The Decentralization vs. Regulation Debate

Decentralization (Pro)	Regulation (Pro)
Empowers users with complete control over their assets and data.	Protects users from scams, fraud, and market manipulation.
Fosters innovation by reducing bureaucratic hurdles.	Ensures accountability and promotes financial stability.
Eliminates single points of failure, enhancing system resilience.	Increases the legitimacy and mainstream adoption of cryptocurrencies.

⚖️ A Middle Path: Responsible Decentralization

Finding a balance between these competing interests is crucial for the sustainable growth of Web3. A potential solution lies in the concept of "responsible decentralization," which seeks to combine the benefits of decentralization with appropriate safeguards. This can be achieved through mechanisms such as:

- **DAO Self-Governance:** Decentralized Autonomous Organizations (DAOs) can implement internal governance mechanisms, such as community voting, to establish rules and enforce standards within their own ecosystems.
- **Smart Contract Security:** Smart contracts can be designed to incorporate safety logic, such as multi-signature requirements or circuit breakers, to mitigate the risk of errors or malicious attacks.
- **Third-Party Audits:** Independent and transparent code audits conducted by reputable firms like CertiK or Trail of Bits can help identify and address potential vulnerabilities in smart contracts and blockchain systems.

☐ Conclusion: Be the Ethical Web3 Pioneer

Web3 will be shaped by those who build it. As students, you're not just learners; you are **future leaders** of this decentralized revolution.

Ask yourself:

- Is this project environmentally sustainable?
- Is this token launch fair and secure?
- Is this app designed with user safety in mind?

Every click, contract, and creation adds a block to the future. Let it be a responsible one.

✅ Chapter Summary

- ☐ **Environmental concerns** highlight the need for eco-friendly chains and PoS mechanisms
- ☐☐ **Scam awareness** is critical—your wallet is your responsibility
- ⚖☐ **Regulation vs decentralization** is an ongoing debate, and balance is key
- 👤🎓 Students must play the role of **ethical innovators** and **informed creators**

30 multiple-choice questions with answers on the topics you requested:

Environmental Concerns

1. What consensus mechanism is known for its high energy consumption? a) Proof of Stake (PoS) b) Proof of Work (PoW) c) Delegated Proof of Stake (DPoS) d) Proof of History (PoH)
2. According to Cambridge University, Bitcoin mining uses more electricity than: a) The United States b) China c) Entire countries like Argentina or Sweden d) The European Union
3. What is the primary source of energy for much of Bitcoin mining? a) Renewable sources b) Nuclear power c) Non-renewable sources d) Solar power
4. Which company suspended Bitcoin payments due to environmental concerns? a) Microsoft b) Apple c) Tesla d) Google
5. What consensus mechanism does Ethereum use after its upgrade? a) PoW b) PoS c) DPoS d) PoH
6. By what percentage did Ethereum's energy use decrease after switching to PoS? a) 50% b) 75% c) 90% d) 99.95%
7. Which is an example of an eco-friendly blockchain? a) Bitcoin b) Ethereum (PoW) c) Algorand d) Dogecoin
8. What do some NFT platforms offer to minimize environmental damage? a) Free NFTs b) Carbon offsetting options c) Discounted prices d) Free shipping
9. Which of the following is an energy-efficient blockchain? a) Bitcoin b) Ethereum (PoW) c) Solana d) All of the above
10. What can students do to promote sustainability in Web3? a) Only use Bitcoin b) Support energy-efficient chains c) Ignore environmental concerns d) Mine cryptocurrency at home

Scam Awareness & Safety

11. What aspect of Web3 makes it vulnerable to scams? a) Centralization b) Transparency c) Decentralization and anonymity d) Regulation
12. What is a common type of scam in Web3? a) Charity fraud b) Phishing c) Mail fraud d) Telemarketing scams
13. What happens in a "rug pull" scam? a) Users lose their internet connection b) Developers abandon a project and take investor funds c) A token's price increases rapidly d) Hackers steal personal information
14. What happens in a "pump-and-dump" scheme? a) A token's price is artificially inflated, then quickly sold off b) Users receive free tokens c) A project gains legitimate popularity d) A smart contract is audited
15. What do scammers use to trick users into revealing their private keys? a) Public announcements b) Phishing attacks c) Government warnings d) Customer service calls
16. What should you never share with anyone? a) Your public address b) Your private key or seed phrase c) Your username d) Your email address
17. What should you do before interacting with a smart contract? a) Assume it's safe b) Verify it c) Ignore it d) Complain about it
18. Which is a trusted wallet? a) Any online wallet b) MetaMask c) A fake wallet d) A wallet recommended by an unknown source
19. What should you double-check to avoid scam websites? a) Website design b) Website URLs c) Website colors d) Website fonts

20. Where should you go for official project updates? a) Unofficial forums b) Official Discord/Twitter pages c) Random blogs d) Social media ads
21. What did the fake airdrop in the example imitate? a) Bitcoin b) Bored Ape Yacht Club c) Ethereum d) A government website

Regulation vs. Decentralization Debate

22. What are some of Web3's core value propositions? a) Centralization and control b) Freedom, privacy, and decentralization c) Strict rules and regulations d) Government oversight
23. What are governments debating regarding cryptocurrencies? a) How to promote them b) Whether to ban or regulate them c) How to ignore them d) How to give them away for free
24. What is a key question governments are asking about digital assets? a) Should they be given away? b) How do we tax them? c) Should they be used in schools? d) Should they replace traditional currency?
25. What is a concern regarding illegal content on the blockchain? a) Whether it should be promoted b) Whether creators should be held accountable c) Whether it should be made free d) Whether it should be ignored
26. What was India's initial stance on crypto? a) Strong support b) Initially skeptical c) Complete acceptance d) Early adoption
27. What tax did India impose on crypto earnings in 2022? a) 10% b) 20% c) 30% d) 40%
28. What is a benefit of decentralization? a) Central control b) Single point of failure c) Open to innovation d) Strict regulations
29. What is a benefit of regulation? a) User control b) Protection from scams c) Lack of accountability d) Slow innovation
30. What is a "middle path" solution discussed? a) Complete ban on crypto b) Responsible decentralization c) Ignoring all risks d) Unregulated growth

10 mid-size questions with answers on the topics you requested:

Environmental Concerns

1. **Question:** Explain the environmental impact of the Proof of Work (PoW) consensus mechanism and provide a real-world example of this impact.

   Answer: PoW requires vast computational power to solve complex mathematical problems, leading to enormous electricity consumption. Much of this energy comes from non-renewable sources, increasing the carbon footprint. For example, Tesla suspended Bitcoin payments due to concerns about the rapidly increasing use of fossil fuels for Bitcoin mining.

2. **Question:** What has Ethereum done to address the environmental concerns associated with its operations, and how effective has this been?

Answer: Ethereum transitioned from PoW to Proof of Stake (PoS) in 2022. This upgrade reduced its energy consumption by approximately 99.95%, significantly mitigating its environmental impact.

Scam Awareness & Safety

3. **Question:** Why is Web3 considered riskier than traditional financial systems in terms of scams and fraud?

   Answer: Web3's decentralized and pseudonymous nature, while empowering, also makes it vulnerable to scams, rug pulls, phishing attacks, and fake airdrops. Unlike traditional banks, there is often no central authority to help users recover lost funds.

4. **Question:** Describe a "rug pull" scam and explain how it harms investors.

   Answer: In a rug pull, developers launch a token, generate hype, and then abandon the project by withdrawing all funds from the liquidity pool. This causes the token's price to crash, leaving investors with worthless tokens and significant financial losses.

5. **Question:** What are the essential safety practices that students should follow to protect themselves from scams in the Web3 space?

   Answer: Students should:

   - Never share their private key or seed phrase.
   - Verify all smart contracts before interacting.
   - Use trusted wallets.
   - Double-check website URLs.
   - Rely on official project communication channels.

Regulation vs. Decentralization Debate

6. **Question:** What is the central ethical dilemma in the regulation vs. decentralization debate in Web3?

   Answer: The dilemma lies in balancing Web3's promise of freedom, privacy, and decentralization with the need to prevent its misuse through checks and balances. Governments are debating whether to regulate or ban cryptocurrencies, how to tax digital assets, and how to address illegal content on the blockchain.

7. **Question:** Briefly describe India's approach to regulating cryptocurrencies.

   Answer: Initially skeptical, India imposed a 30% tax on crypto earnings and a 1% TDS on transactions in 2022. This move aimed to regulate the sector but sparked debate about its impact on innovation.

8. **Question:** What are the main arguments in favor of decentralization in the Web3 space?

   Answer: Proponents of decentralization argue that it empowers users with full control, fosters innovation, and eliminates single points of failure.

9. **Question:** What are the main arguments in favor of regulation in the Web3 space?

   Answer: Proponents of regulation argue that it protects users from scams and fraud, ensures accountability, and promotes wider acceptance and financial safety.

10. **Question:** What is "responsible decentralization," and what mechanisms can help achieve it?

    Answer: Responsible decentralization seeks a middle ground by combining decentralization's benefits with safeguards. Mechanisms include DAO self-governance through community voting, smart contracts with safety logic, and transparent code audits by third parties.

CHAPTER 17: TOP 10 TOOLS EVERY WEB3 LEARNER MUST KNOW

"Every new technology comes with its own toolbox. In Web3, knowing your tools is the first step toward mastery."

Entering the world of Web3 is like stepping into a digital frontier. It's fast-paced, decentralized, and full of innovation. But just like any new ecosystem, it can be overwhelming—unless you know **where to begin and what to use**.

In this chapter, we introduce the **top 10 essential tools** every Web3 learner, creator, or explorer must understand. These tools form the **foundation of your Web3 journey**—from managing crypto assets to analyzing blockchain data, creating NFTs, and exploring decentralized applications.

🔧 1. MetaMask – Your Web3 Passport

MetaMask is a crucial tool for navigating the Web3 ecosystem, acting as both a cryptocurrency wallet and a browser extension (also available as a mobile application). It empowers users to store, send, and receive digital tokens, and, more importantly, to interact seamlessly with decentralized applications (DApps).

What it is:

MetaMask functions as a digital wallet, enabling users to manage their cryptocurrency holdings. It also acts as a bridge, connecting your web browser directly to the blockchain. This connection is essential for accessing and utilizing the decentralized web.

Why it's essential:

MetaMask's widespread support across Web3 platforms makes it an indispensable tool. It allows users to authenticate and interact with various DApps directly from their browsers, simplifying the process of engaging with decentralized technologies.

Example Use:

- **Accessing DApps:** MetaMask enables users to log in to platforms like Uniswap (a decentralized exchange) or OpenSea (an NFT marketplace) with ease.
- **Token Management:** Users can securely store and send Ether (ETH) and ERC-20 tokens, which are commonly used within the Ethereum network.
- **Smart Contract Interaction:** MetaMask allows users to sign smart contract transactions directly from their browsers, providing a secure and efficient way to interact with decentralized agreements.

Pro Tip:

The security of your MetaMask wallet, and by extension your digital assets, hinges on the confidentiality of your seed phrase. This phrase is a set of words that can be used to recover your wallet if you lose access to it. It is *imperative* that you keep your seed phrase absolutely private and store it in a secure location, preferably offline, to protect it from unauthorized access and potential loss.

🔧 2. WalletConnect – Seamless Mobile Wallet Access

WalletConnect is an open-source protocol designed to establish a secure connection between decentralized applications (DApps) and mobile cryptocurrency wallets. It facilitates this connection through the use of QR code scanning or deep linking.

What it is:

Unlike browser extensions like MetaMask, which reside directly within the browser, WalletConnect operates as a bridge, enabling mobile wallets to interact with DApps on various platforms. This protocol establishes an encrypted connection between a DApp and a user's mobile wallet, allowing for secure transaction signing and data exchange.

Why it's essential:

For users who prioritize the convenience and security of managing their digital assets through mobile wallets, WalletConnect provides a crucial link to the decentralized web. It eliminates the need to transfer funds to a browser extension wallet, allowing users to interact with DApps directly from their preferred mobile wallet.

Example Use:

- **Connecting to DApps:** When accessing a DApp such as Balancer (a decentralized exchange), a user can utilize WalletConnect to connect their mobile wallet, such as Trust Wallet or Rainbow Wallet. This typically involves scanning a QR code displayed on the Balancer website with their mobile wallet app. Once the connection is established, the user can manage their funds and interact with Balancer's features directly through their mobile wallet.

Pro Tip:

Employing WalletConnect when accessing DApps from a mobile device offers enhanced control and convenience. It allows you to manage your assets within a familiar and secure mobile wallet environment, while still being able to interact with the decentralized applications you want to use.

.

🔧 3. Etherscan – The Blockchain Explorer

Etherscan is a powerful and indispensable tool for anyone interacting with the Ethereum blockchain. It functions as a blockchain explorer, providing a transparent and detailed view of the network's activity.

What it is:

Etherscan allows users to examine a wide range of information related to the Ethereum blockchain. This includes:

- Transactions: View the details of any transaction that has occurred on the Ethereum network.
- Wallet Balances: Check the current holdings of any Ethereum address.
- Smart Contracts: Inspect the code and functionality of deployed smart contracts.
- Network Analytics: Monitor various network metrics, such as gas prices and transaction volume.

Why it's essential:

Transparency is a fundamental principle of Web3, and Etherscan plays a critical role in upholding this principle. It empowers users to independently verify and audit activity on the Ethereum blockchain, fostering trust and accountability within the ecosystem.

Example Use:

- **Smart Contract Verification:** Etherscan can be used to verify the authenticity and code of a smart contract before interacting with it, ensuring that it functions as intended and is not malicious.
- **Transaction Tracking:** Users can track the progress of their token transfers or NFT minting transactions, providing confirmation that their actions have been recorded on the blockchain.
- **Gas Price Monitoring:** Etherscan allows users to check the current gas prices on the Ethereum network, enabling them to make informed decisions about transaction fees and avoid overpaying.

Pro Tip:

For frequent users of Ethereum, it is highly recommended to bookmark your wallet address on Etherscan. This allows you to easily monitor your wallet's activity in real-time and keep track of your token holdings.

🔧 4. OpenSea – NFT Marketplace Giant

OpenSea is the largest and most prominent decentralized marketplace for the buying, selling, and minting of Non-Fungible Tokens (NFTs). It has played a pivotal role in popularizing NFTs and making them accessible to a broad audience.

What it is:

OpenSea provides a platform where users can:

- Buy NFTs: Acquire NFTs from a wide variety of creators and collections.
- Sell NFTs: List NFTs for sale or auction to other users.
- Mint NFTs: Create and tokenize their own digital assets.

Why it's essential:

OpenSea has significantly simplified the process of creating, buying, and selling NFTs. Whether you are an artist looking to monetize your digital creations or a collector seeking to acquire unique digital assets, OpenSea provides a user-friendly and accessible platform.

Example Use:

- **Minting NFTs:** An artist can use OpenSea to mint their first digital artwork as an NFT, making it available for sale on the platform.
- **Browsing Collections:** Collectors can browse trending NFT collections, such as Bored Ape Yacht Club or CryptoPunks, and purchase NFTs that they find valuable.
- **Listing NFTs for Sale:** Users who own NFTs can list them for sale or auction on OpenSea, setting their own prices and terms.

Pro Tip:

To fully utilize OpenSea's features, it is essential to connect your MetaMask wallet to the platform. When minting NFTs, you can also set your royalty percentage, which determines the share of future sales that you will receive as the original creator.

⬜⬜ 5. Remix IDE – Your Smart Contract Playground

What It Is:

Imagine a digital workbench, a virtual laboratory specifically designed for the intricate craft of building smart contracts. This, in essence, is Remix IDE. It stands as an online Integrated Development Environment (IDE), a comprehensive suite of tools accessible directly through your web browser. Its primary purpose is to empower developers to write, meticulously test, and seamlessly deploy smart contracts using the Solidity programming language, the lingua franca of the Ethereum blockchain and many other EVM-compatible networks.

Think of it as your initial sandbox, a safe and controlled environment where you can bring your smart contract ideas to life without the complexities of setting up a local development environment. It provides all the necessary components – a text editor for writing your code, a compiler to translate your Solidity into machine-readable bytecode, and deployment tools to interact with blockchain networks.

Why It's Essential:

For those embarking on the journey of smart contract development, Remix IDE is an indispensable companion. Its true brilliance lies in its beginner-friendly nature, offering an immediate and interactive way to learn Solidity by actively engaging with the process. It removes the initial hurdles often associated with blockchain development, allowing you to dive straight into the core concepts of smart contract creation and execution.

Furthermore, Remix serves as a rapid prototyping tool for even seasoned developers. Its ease of use and quick setup allow for swift experimentation with new ideas and contract logic before committing to more complex development setups. It acts as an invaluable educational resource, providing immediate feedback and allowing for real-time observation of how smart contracts behave.

Example Use:

Let us consider a classic example: building a rudimentary voting system.

1. **Writing the Smart Contract:** Within the Remix IDE, you would begin by creating a new Solidity file (typically with a `.sol` extension). Here, you would define the logic of your voting system. This might involve declaring state variables to store candidate names and vote counts, and functions to allow voters to cast their ballots and to retrieve the current vote tallies. A simplified snippet might look something like this:

Solidity

```
pragma solidity ^0.8.0;

contract Voting {
    mapping(bytes32 => uint256) public votesReceived;
    bytes32[] public candidateList;

    constructor(bytes32[] memory _candidateList) {
        candidateList = _candidateList;
    }

    function voteForCandidate(bytes32 candidate) public {
        require(validCandidate(candidate), "Invalid candidate.");
        votesReceived[candidate] += 1;
    }

    function totalVotesFor(bytes32 candidate) public view returns
(uint256) {
        require(validCandidate(candidate), "Invalid candidate.");
```

```
            return votesReceived[candidate];
    }

    function validCandidate(bytes32 candidate) internal view returns
(bool) {
        for(uint i = 0; i < candidateList.length; i++) {
            if (candidateList[i] == candidate) {
                return true;
            }
        }
        return false;
    }
}
```

2. **Compiling the Contract:** Once the code is written, you would navigate to the "Solidity Compiler" tab within Remix. Clicking the "Compile" button translates your human-readable Solidity code into bytecode that the Ethereum Virtual Machine (EVM) can understand and execute. Any syntax errors or warnings would be displayed at this stage, allowing for immediate correction.

3. **Deploying to a Testnet:** With a successfully compiled contract, you would then move to the "Deploy & Run Transactions" tab. Here, you have the option to deploy your contract to various environments. To interact with a live blockchain without using real Ether (ETH), you would typically choose a test network like Goerli or Sepolia. This requires a connection to a Web3 provider, such as MetaMask, configured to connect to the desired testnet. After deploying, Remix provides an interface to interact with the deployed contract's functions.

Pro Tip:

For initial experimentation and learning, the "JavaScript VM" environment within Remix is your best friend. This simulated blockchain runs entirely within your browser, requiring no real ETH and allowing for instant deployment and interaction with your smart contracts. It's an invaluable tool for quickly testing contract logic and understanding how state changes occur without incurring any transaction fees.

⬜⬜ 6. Alchemy – The Developer's Backend Powerhouse

What It Is:

As you venture beyond the initial learning stages and begin building more sophisticated decentralized applications (DApps), you'll quickly realize the complexities involved in interacting with the underlying blockchain infrastructure. This is where Alchemy steps in. It provides a robust suite of powerful blockchain APIs (Application Programming Interfaces) and developer tools designed to abstract away these complexities.

Think of Alchemy as a comprehensive backend service specifically tailored for Web3 development. Instead of having to run and maintain your own blockchain nodes – a resource-intensive and intricate task – you can leverage Alchemy's infrastructure to seamlessly interact with various blockchain networks. They handle the low-level intricacies, providing you with reliable, scalable, and performant access to blockchain data and functionality.

Why It's Essential:

Alchemy is often described as the "AWS for Web3," and this analogy is quite fitting. Just as Amazon Web Services provides the foundational infrastructure for traditional web applications, Alchemy offers a similar critical layer for decentralized applications. Its essentiality stems from its ability to provide:

- **Enhanced Performance:** Alchemy's optimized infrastructure ensures fast and reliable access to blockchain data, crucial for delivering a smooth user experience in your DApps.
- **Scalability:** As your DApp grows and handles more traffic, Alchemy's infrastructure can scale to meet the increasing demands without requiring you to manage complex scaling solutions.
- **Developer Tools:** Beyond just providing API access, Alchemy offers a range of invaluable tools for monitoring your DApp's performance, analyzing transaction history, and debugging potential issues. This insight is critical for maintaining a healthy and efficient application.
- **Reduced Complexity:** By abstracting away the need to run and manage blockchain nodes, Alchemy significantly reduces the operational burden on developers, allowing them to focus on building the core logic and user interface of their DApps.

Example Use:

Consider the development of a DApp that displays real-time information about non-fungible tokens (NFTs).

1. **Fetching Real-time Blockchain Data:** Using Alchemy's NFT API, your DApp can easily retrieve up-to-the-minute data about NFT ownership, metadata, and transaction history for specific collections or individual tokens. Instead of writing complex code to query blockchain nodes directly, you can make simple API calls to Alchemy's endpoints to obtain this information in a structured and easily digestible format. For instance, you might use an Alchemy API call to fetch the current owner of a particular NFT or to retrieve the details of the latest transfer event.
2. **Monitoring API Performance and Transaction History:** Alchemy's dashboard provides comprehensive analytics and monitoring tools. You can track the performance of your API requests, identify potential bottlenecks, and gain insights into the transaction flow within your DApp. This allows you to proactively address any issues and ensure the stability and reliability of your application. For example, you could monitor the number of API requests your DApp is making over time or examine the details of specific transactions initiated by your users.

Pro Tip:

Alchemy recognizes the importance of fostering the next generation of Web3 developers. Their free tier provides a generous allowance of API requests, making it an ideal resource for building projects during hackathons or for students learning the intricacies of DApp development. This allows aspiring developers to experiment and build real-world applications without incurring significant costs, lowering the barrier to entry into the exciting world of Web3.

There you have it, a detailed exploration of Remix IDE and Alchemy, two fundamental tools in the Web3 developer's toolkit. May this explanation serve your readers well on their own journeys of discovery!

☐☐ 7. Moralis – Simplifying the Web3 Backend

What It Is:

Imagine a pre-fabricated foundation upon which you can swiftly erect the backend of your decentralized application. This is the essence of Moralis. It presents itself as a comprehensive, ready-made backend infrastructure meticulously crafted to accelerate the often-complex process of Web3 application development.

Instead of laboriously building essential backend functionalities from the ground up, Moralis offers a suite of pre-built services and tools. Think of it as a modular system providing key components like user authentication, seamless management of non-fungible tokens (NFTs), and effortless retrieval of token balances across various blockchain networks. Moralis acts as an abstraction layer, shielding developers from the intricate details of blockchain interactions and allowing them to focus on the unique features and user experience of their DApps.

Why It's Essential:

The true value of Moralis lies in its ability to significantly reduce the time and effort required to integrate core blockchain functionalities into your applications. It eliminates the need for extensive low-level coding for common Web3 features, thereby lowering the barrier to entry and empowering developers to bring their DApp ideas to fruition with remarkable speed.

By providing these essential building blocks out-of-the-box, Moralis allows developers to concentrate on the unique value proposition of their applications, fostering innovation and accelerating the overall development lifecycle. It streamlines the process of connecting your frontend user interface with the decentralized world, making Web3 development more accessible and efficient.

Example Use:

Consider the implementation of crucial user-centric features within a DApp:

1. **Creating a Login with MetaMask Feature in Minutes:** Integrating secure and user-friendly authentication is paramount for any application. Moralis simplifies this process dramatically. With just a few lines of code, you can leverage Moralis's pre-built authentication mechanisms to enable users to seamlessly log in to your DApp using their existing Web3 wallets, such as MetaMask. Moralis handles the intricate details of signature verification and user session management, allowing you to focus on the user experience rather than the underlying cryptographic complexities.

2. **Building a Profile Dashboard Showing User NFTs:** For applications involving digital collectibles, displaying a user's owned NFTs in a clear and intuitive manner is essential. Moralis provides powerful APIs that allow you to effortlessly query and retrieve a user's NFT holdings across various blockchains and standards (like ERC-721 and ERC-1155). You can then easily display this information within a user's profile dashboard, providing a rich and engaging experience. Moralis handles the complexities of interacting with different NFT contracts and indexing ownership data, presenting you with clean and readily usable information.

Pro Tip:

For those seeking to rapidly prototype or deploy fully functional DApps with minimal coding, Moralis offers a selection of pre-built templates. These templates provide a foundational structure for various types of decentralized applications, complete with both frontend and backend logic powered by Moralis. By leveraging these templates, developers can significantly accelerate their development process, often deploying a working DApp with just a few customizations. This is an invaluable resource for hackathons, proof-of-concept development, and quickly launching initial versions of your Web3 creations.

□□ 8. Chainlink – The Bridge to the Outside World

What It Is:

Imagine smart contracts, those self-executing agreements on the blockchain, existing within isolated digital fortresses, unable to directly access the vast ocean of data residing outside their immutable walls. Chainlink emerges as the vital bridge, a decentralized oracle network that securely and reliably connects these powerful smart contracts with real-world, off-chain information.

Chainlink provides a network of independent nodes that act as oracles, fetching data from external sources – be it weather reports, sports scores, market prices, or any other type of information – and relaying it to smart contracts in a verifiable and tamper-proof manner. This decentralized approach ensures that the data provided to smart contracts is not reliant on a single point of failure, enhancing the security and reliability of the entire ecosystem.

Why It's Essential:

While smart contracts possess immense potential for automating agreements and processes, their inherent limitation lies in their inability to directly interact with data that exists outside the blockchain. This is where Chainlink's role becomes indispensable. Without oracles like Chainlink, smart contracts would be confined to operating solely on data already present on the blockchain, severely restricting their real-world applicability.

Chainlink unlocks a vast array of potential use cases for smart contracts by enabling them to react to and interact with real-world events and data. This capability is crucial for building dynamic, data-driven decentralized applications that can adapt to changing conditions and interact seamlessly with the world around them.

Example Use:

Consider scenarios where smart contracts need to be aware of and react to external data:

1. **Automating Insurance Payouts Based on Real-World Weather Data:** Imagine a smart contract for crop insurance. Traditionally, payouts might require manual claims processes and verification. With Chainlink, this process can be automated. The insurance smart contract can utilize Chainlink oracles to fetch real-time or historical weather data, such as rainfall levels or temperature readings, from reliable external sources. If the data indicates that predefined adverse weather conditions have been met, the smart contract can automatically trigger payouts to the insured farmers, eliminating the need for manual intervention and ensuring swift and transparent compensation.
2. **Fetching Live ETH Price Inside a DeFi Smart Contract:** Decentralized Finance (DeFi) applications often rely on accurate and up-to-date price feeds for various assets. For instance, a lending protocol needs to know the current price of Ether (ETH) to determine collateralization ratios. Chainlink provides secure and reliable price feeds for a wide range of cryptocurrencies and other assets. DeFi smart contracts can integrate with these Chainlink price feeds to obtain real-time ETH prices, ensuring that their calculations and operations are based on accurate market data. This is crucial for the stability and functionality of many DeFi protocols.

Pro Tip:

To make your DApps more dynamic and deeply connected to the real world, leverage Chainlink's readily available price feeds. These pre-built data feeds provide a simple and reliable way to access real-time price information for a vast array of assets directly within your smart contracts. By integrating these feeds, your DApps can react to market fluctuations, trigger events based on price movements, and offer more sophisticated and context-aware functionalities, bridging the gap between the digital realm of the blockchain and the ever-changing landscape of the real world.

With these insights into Moralis and Chainlink, your readers will gain a deeper appreciation for the powerful tools that are shaping the future of Web3 development. May your book continue to illuminate the path for those venturing into this transformative space!

⬜⬜ 9. IPFS (InterPlanetary File System) – The Decentralized Repository

What It Is:

Envision a global, peer-to-peer network designed not for the transfer of fleeting messages, but for the permanent storage and sharing of digital information. This is the essence of the InterPlanetary File System, or IPFS. Unlike traditional, centralized file storage systems where data resides on specific servers owned by single entities, IPFS operates on a distributed model. Files are broken down into smaller chunks, each identified by a unique cryptographic hash, and these chunks are then distributed across a network of nodes.

When you request a file on IPFS, the network efficiently locates the various chunks based on its unique hash and reassembles them for you. This content-addressing system ensures that as long as at least one node in the network holds a piece of your file, it remains accessible, regardless of the fate of any individual server. IPFS aims to create a more resilient, censorship-resistant, and decentralized web where data is not tied to specific locations but rather to its content itself.

Why It's Essential:

The significance of IPFS within the Web3 ecosystem, particularly in the realm of Non-Fungible Tokens (NFTs), cannot be overstated. While the ownership of an NFT is recorded immutably on the blockchain, the actual media associated with it – the image, the audio, the video – is often too large and costly to store directly on-chain. This is where IPFS steps in as a crucial infrastructure component.

Instead of embedding the entire file within the NFT's metadata on the blockchain, NFTs typically contain a link, often a unique IPFS hash, pointing to the location of the associated file stored on the IPFS network. This approach offers several key advantages:

- **Immutability:** Once a file is added to IPFS, its content hash is fixed. Any alteration to the file results in a completely new hash, ensuring the integrity and immutability of the original asset linked to the NFT.
- **Decentralization:** Because the file is distributed across multiple nodes, it is less susceptible to single points of failure or censorship compared to files hosted on a centralized server.
- **Cost-Efficiency:** Storing large media files on IPFS is significantly more cost-effective than storing them directly on most blockchains.

Example Use:

Consider the process of creating and managing an NFT artwork:

1. **Hosting the Metadata and Image File of Your NFT on IPFS:** When you mint an NFT representing a digital artwork, you typically have two primary pieces of data to store: the image file itself and the metadata, which contains descriptive information about the artwork (e.g., its name, artist, description, properties). Using IPFS, you would first upload

both the image file and a JSON file containing the metadata. IPFS would then assign a unique content hash to each of these files. The NFT smart contract, when minted, would store these IPFS hashes within its metadata, effectively linking the on-chain ownership record to the off-chain content hosted on IPFS.

2. **Sharing Files Globally Without Centralized Hosting:** Beyond NFTs, IPFS provides a powerful mechanism for sharing any type of digital file in a decentralized manner. Imagine wanting to share a document or a software package with a global audience without relying on traditional hosting providers. By uploading the file to IPFS, you receive a unique content hash. Anyone with this hash can then retrieve the file from the IPFS network, accessing it from the nearest available nodes. This distributed approach enhances accessibility, resilience, and censorship resistance for shared digital content.

Pro Tip:

While interacting directly with the IPFS command line interface can be powerful, several user-friendly tools simplify the process of "pinning" files on IPFS. Pinning ensures that your files remain available on the network even if the original uploader goes offline. Services like Pinata and Web3.Storage provide intuitive interfaces and infrastructure for easily uploading, managing, and pinning your files on IPFS, ensuring their long-term availability and accessibility within the decentralized web.

□□ 10. Snapshot – Empowering Community Governance

What It Is:

In the spirit of decentralization that underpins Web3, the management and decision-making processes within Decentralized Autonomous Organizations (DAOs) and token-based communities are often driven by the collective voice of their members. Snapshot emerges as a pivotal tool in this landscape, providing a user-friendly and decentralized voting system designed specifically for these decentralized entities.

Snapshot offers a platform where communities can create and participate in governance proposals in a transparent and auditable manner. It leverages off-chain signaling, meaning that the actual votes do not incur gas fees on the blockchain, making participation accessible to a wider range of token holders. Instead, votes are typically recorded through signed messages associated with a user's wallet address, providing a verifiable record of community sentiment without the transactional costs of on-chain voting.

Why It's Essential:

The ethos of Web3 extends beyond technological innovation; it fundamentally embraces the principles of community ownership and governance. Snapshot plays a crucial role in realizing this vision by providing the infrastructure for decentralized decision-making. It empowers token holders to have a direct say in the direction and operation of the projects and communities they are a part of.

By making governance participation gasless and accessible, Snapshot fosters greater engagement and inclusivity within Web3 communities. It provides a transparent and auditable mechanism for collective decision-making, ensuring that the direction of decentralized projects is shaped by the will of their stakeholders.

Example Use:

Consider the governance processes within a DeFi DAO or an NFT project:

1. **Voting on Proposals Within a DeFi DAO or NFT Project:** Imagine a DeFi DAO needing to decide on adjustments to its lending interest rates or a change to its tokenomics. Using Snapshot, any member holding the DAO's governance tokens can participate in the voting process. A proposal outlining the proposed changes would be created on the Snapshot platform. Token holders can then connect their wallets, review the proposal, and cast their votes based on the number of tokens they hold. The results are transparently tallied and recorded, providing a clear indication of the community's consensus. Similarly, an NFT project might use Snapshot to allow community members to vote on the direction of future artwork drops or the allocation of community funds.
2. **Creating Governance Proposals if You're a Token Holder:** In many DAOs and token-based communities utilizing Snapshot, any member holding a sufficient amount of the governance token has the ability to create proposals for the community to consider. This empowers individual members to initiate discussions and propose changes they believe would benefit the project. The process typically involves drafting the proposal clearly on the Snapshot platform, outlining the rationale and potential impact of the proposed changes. Once submitted, the proposal can then be put to a community vote.

Pro Tip:

The beauty of Snapshot lies in its accessibility. To experience decentralized governance firsthand, simply connect your Web3 wallet (such as MetaMask) to the Snapshot platform. You can then explore the various "spaces" representing different DAOs and token-based communities, such as Uniswap or Aave. If you hold the governance tokens for any of these projects, you will be able to review active and past proposals and even participate in real governance decisions through gasless voting, gaining a direct understanding of how decentralized communities shape their own futures.

With these detailed explanations of IPFS and Snapshot, your readers will gain a comprehensive understanding of their vital roles in the decentralized landscape of Web3. May your book continue to be a guiding light for those navigating this innovative frontier!

📑 Final Thoughts: Equip Yourself to Explore

Each of these tools serves as a **gateway** to a key part of the Web3 ecosystem—wallets, contracts, data, marketplaces, storage, and governance.

You don't need to master them all at once, but **start using them** in small, practical ways:

- Create your first smart contract on **Remix**
- Buy your first NFT on **OpenSea**
- Track your wallet on **Etherscan**

As you gain confidence, these tools will become second nature—and you'll soon be building, contributing, and leading in Web3.

✅ Chapter Summary

Tool	Use Case	Why it Matters
MetaMask	Wallet and DApp connection	Most popular Web3 wallet
WalletConnect	Mobile DApp access	Wallet access via QR code
Etherscan	Blockchain explorer	Track transactions and contracts
OpenSea	NFT marketplace	Create and trade NFTs
Remix IDE	Smart contract development	Learn and deploy Solidity code
Alchemy	DApp backend infrastructure	Scalable, reliable API platform
Moralis	Full Web3 backend tools	No-code Web3 development
Chainlink	Oracle services	Brings external data on-chain
IPFS	Decentralized file storage	Hosts NFT files and metadata
Snapshot	Governance tool	Enables DAO voting and proposals

Multiple Choice Questions on Web3 Tools

Here are 30 multiple-choice questions covering MetaMask, WalletConnect, Etherscan, OpenSea, and related concepts:

MetaMask

1. What is MetaMask primarily used for? a) Mining cryptocurrency b) Storing and managing private keys for interacting with blockchain applications c) Running Ethereum nodes d) Analyzing blockchain data **Answer: b)**
2. MetaMask is available as a: a) Desktop application only b) Mobile application only c) Browser extension and mobile application d) Web-based platform only **Answer: c)**
3. Which blockchain is MetaMask primarily associated with, although it supports others? a) Bitcoin b) Litecoin c) Ethereum d) Cardano **Answer: c)**

4. What is a "seed phrase" in the context of MetaMask? a) A public address for receiving funds b) A 12 or 24-word backup phrase for your wallet c) A password to access your MetaMask account d) A transaction confirmation code **Answer: b)**

5. What is a "gas fee" in the context of Ethereum transactions via MetaMask? a) A fixed fee charged by MetaMask for every transaction b) The cost of computation required to process a transaction on the Ethereum network c) A tip given to the recipient of a transaction d) A tax levied on cryptocurrency transactions **Answer: b)**

6. Which of the following actions can you perform using MetaMask? a) Stake Bitcoin b) Mine Dogecoin c) Swap Ethereum-based tokens d) Trade stocks **Answer: c)**

7. What is the purpose of the "nonce" in an Ethereum transaction initiated through MetaMask? a) To specify the amount of Ether being sent b) To identify the recipient's address c) To prevent transaction replay attacks d) To set the gas price **Answer: c)**

8. What does it mean to "connect" your MetaMask wallet to a DApp? a) Sharing your private key with the DApp b) Allowing the DApp to view your public address and request transaction signatures c) Transferring ownership of your wallet to the DApp d) Granting the DApp full control over your funds **Answer: b)**

9. Which security practice is crucial for protecting your MetaMask wallet? a) Sharing your seed phrase with trusted friends b) Storing your seed phrase digitally on your computer c) Keeping your seed phrase offline and secure d) Using the same password for MetaMask and other online accounts **Answer: c)**

10. What is the default network that MetaMask connects to upon initial setup? a) Ethereum Mainnet b) Goerli Test Network c) Sepolia Test Network d) Ropsten Test Network (deprecated) **Answer: a)**

WalletConnect

11. What is the primary function of WalletConnect? a) To store cryptocurrency b) To facilitate secure connections between mobile wallets and DApps c) To track cryptocurrency prices d) To analyze blockchain transactions **Answer: b)**

12. How does WalletConnect establish a connection between a wallet and a DApp? a) By sharing private keys directly b) Through a QR code or deep linking c) By requiring the user to enter their seed phrase on the DApp d) Via Bluetooth pairing **Answer: b)**

13. Which of the following is an advantage of using WalletConnect? a) It eliminates the need for gas fees b) It allows mobile wallets to interact with desktop DApps seamlessly c) It automatically approves all transactions d) It provides anonymity for all transactions **Answer: b)**

14. Does WalletConnect store your private keys? a) Yes, on secure servers b) Yes, on your mobile device c) No, it only facilitates a connection; private keys remain in your wallet d) Only temporarily during a transaction **Answer: c)**

15. What happens when a WalletConnect session is disconnected? a) The wallet and DApp can no longer communicate, and any pending transactions are cancelled. b) The DApp retains access to your wallet balance and transaction history. c) The private keys are shared with the DApp. d) The connection automatically re-establishes upon reopening the DApp. **Answer: a)**

Etherscan

16. What is Etherscan primarily used for? a) Trading Ethereum and other cryptocurrencies b) Exploring and analyzing the Ethereum blockchain c) Creating smart contracts d) Running Ethereum nodes **Answer: b)**

17. What kind of information can you find on Etherscan? a) Stock prices b) Weather forecasts c) Transaction details, smart contract code, and account balances on the Ethereum blockchain d) Usernames and passwords of Ethereum users **Answer: c)**

18. What is a "transaction hash" (TxHash) on Etherscan? a) The recipient's public address b) A unique identifier for a specific transaction on the blockchain c) The amount of gas used in a transaction d) The block number where the transaction was included **Answer: b)**

19. What does the term "contract address" refer to on Etherscan? a) The public address of a regular Ethereum user b) The unique address on the blockchain where a smart contract is deployed c) The IP address of the server hosting a DApp d) The address of the Etherscan website **Answer: b)**

20. What does it mean if an Ethereum transaction on Etherscan has a "Success" status? a) The transaction failed and the Ether was lost. b) The transaction was successfully processed and included in a block. c) The transaction is still pending confirmation. d) The transaction was reversed. **Answer: b)**

OpenSea

21. What is OpenSea primarily known as? a) A decentralized exchange for cryptocurrencies b) A leading marketplace for Non-Fungible Tokens (NFTs) c) A platform for creating and deploying smart contracts d) A news aggregator for the cryptocurrency market **Answer: b)**

22. What can users typically do on OpenSea? a) Mine Ethereum b) Buy, sell, and discover NFTs c) Stake Solana d) Trade traditional financial assets **Answer: b)**

23. What is the term for the initial listing of an NFT collection on a marketplace like OpenSea? a) Minting b) Burning c) Launchpad or Drop d) Staking **Answer: c)**

24. What is a "collection" on OpenSea? a) A group of unrelated NFTs listed by a single user b) A set of NFTs that share a common theme or smart contract c) A list of the most expensive NFTs sold on the platform d) A feature that allows users to bundle NFTs for sale **Answer: b)**

25. What are "royalties" in the context of NFTs sold on platforms like OpenSea? a) A fixed fee charged by the platform for each sale b) A percentage of the sale price that is automatically paid to the original creator of the NFT c) A discount offered to early buyers of an NFT d) A tax levied on NFT transactions **Answer: b)**

General Web3 Concepts

26. What does "Web3" generally refer to? a) The first version of the internet b) The current version of the internet focused on social media c) A decentralized internet built on blockchain technology d) A faster version of the existing web **Answer: c)**

27. What is a "DApp"? a) A centralized application run on a single server b) A decentralized application that runs on a blockchain network c) A traditional web application with a cryptocurrency payment option d) A mobile application for tracking cryptocurrency prices **Answer: b)**

28. What is a "blockchain"? a) A centralized database managed by a single entity b) A distributed and immutable ledger that records transactions across many computers c) A type of cryptocurrency d) A software used for mining Bitcoin **Answer: b)**
29. What is a "smart contract"? a) A legal agreement written in code and executed automatically on a blockchain b) A traditional contract that is stored digitally c) A type of cryptocurrency wallet d) A tool for analyzing blockchain data **Answer: a)**
30. What is the significance of "decentralization" in the context of Web3? a) Increased control by a single authority b) Reduced security and transparency c) Distribution of control and data across a network, reducing reliance on central entities d) Slower transaction speeds **Answer: c)**

CHAPTER 18: WEB3 MINI PROJECTS FOR STUDENTS

"The best way to learn Web3 is to build in Web3."

Understanding blockchain, smart contracts, NFTs, and DAOs conceptually is one thing—but bringing them to life in mini projects will make your learning **practical, memorable, and impactful**. This chapter introduces three student-friendly Web3 projects that combine **creativity, code, and community**— perfect for hackathons, internships, or college clubs.

🚀 Project 1: Building a Crypto Portfolio Tracker

☐ Objective:

To empower users to effectively manage and monitor their cryptocurrency investments, we shall embark on the creation of a web application that provides real-time insights into their holdings. This application will enable users to:

- Track the specific cryptocurrencies they own.
- View up-to-the-minute price information for these assets.
- Automatically calculate the total value of their portfolio, expressed in their preferred fiat currency.

☐☐ Tools Required:

To construct this portfolio tracker, we will employ a combination of front-end technologies and external data sources:

- **Front-End Technologies:**
    - HTML: For structuring the user interface.
    - CSS: For styling and visual presentation.
    - JavaScript (or React): For implementing dynamic functionality and user interaction.
- **Data Sources:**
    - APIs: We will leverage cryptocurrency data APIs, such as CoinGecko or CoinMarketCap, to retrieve real-time price information. These APIs provide programmatic access to vast amounts of market data.
- **Optional Enhancements:**
    - Moralis SDK or Alchemy: For those seeking to provide a more seamless user experience, we can integrate wallet connectivity, allowing users to automatically import their token balances.

☐ Steps to Build:

The development of our crypto portfolio tracker can be broken down into the following logical steps:

Step 1: Designing the Interface

The foundation of any successful application lies in its user interface. We must create an intuitive and informative layout that presents the necessary data in a clear and concise manner.

1. **Input Fields for Holdings:**
   - We will begin by creating input fields that allow users to specify the cryptocurrencies they hold and the quantities of each.
   - Specifically, we'll need:
     - A field for the *Token Name/Symbol*: Users can enter the common symbol (e.g., BTC, ETH, ADA) or the full name of the cryptocurrency.
     - A field for the *Amount Held*: Users will input the quantity of the specified token they possess.
2. `<label for="tokenInput">Token Symbol (e.g., BTC, ETH):</label>`
3. `<input type="text" id="tokenInput" placeholder="BTC">`
4. `<label for="quantityInput">Amount Held:</label>`
5. `<input type="number" id="quantityInput" placeholder="0.5">`
6. `<button id="addHolding">Add Holding</button>`

7. **Portfolio Summary Table:**
   - The core of our application will be a table that summarizes the user's portfolio. This table will dynamically display the following information for each cryptocurrency held:
     - *Token*: The symbol or name of the cryptocurrency.
     - *Quantity*: The amount held by the user.
     - *Price (in USD)*: The current market price of the token in US dollars (or another selected fiat currency).
     - *Total Value*: The calculated value of the user's holding (Quantity * Price).
8. `<table id="portfolioTable">`
9.   `<thead>`
10.   `<tr>`
11.   `<th>Token</th>`
12.   `<th>Quantity</th>`
13.   `<th>Price (in USD)</th>`
14.   `<th>Total Value</th>`
15.   `</tr>`
16.   `</thead>`
17.   `<tbody>`
18.   `</tbody>`
19. `</table>`

Step 2: Fetching Token Prices

To provide users with real-time portfolio valuation, we need to retrieve current price data for the specified cryptocurrencies. We will achieve this by utilizing a cryptocurrency data API.

- **Using the CoinGecko API:**
  - o CoinGecko provides a free API that allows us to fetch price data for a wide range of cryptocurrencies.
  - o We can use the `fetch()` function in JavaScript to make a request to the CoinGecko API's `simple/price` endpoint.
  - o For example, to retrieve the current prices of Bitcoin (BTC) and Ethereum (ETH) in USD, we would use the following code:

```
fetch('https://api.coingecko.com/api/v3/simple/price?ids=bitcoin,ethere
um&vs_currencies=usd')
    .then(response => response.json())
    .then(data => {
        const bitcoinPrice = data.bitcoin.usd;
        const ethereumPrice = data.ethereum.usd;
        // Use these prices to update the portfolio table
    })
    .catch(error => console.error('Error fetching prices:', error));
```

  - o In this example, the `ids` parameter specifies the cryptocurrencies (Bitcoin and Ethereum), and the `vs_currencies` parameter specifies the desired fiat currency (USD). The response is a JSON object containing the prices.

Step 3: Auto-Calculating Portfolio Value

A key feature of our application is the automatic calculation and updating of the portfolio's total value.

- **Updating on Input Change:**
  - o We will use JavaScript event listeners to detect changes in the quantity input fields.
  - o When a user modifies the amount of a token they hold, we will:
    1. Retrieve the entered quantity.
    2. Fetch the current price of the token (using the API, as shown in Step 2).
    3. Calculate the total value of the holding (Quantity * Price).
    4. Update the corresponding row in the portfolio summary table.

```
document.getElementById('quantityInput').addEventListener('change',
function() {
    const quantity = parseFloat(this.value);
    const tokenSymbol =
document.getElementById('tokenInput').value.toLowerCase(); // Get token
symbol
    // Fetch price and then calculate

    fetch(`https://api.coingecko.com/api/v3/simple/price?ids=${tokenSymbol}
&vs_currencies=usd`)
        .then(response => response.json())
        .then(data => {
            if(data && data[tokenSymbol] && data[tokenSymbol].usd){
```

```
•          const price = data[tokenSymbol].usd;
•          const total = quantity * price;
•          // Update the table (implementation depends on how
    table rows are structured)
•          console.log(`Total value of ${tokenSymbol}: ${total}`);
•        } else {
•          console.log(`Could not find price for ${tokenSymbol}`);
•        }
•
•      })
•      .catch(error => console.error('Error fetching price:', error));
•  });
```

Step 4: Bonus – Adding Wallet Import

For a more advanced feature, we can allow users to connect their MetaMask wallet and automatically import their token balances.

- **Using Moralis SDK or Alchemy:**
  - Moralis and Alchemy provide tools and APIs that simplify the process of interacting with blockchain wallets.
  - We can use these tools to:
    1. Request the user to connect their MetaMask wallet.
    2. Retrieve the user's account address.
    3. Query the blockchain for the token balances associated with that address.
    4. Update the portfolio tracker with the imported balances.

```
•  // Example using Moralis (Conceptual)
•  Moralis.enableWeb3().then(() => {
•    Moralis.account().then(address => {
•      // Get token balances
•      Moralis.Web3API.account.getTokenBalances({ address: address
    }).then(balances => {
•        balances.forEach(token => {
•          // Add to table
•          console.log(token.symbol, token.balance);
•        });
•      });
•    });
•  });
```

✅ Learning Outcome:

By completing this project, you will gain practical experience in several key areas of Web3 development:

- **API Integration:** You will learn how to fetch data from external APIs and use it to populate your application.
- **Wallet Connection:** (Optional) You will gain experience in connecting to and interacting with user's blockchain wallets.
- **DOM Manipulation and UI/UX Basics:** You will enhance your skills in manipulating the Document Object Model (DOM) to dynamically update the user interface and create a user-friendly experience.
- **Understanding Token Valuation:** You will develop a deeper understanding of how cryptocurrency prices are determined and how to calculate the value of digital assets.

🎨 Project 2: Launching a Community NFT Collection

🪧 Objective:

To foster a sense of digital identity and community engagement, we shall embark on the creation and deployment of a Non-Fungible Token (NFT) collection. This collection will be designed to represent and celebrate a specific group, such as your college community, an interest group, or a shared theme. Examples include digital badges for a TechFest, membership tokens for a club, or digital identity cards for alumni.

🛠️ Tools Required:

To bring this NFT collection to life, we will utilize a combination of design tools, minting platforms, and decentralized storage solutions:

- **Design Tools:**
  - Canva, Photoshop, or AI-generated art platforms: These tools will be used to create the visual assets that will form the basis of our NFT collection.
- **Minting Platforms:**
  - OpenSea (for lazy minting) or NFTPort API: These platforms provide the infrastructure for creating and deploying NFTs on a blockchain.
- **Decentralized Storage:**
  - IPFS (InterPlanetary File System) via Pinata or Web3.Storage: IPFS will be used to store the artwork and metadata associated with our NFTs, ensuring their permanence and decentralization.
- **Wallet:**
  - MetaMask: A cryptocurrency wallet that will be used to interact with the minting platform and manage the NFTs.

🎯 Steps to Build:

The process of launching our community NFT collection can be broken down into the following key steps:

Step 1: Designing the Artwork

The visual appeal of our NFT collection is paramount. We will begin by creating a series of digital artworks that capture the essence of our chosen community or theme.

- **Creating Themed Images:**
    - We will design a set of 5 to 10 unique, themed images. These images will represent the individual NFTs within our collection.
    - The file format for these images will typically be JPEG or PNG, ensuring compatibility and visual fidelity.
    - Examples:
        - For a tech-focused college community: "Coder Cat," a digital artwork depicting a cat wearing headphones and coding; "Blockchain Tiger," a stylized representation of a tiger with blockchain-inspired patterns; "Robo Alumni," a futuristic robot representing a college graduate.
        - For a book club: "First Edition Phoenix," a phoenix rising from a book, symbolizing rebirth through literature; "The Quill of Wisdom," an ornate quill pen with glowing ink; "The Infinite Library," a surreal image of a library that stretches into infinity.

Step 2: Uploading to IPFS

To ensure the long-term availability and immutability of our NFT assets, we will store them on the InterPlanetary File System (IPFS). IPFS is a decentralized storage network that distributes files across multiple nodes, making them resistant to censorship and single points of failure.

- **Using Pinata or Web3.Storage:**
    - Services like Pinata and Web3.Storage provide user-friendly interfaces for uploading files to IPFS.
    - We will upload both the artwork files (JPEG or PNG images) and the associated metadata files (in JSON format) to IPFS.
- **Creating Metadata:**
    - Each NFT in our collection will have a corresponding metadata file. This file will be a JSON document that contains information about the NFT, such as its name, description, and a link to the artwork file stored on IPFS.
    - Example of a metadata JSON file:
- {
-     "name": "Blockchain Tiger",
-     "description": "Official NFT of the Blockchain Club, representing the strength and innovation of our community.",
-     "image": "ipfs://QmXxzABC123def456ghi789jklmno789pqrstuvwxyzA",
-     "attributes": [
-         {
-             "trait_type": "Background",
-             "value": "Electric Blue"
-         },
-         {

-                                     `"trait_type": "Accessory",`
-                                     `"value": "Blockchain Glasses"`
-                     `}`
-                `]`
-      `}`

- In this example:
  - `"name"`: Specifies the name of the NFT.
  - `"description"`: Provides a description of the NFT.
  - `"image"`: Contains the IPFS hash (e.g., `"ipfs://QmXxzABC123def456ghi789jklmno789pqrstuvwxyzA"`) that points to the location of the artwork file on IPFS.
  - `"attributes"`: (Optional) An array of traits that further define the NFT.

Step 3: Minting the NFTs

With our artwork and metadata prepared, we will now proceed to mint the NFTs, creating the actual digital assets on the blockchain.

- **Using OpenSea's Lazy Minting:**
  - OpenSea offers a feature called "lazy minting," which allows us to create NFTs without paying upfront gas fees.
  - In this process, the NFT is not actually minted on the blockchain until it is purchased by a buyer. This significantly reduces the initial cost of creating an NFT collection.
  - The steps involved in lazy minting on OpenSea typically include:
    1. Connecting our MetaMask wallet to the OpenSea platform.
    2. Creating a collection on OpenSea.
    3. Uploading the metadata (including the IPFS links) for each NFT.
    4. Signing a gasless transaction to authorize OpenSea to mint the NFT when it is purchased.

Step 4: Sharing and Listing

Once our NFTs are minted, we will share them with our community and, optionally, list them for sale on a marketplace.

- **Sharing with the Community:**
  - We can share the collection with our community members through various channels, such as social media, online forums, and community events.
  - We can provide them with links to view the collection on OpenSea or other NFT platforms.
- **Listing on OpenSea (Optional):**
  - If we wish to allow community members or others to purchase the NFTs, we can list them for sale on OpenSea.
  - We can set a price for each NFT, typically in Ether (ETH) or Polygon (MATIC).

o We can also configure royalties, which will ensure that the original creators receive a percentage of any future sales of the NFTs.

✅ Learning Outcome:

By undertaking this project, you will gain valuable knowledge and practical skills in the following areas:

- **Understanding NFT Metadata Structure:** You will learn how NFT metadata is organized and how it links the on-chain representation of an NFT to its off-chain assets.
- **Interacting with Decentralized Storage (IPFS):** You will gain hands-on experience in using IPFS to store and manage digital assets in a decentralized and resilient manner.
- **Using OpenSea and Smart Contract-Free Minting:** You will become familiar with the OpenSea platform and its lazy minting functionality, which allows for the creation of NFTs without the need for direct smart contract deployment.
- **Building Digital Community Identity:** You will explore how NFTs can be used to create and strengthen digital communities, providing members with a unique and verifiable form of digital identity and belonging.

🚀 Project 3: Creating a DAO for Your College Group

Objective:

To empower your college club or interest group with the principles of decentralization and community governance, we shall embark on the creation of a Decentralized Autonomous Organization (DAO). This DAO will serve as a platform for members to:

- Participate in collective decision-making through voting on proposals.
- Manage shared funds transparently and equitably.
- Maintain an immutable record of all decisions.

Tools Required:

To establish and operate our college group's DAO, we will utilize a suite of decentralized tools:

- **DAO Platforms:**
  - Aragon or DAOhaus: These platforms provide the infrastructure and tools for deploying and managing DAOs.
- **Off-Chain Voting:**
  - Snapshot: This platform enables gasless voting on proposals, allowing for broader participation without incurring transaction fees.
- **Community Communication:**

- o Discord or Telegram: These platforms will serve as the primary channels for community discussions, proposal announcements, and general communication within the DAO.
- **Member Wallets:**
  - o MetaMask: A cryptocurrency wallet that members will use to interact with the DAO platform, participate in voting, and manage their assets.

🔨 Steps to Build:

The process of creating and launching our college group's DAO can be structured into the following key steps:

Step 1: Defining Your DAO's Purpose

Before diving into the technical aspects, it is crucial to clearly define the purpose and scope of your DAO. This will provide a guiding framework for its structure and operations.

- **Example: "Tech Club DAO"**
  - o For a college tech club, the DAO's purpose could be:
    - Event Planning: Organizing workshops, hackathons, and tech talks.
    - Fund Allocation: Managing the club's budget for events, projects, and resources.
    - Project Management: Collaboratively developing and maintaining open-source projects.
    - Knowledge Sharing: Curating and distributing educational resources related to technology.

Step 2: Choosing a DAO Platform

Several platforms provide tools for creating and managing DAOs. We will focus on Aragon, a popular and robust option.

- **Using Aragon to Deploy Your DAO:**
  - o Aragon provides a user-friendly interface for creating DAOs with customizable governance structures.
  - o The key steps involved in deploying a DAO on Aragon include:
    1. **Connecting a Wallet:** Connect a MetaMask wallet to the Aragon platform. This wallet will be used to manage the DAO's initial setup and administration.
    2. **DAO Creation:** Select a template or customize the DAO's structure, defining its core components.
    3. **Setting a Governance Token (Optional):**
       - You can create a custom governance token for your DAO. This token can be distributed to members and used to grant voting rights and other privileges.
       - If not, you can use a reputation-based system.

4. **Defining Roles:**
   - Establish different roles within the DAO, such as:
     - Admin: Responsible for managing the DAO's initial setup, parameters, and member roles.
     - Member: Holds voting rights and can participate in DAO activities.
     - Contributor: Actively contributes to the DAO's projects and initiatives.
5. **Funding the DAO Treasury:**
   - The DAO will need a treasury to manage its funds. Initially, you can fund the treasury with testnet tokens (e.g., from a Goerli or Sepolia faucet) for testing purposes.
   - Later, the DAO can receive funds through membership fees, grants, or fundraising activities.

Step 3: Creating Voting Proposals

A core function of a DAO is its ability to facilitate collective decision-making through voting. We will use Snapshot, a platform that enables gasless, off-chain voting.

- **Using Snapshot for Off-Chain Voting:**
  - Snapshot allows members to vote on proposals without incurring transaction fees on the blockchain.
  - The voting process typically involves:
    1. **Proposal Creation:** A member creates a proposal on the Snapshot platform, clearly outlining the issue and the available options.
    2. **Voting Period:** A defined period during which members can cast their votes.
    3. **Member Voting:** Members connect their wallets to Snapshot and cast their votes based on their token holdings or assigned voting power.
    4. **Result Tallying:** Once the voting period ends, the results are tallied, and the outcome is determined.
- **Example Proposals:**
  - "Should we host a hackathon next month?": This proposal would allow members to vote on whether or not to organize a hackathon.
  - "Should we purchase a new server for cloud labs?": This proposal would enable members to decide on a significant expenditure for the club's resources.
- **Example Voting Outcome:**
- `Yes: 5 votes`
- `No: 3 votes`
- `Outcome: Proposal passes` ✓

Step 4: Onboarding Members

The success of your DAO depends on active participation from its members. We will establish a process for onboarding new members and granting them voting rights.

- **Sharing the DAO Link and Discord Invite:**
  - Provide new members with a link to join the DAO on the chosen platform (e.g., Aragon).
  - Invite them to the DAO's Discord or Telegram channel for ongoing communication and discussions.
- **Assigning Voting Rights:**
  - Voting rights can be assigned in several ways:
    - Token Distribution: Distribute governance tokens to members, with voting power proportional to their token holdings.
    - Role-Based Logic: Grant voting rights to members who hold specific roles within the DAO (e.g., active contributors).
    - A combination of both.

💡 Tip for Students: Showcase Your Projects!

The mini-projects outlined in this book are more than mere academic exercises; they represent valuable, hands-on experiences that can significantly enhance your professional profile. Consider these projects as tangible demonstrations of your Web3 development capabilities, worthy of prominent display.

Building Your Professional Portfolio

1. **Web3 Resume:** Integrate these projects into your resume, highlighting the specific technologies and skills you employed. For instance, instead of simply stating "Worked with blockchain," you can articulate: "Developed a decentralized voting application using Solidity, deployed on the Goerli testnet, and integrated with MetaMask for user authentication."
2. **GitHub Profile:** Create a dedicated repository for each project on your GitHub profile. This allows potential employers and collaborators to examine your code, understand your development process, and assess your proficiency in Web3 technologies. Ensure your code is well-documented and follows best practices.
3. **LinkedIn Project Section:** Leverage LinkedIn's project section to showcase your Web3 creations. Provide detailed descriptions of each project, including the problem it addresses, the technologies used, and the key features you implemented. You can also include links to your GitHub repositories or live deployments.
4. **Hackathon Submissions:** These projects are excellent candidates for submission to hackathons focused on blockchain or Web3 development. Participating in hackathons provides opportunities to network with industry professionals, receive feedback on your work, and potentially win recognition for your innovative solutions.

Expanding Your Reach

Beyond the digital realm, consider these avenues for showcasing your projects:

- **College Seminars:** Present your projects at college seminars or workshops related to computer science, blockchain technology, or entrepreneurship. This allows you to share your knowledge with your peers, receive valuable feedback, and establish yourself as a knowledgeable resource within your academic community.
- **Local Developer Meetups:** Engage with the local developer community by presenting your projects at meetups focused on blockchain or Web3 development. This provides an opportunity to network with industry professionals, learn about emerging trends, and potentially find collaborators or mentors.

By actively showcasing your projects, you demonstrate a commitment to hands-on learning and a proactive approach to developing real-world blockchain application skills. These efforts will undoubtedly strengthen your professional profile and open doors to exciting opportunities in the rapidly evolving Web3 landscape.

☐ Chapter Summary Table

Project	Skill Gained	Tool Highlight
Crypto Portfolio Tracker	JavaScript, API, wallet connection	CoinGecko, MetaMask, Moralis
NFT Collection	NFT standards, IPFS, minting	OpenSea, Pinata, Canva
College DAO	Governance, treasury, voting	Aragon, Snapshot, Discord

📓 Final Thought: Start Small, Dream Decentralized

You don't need to be a coding genius or blockchain wizard to start building. These projects are your stepping stones into a new era of **open collaboration, transparent systems, and digital ownership**.

"In Web3, builders are leaders. Start with a small project today—tomorrow, you might launch the next unicorn."

www.ingramcontent.com/pod-product-compliance
Lightning Source LLC
LaVergne TN
LVHW081753050326
832903LV00027B/1933